Gender, Diversity and Innovation

Gender, Diversity and Innovation

Concepts, Policies and Practice

Edited by

Beldina Owalla

Research Fellow, Faculty of Business and Law, University of Portsmouth, UK

Tim Vorley

Pro Vice-Chancellor and Dean, Oxford Brookes Business School, Oxford Brookes University, UK

Helen Lawton Smith

Professor of Entrepreneurship and Director of the Centre for Innovation Management Research, Birkbeck University of London, UK

 Edward Elgar
PUBLISHING

Cheltenham, UK • Northampton, MA, USA

Published by
Edward Elgar Publishing Limited
The Lypiatts
15 Lansdown Road
Cheltenham
Glos GL50 2JA
UK

Edward Elgar Publishing, Inc.
William Pratt House
9 Dewey Court
Northampton
Massachusetts 01060
USA

A catalogue record for this book
is available from the British Library

Library of Congress Control Number: 2022932892

This book is available electronically in the **Elgar**online
Business subject collection
http://dx.doi.org/10.4337/9781800377462

ISBN 978 1 80037 745 5 (cased)
ISBN 978 1 80037 746 2 (eBook)

Printed and bound by CPI Group (UK) Ltd, Croydon, CR0 4YY

Contents

Contributors

James Bort is Assistant Professor of Entrepreneurship at the University of Missouri. His research is largely inspired by his experiences as an early stage employee, entrepreneur, and musician. These interests include well-being, the entrepreneurial workforce, crowdfunding, and computational social science. He received his PhD in Business Administration from Syracuse University.

Silvia Cervia, PhD in Sociology, is Assistant Professor in the Sociology of Cultural and Communicative Processes, Department of Political Science, University of Pisa, Italy. Her research focuses on gender issues, female participation in science and on inclusion/exclusion dynamics in social and educational processes. She has been involved in many research activities, such as projects funded by the European Commission, the Ministry of Education, University and Research (MIUR) and the Presidency of the Council of Ministers.

Wendy Cukier is Professor at Ryerson University, Diversity Institute Founder, Academic Director of the Women Entrepreneurship Knowledge Hub and Research Lead of the Future Skills Centre. She is the co-author of the bestseller, *Innovation Nation: Canadian Leadership from Java to Jurassic* (Wiley 2002) and former VP of Research and Innovation.

Cecelia Dotzler is an MBA graduate with over 15 years of professional experience working in various roles including physician clinical training, project management, sales, marketing, and human resources. Currently, she is a doctoral student in Organizational Psychology at Claremont Graduate University where she focuses her research on women's thriving in multiple contexts and workplaces.

Cynthia Forson is Associate Professor and Deputy Provost at Lancaster University Ghana. Academic and research interests focus on organisational behaviour and the work, leadership and management experiences of women (and other minority groups) in the labour market, entrepreneurship and organisations.

Jodi-Ann Francis, PhD (ABD), is a Senior Research Associate at the Diversity Institute. Her research focuses on development of hybrid immigration policies, such as the Atlantic Immigration Pilot. Her main research interests include immigration policy development, power structure and hierarchy. Jodi-Ann is also the principal immigration consultant at Dalrymple Immigration Consulting.

M. Gloria González-Morales is Associate Professor of Organizational Psychology at Claremont Graduate University. Her research areas are occupational health psychology, diversity and respect in workplaces and organisational interventions to enhance well-being. Her research has been funded with scholarships and grants, including Fulbright, SSHRC and the Canadian Foundation for Innovation.

Heather Griffiths is a Lecturer in Business Intelligence and Analytics at Oxford Brookes Business School. She is also affiliated to the Centre for Diversity Policy Research and Practice at Oxford Brookes where she previously worked as a Postdoctoral Research Assistant on the EPSRC project looking at women's under-representation in university spinouts. Her ESRC-funded doctorate at the University of Warwick explored how gender is embedded in flexible working practices. Heather's wider research interests are around gender and work, work–life balance and feminist organisational theory.

Helen Lawton Smith is Professor of Entrepreneurship, Department of Management, Birkbeck, University of London, and is the Director of the Centre for Innovation Management Research. Her research interests are in entrepreneurship, innovation, public policy and regional development in national and international contexts. She has authored two monographs, edited ten books, numerous book chapters, and is widely published in academic journals.

Simonetta Manfredi is Professor of Equality and Diversity Management, Associate Dean for Research and Knowledge Exchange (ADRKE), and Founding Director of the Centre for Diversity Policy Research and Practice at Oxford Brookes University. She has led a number of studies and knowledge exchange initiatives on women's careers and participation in leadership roles in HE. These include a project on Women and Spinouts: A case for Action, funded by the EPSRC under their Inclusion Matters programme.

Azzurra Meoli is Assistant Professor in Entrepreneurship at the University of Bologna. Her research interests fall primarily within the area entrepreneurship and innovation. In particular, she focuses on new venture creation and crowdfunding. She earned a PhD in Management at the University of Bologna in March 2018.

Rosa Morales is Associate Professor at the Department of Economics, UDEM Business School, Universidad de Monterrey. She holds a BA in Economics from Universidad de Carabobo (Venezuela) and a PhD in Economics from

Claremont Graduate University. She researches on innovation, patents, and gender in Latin America, with publications in *Scientometrics*, the *Journal of Economic Behaviour and Organizations*, and the *Brazilian Journal of Innovation*.

Elvis Nyanzu is a Research Associate at Oxford Brookes Business School. His research interest focuses on understanding spatial productivity patterns, socio-economic inequality and urban and regional policies. He has worked on several projects including the production of the English Atlas of Inequality. He is currently working on a research project focused on the functional relationships between city centres and their hinterlands as well as the relative benefits of industrial specialisation and/or diversification across space.

Anthony N-Yelkabong is Research and Engagement Officer of the GCRF-funded RECIRCULATE Project at Lancaster University, Ghana, supporting new partnership-based approaches and enabling African researchers to grow transformational impact working with, in and for their communities. He co-develops and co-delivers training modules to stimulate entrepreneurial thinking among academics in Africa.

Priscilla Otuo is a Research Associate in Entrepreneurship and Innovation. She works on the UKRI/GCRF RECIRCULATE Project at Lancaster University Ghana. Her research focuses on issues regarding firm growth and innovation in African economies.

Beldina Owalla is a Research Fellow at the Faculty of Business and Law, University of Portsmouth. Her research focuses on understanding the impact of gender and culture on entrepreneurship and innovation activities in different geographical contexts. She has worked on projects on SME productivity, diversity and inclusion in business innovation, and growth strategies of community businesses. Her other research interests are in women's entrepreneurship, entrepreneurship education, leadership, SME growth and venture finance.

Afua Owusu-Kwarteng is a Doctoral Researcher completing a Lancaster University funded PhD contributing to the Entrepreneurship and Innovation strand of the GCRF-funded RECIRCULATE Project supporting new partnership-based approaches and enabling African researchers to grow transformational impact working with, in and for their communities. Her PhD examines gender dimensions of industry/academia knowledge exchange practices.

Ilenia Picardi is Assistant Professor in Sociology at the University of Naples Federico II (UNINA), Italy. She holds a PhD in Mind Gender Language and a PhD in Physics. Her research activity focuses on Social Studies of

Science and Technology, mainly on issues related to the social impact of techno-science, environmental sustainability, intersectionality in scientific research and academia. Currently she is in charge of the Gender Studies in Science and Technology area at the Gender Observatory on university and research at UNIN.

Vishal Rituraj is a Doctoral student in the Strategy area at the Smith School of Business, Queen's University. He holds an MBA from SP Jain School of Global Management and holds an undergraduate degree in engineering from Birla Institute of Technology Mesra in India. His research interests lie in the field of strategic and public policy research in the domain of the Fourth Industrial Revolution.

Katindi Sivi is an African Futurist, working with individuals, organisations and governments to unpack complexity and make sense of future possibilities for strategic change in an uncertain and rapidly changing world, through research, policy analysis, strategic foresight and training. She has published work in, among other areas, Africa's youth demographics and the future of African women and contributed to various policy frameworks.

Alexis Still completed her MSc in Social Anthropology from the University of Oxford in 2018, and has a particular interest in cultural constructions of gender, migration, social justice and mental health. She is currently undertaking an ESRC-funded doctorate exploring the effects of cultural dislocation on mental health treatment in the Ghanaian diaspora.

Besrat Tesfaye is Associate Professor of Business Administration and works as senior lecturer at Södertörn University in Stockholm, Sweden. Her research interests lie within the areas of entrepreneurship and innovation. Her current research focuses on the patent system and the SMEs, high-technology entrepreneurship in the suburbs, and women in entrepreneurship in low income economies.

Victoria Tonks is a regional partnerships manager at the University of West London with a keen interest in gender issues, particularly female entrepreneurship, having launched and run her own business in the 1990s. In 2014 she applied for a charity job to raise corporate sponsorship for a project supporting entrepreneurial projects in Central Africa. Victoria completed an MSc in Management at Birkbeck College which enabled her to conduct research with female entrepreneurs in the Democratic Republic of Congo.

Charikleia Tzanakou is a Senior Lecturer in Human Resource Management, at Oxford Brookes Business School. She is affiliated with the Centre for Diversity Policy Research and Practice at Oxford Brookes University where she has led and co-led various projects focusing on: women and spinouts; Europe-wide gender certification systems, gender and structural change; impact of Covid-19 on inequalities. She is an expert on organisational change and gender equality with a focus on higher education. Her wider research interests fall within gender and diversity in organisations and professions, highly skilled migration and transitions from education to employment.

Vidhula Venugopal is Assistant Professor in the Strategy and Entrepreneurship area at the Indian Institute of Management Nagpur (IIMN). Her research interest spans the areas of entrepreneurship, strategy, gender, and migration. She has published her research in top ranked peer-reviewed journals in her area. She teaches courses on entrepreneurship and future of work & strategy and also leads the Centre for Entrepreneurship at IIMN.

Allan Villegas-Mateos is a Postdoctoral Researcher at HEC Paris in Qatar and holds a PhD in Business Administration from EGADE Business School, Tecnologico de Monterrey (Mexico). His research is focused on understanding the local entrepreneurial ecosystem. He is a member of the National System of Researchers (Mexico) and of Beta Gamma Sigma honor society.

Tim Vorley is Pro Vice-Chancellor and Dean of Oxford Brookes Business School, Oxford Brookes University. He is Professor of Industry, Enterprise and Innovation and convenes the ESRC/Innovate UK funded Innovation Caucus. His academic interests are broadly in the policy and practice of entrepreneurship and innovation. He has written and edited several books and published widely in academic journals.

Christina Wainikka is a policy expert and researcher in the areas of innovation and intellectual property rights. She has not only covered the legal rules as such but also the impact of different types of rules. She has written six books and published several articles and book chapters.

Guang Ying Mo is Senior Research Associate at Ryerson University and obtained her PhD in Sociology from the University of Toronto. Her research fields are organisational communication, collaboration and innovation, social support for underrepresented groups, and social media. Her current work is focusing on entrepreneurship and employment equity for underrepresented groups.

Foreword by Dr Emily Nott

We live in a richly multicultural world, and it is widely accepted that diversity and inclusion not only matter, but also actively enhance economic and societal outcomes. When thinking about diversity, a lot of attention has been given to gender, age and ethnicity.

Of course, diversity extends well beyond these three categories. In addition to the nine protected characteristics, it is important to consider different educations and different socio-economic backgrounds. However, even when considering these three characteristics, they can rarely be considered independently. The importance of intersectionality has implications for the lives and experience of individuals, whether an individual is a black/white, young/old, man/woman.

The language of diversity and inclusion has become widespread and is now a prominent focus for many organisations. Beyond the moral imperative, the benefits of diversity mean that it is not just 'a nice to have' but increasingly a critical success factor for businesses. Academic researchers and business leaders alike continue to recognise the value of a diverse and inclusive workforce as a source of competitive advantage.

Further to diversity being generally regarded as good for business, the importance of a diverse workforce has been shown as a key driver in harnessing innovation. Building diverse teams and promoting diversity among aspiring innovators and entrepreneurs is key to stimulating the creation of new products, processes and services. Given the importance of innovation to the competitiveness of the economy and growth of individual firms, it is imperative that the value and importance of diversity is both understood and embraced.

Beyond business, there is an onus on governments and innovation agencies to promote the inclusive innovation agenda. We have seen a growing number of examples, with innovation agencies targeting underrepresented groups, for example women in innovation. There have also been initiatives to encourage young innovators, ethnic minority innovators, and disabled innovators, in order to promote awareness and engagement of innovation opportunities beyond the usual suspects.

Progress continues to be made in promoting diversity, but there is still much more that needs to be done and barriers to overcome. There is of course an imperative on businesses, who are likely to be the direct beneficiaries of more diverse teams. However, there remain systemic and structural challenges that require changes to policy and practice, institutional and societal structures. While this is beyond the scope of any single business or government, everyone needs to be a part of the solution.

If individuals, businesses, and economies are to realise their innovation goals, there is a need to embrace and promote the wider equality, diversity, and inclusion agendas in the coming years. In reading this edited collection, many of the key issues we need to address in harnessing innovation are identified through the different cases. In thinking specifically about the importance of context, the barriers facing diversity and the challenges of intersectionality, the contributors to this book raise important observations and reflections on the concepts, policies, and practices fundamental to promoting inclusive innovation.

Dr Emily Nott
Head of Diversity and Inclusion Programmes
Innovate UK-UKRI

Acknowledgements

As editors we are extremely grateful to the chapter authors for their excellent and insightful contributions. Without their efforts this book would not have been possible.

The idea for this book came from an Innovation Caucus project on Equality, Diversity and Inclusion among innovators, and we are grateful to the Economic and Social Research Council (ESRC) and Innovate UK for the grant funding (ES/T000570/2).

We are also grateful for the support of the Global Women's Entrepreneurship Policy (Global WEP) network, which includes over 40 research scholars from 35 countries, who critically review and compare women's entrepreneurship policy from a gender perspective.

We would also like to thank the team at Edward Elgar Publishing for their patience and guidance throughout the publishing process, and especially as we prepared the final manuscript.

1. Introduction: promoting inclusive innovation

Tim Vorley, Helen Lawton Smith and Beldina Owalla

1. INTRODUCTION

Entrepreneurship and innovation are pervasive concepts in academic and policy discourses. The potential impact of entrepreneurship and innovation on societal and economic growth, recovery and sustainability is globally recognized. This has led to the proliferation of policies and initiatives aimed at increasing the level of innovation activity in the UK and globally (Pettersson and Lindberg, 2013). However, until recently, these policies mainly targeted product development and focused on sectors primarily dominated by men, like manufacturing and technology industries (Lindberg et al., 2015). Despite the broadened focus, many innovation policies and initiatives still adopt a gender-blind perspective that assumes equal outcomes in science and technology (Lee and Pollitzer, 2016).

Gender blindness conceals the gendered nature of the innovation processes (Pecis, 2016). By focusing on innovation products, processes and systems, the role of the innovator has been overlooked (Alsos et al., 2013). Therefore, while the positive impact of gender diversity on creativity and innovation is well-evidenced (Bouncken, 2004; Dai et al., 2019; Díaz-García et al., 2013), the role of diversity in innovation processes within the lens of entrepreneurship, that is, how individuals mobilize resources and processes in creating value through innovation, remains under-explored. Thus, the implications of an under-utilization of the full range of talent, potential and creativity available in the workforce are missed (Etzkowitz et al., 2020) and need to be addressed. The role of place (geographic context) in influencing the distribution of capital, access to networks, and recognition/creation of innovation opportunities also needs to be further explored (Blake and Hanson, 2005).

Innovation and technological development are highly gender-skewed. For example, studies highlight the under-representation of women in STEM fields regardless of whether the population considered is students, faculty members, graduates, top managers or entrepreneurs (Kuschel et al., 2020). Even though several studies have been carried out in this area, it is unclear as to how to address these inequalities (Gorbacheva et al., 2019). While the gendered nature of entrepreneurship is more widely acknowledged (Jennings and Brush, 2013), policies still tend to adopt neo-liberal perspectives that subordinate women to the economic agenda and focus on their inadequacies or extraordinariness (Ahl and Nelson, 2015; Coleman et al., 2019). The challenges in reaction to innovation policies are more acute, with less awareness and fewer initiatives aimed at promoting the participation of under-represented groups.

Achieving inclusive innovation, that is, a view of innovation that embraces both the diversity of the actors and the activities involved, therefore requires a holistic understanding of the heterogeneity of innovators involved, as well as the broader structural factors (e.g. societal expectations, cultural norms, regulations, politics, place, religion, etc.) that influence their activities within ecosystems (Brush et al., 2019; Foss et al., 2019; Henry et al., 2017). Central to this is understanding the intersectionality of socio-demographic categories such as age, race, ethnicity, class, ability status and so on, which have been consistently shown to create additional barriers for under-represented groups (Carter et al., 2015; Marlow and Martinez Dy, 2018; Vorley et al., 2020), in order to formulate more effective interventions and in promoting system change.

In addition to exploring the gendered aspects of innovation, this book provides insights into the diversity of innovators and how to promote greater inclusive innovation. It focuses on the heterogeneity of women entrepreneurs and the intersecting social categories such as age, gender, race, ethnicity, ability status, social status and so on that influence their participation in innovation activities. It also addresses the broader contextual and institutional factors within the ecosystem that act as enablers or inhibitors of women entrepreneurs' innovation activities. The book contributes to a more comprehensive understanding of how policies and interventions can effectively support diversity and inclusion within business innovation. It develops themes picked up in the GWEP-OECD Report, and looks to explore different dimensions of gender, diversity and inclusive innovation. The remainder of this introductory chapter focuses first on the concepts of gender, diversity and innovation, before outlining the structure of the book and the contributions of the twenty-nine contributors.

2.   GENDER, DIVERSITY AND INNOVATION IN FOCUS

Active participation in entrepreneurship, and particularly innovative entrepreneurship with growth aspects, remains elusive for many social groups including, but not limited to, women, youth and immigrants. The aim of inclusive entrepreneurship and innovation research, policies and practice is therefore to ensure that entrepreneurship and innovation is a feasible option for all, regardless of their gender, age, place of birth, or other personal characteristics (OECD, 2019). Women have been one of the key targets of many of these initiatives, given the persistent gender gaps in all areas of social and economic life.

However, while women have been involved in enterprise and owned/ managed businesses for decades, they only became 'visible' in academia in the late 1970s/early 1980s (Jennings and Brush, 2013). A number of major milestones were then reached in the late 1990s/2000s. These included: the first academic special issue (i.e. *Entrepreneurship and Regional Development* journal) in 1997; the first dedicated policy (i.e. OECD) and academic-oriented (i.e. Diana International) conferences held in 1998 and 2003 respectively; and the first speciality journal (i.e. *International Journal of Gender and Entrepreneurship*) launched in 2009 (Jennings and Brush, 2013). Since then, growing attention to the phenomenon of women's entrepreneurship has been largely driven by its importance for economic growth and societal well-being (Brush et al., 2009; Poggesi et al., 2016; Wilson et al., 2007).

2.1 Background to Gender Research in Entrepreneurship and Innovation

Women's entrepreneurship research derives its intellectual origins from two broader areas of scholarship, that is, the gender and occupations literature, and feminist theory research (Jennings and Brush, 2013). Studies on women in the labour force found that despite the increase in women's employment since the 1960s, the workforce remained sharply segregated, and clearly stratified with women occupying the lower ranks (Jennings and Brush, 2013). Feminist theories have also been used to address issues of gender within entrepreneurship. These can be categorized into three main groups: (a) the liberal feminist theory which views men and women as essentially similar; (b) the social feminist theory which views both sexes as essentially different, but equally valid and legitimate; and (c) the social constructionist feminist theory which views masculinity and femininity as socially constructed (Ahl, 2006; Fischer et al., 1993).

Similar to research on women in the labour force, research on women entrepreneurs has largely focused on comparing them to their male counterparts. These studies mainly highlighted the discrepancies between the two groups in terms of the type of firms they start up, access to networks, access to capital, and the level of societal support received (Henry et al., 2015; Ljunggren and Kolvereid, 1996; OECD, 2017). Other common themes were related to differences in personality or psychological traits such as levels of self-efficacy, self-perception, risk taking propensity, desire for autonomy or entrepreneurial intentions (Delmar and Holmquist, 2004; Gatewood et al., 1995; Lo et al., 2012; Sexton and Bowman-Upton, 1990; Verheul and Thurik, 2001). While collectively this research made major contributions in advancing the field of women's entrepreneurship as well as in highlighting the gendered aspects of the entrepreneurship phenomenon (Jennings and Brush, 2013), the constant comparison to male entrepreneurs inadvertently also contributed to the highly gendered perception of women entrepreneurs as being somewhat inferior to their male counterparts (Ahl, 2006).

Entrepreneurship was constructed as a manly pursuit, with women's entrepreneurship portrayed as 'the other' (Ahl, 2007; Nilsson, 1997; Smith, 2010). Furthermore, by rendering the masculine component of gender invisible, research and policies continue to perpetuate the assumption of the male model as the norm, with any deviations being viewed as anomalies (Kimmel, 2008). As a result, that which is associated with the feminine is portrayed as being in contrast to the dominant entrepreneurial characterization (Bruni et al., 2004; Marlow and McAdam, 2012). Likewise, studies of the gendered aspects of innovation research, policies and practice highlight a pattern of segregation between female- and male-dominated sectors, with higher importance being ascribed to the male-dominated manufacturing and high-tech industries, compared to feminized sectors such as education, the public sector or services industries (Alsos et al., 2013; Lindberg et al., 2015).

The under-representation of women in innovation-driven start-ups makes visible the double masculinity that exists at the intersections of innovation and entrepreneurship fields (Kuschel et al., 2020). Despite comparability with male colleagues in terms of qualifications and accomplishments, there is a continuing marginalization of women in science, technology, engineering and mathematics (STEM) fields that are notably important for innovation and technological development (Kuschel et al., 2020; Walters and McNeely, 2010). The causes of these inequalities are largely attributed to either psychological factors such as gender stereotypes and perceptions of STEM fields as masculine, or to structural factors such as the lack of role models, limited access to networks and organization cultures (Botella et al., 2019; Hardey, 2019; Vitores and Gil-Juárez, 2016).

2.2   Focus on Diversity within Gender

Over time, there has been a shift from solely considering gender as a variable, to viewing gender as a social construct that subordinates the female and presents gender-related barriers to women's entrepreneurship and innovation (Brush et al., 2009; Carter et al., 2012). However, there is still a need to understand the root causes for existing gender inequalities, and how policy interventions can most effectively address these issues (Gorbacheva et al., 2019; Henry et al., 2017). Furthermore, studies also argue for the need to pay greater attention to the differences among women entrepreneurs/innovators in terms of their gender, race, class, and so on, in order to avoid portraying women as a homogeneous group and reproducing hegemonic feminism (Knight, 2016; Marlow, 2014; Pettersson and Lindberg, 2013).

The concept of diversity is broadly defined as any observable (gender, ethnicity, age) and non-observable (cognitive, personality types, education) traits that are used to differentiate one individual from the other (Roberson, 2006). Diversity management research mainly focuses on understanding how systems and practices within organizations can be improved to ensure better outcomes from marginalized groups (Leslie, 2019). In entrepreneurship and innovation research, intersectionality has been viewed as a useful lens through which to view diversity and inclusion. As a critical theory, intersectionality conceptualizes knowledge as situated, contextual, relational and reflective of political and economic power (Atewologun, 2018). It defines the interactions between social categories of difference such as age, gender, race, class and so on, in individual lives, social practices, cultural ideologies, and institutional arrangements, and the subsequent outcomes of these interactions in terms of power (Davis, 2008; Samuels and Ross-Sheriff, 2008). Adopting an intersectional perspective therefore provides us with a framework to analyse the interconnections and interdependencies between social categories and structural systems, which reproduce a given group's social positioning and impacts their ability to mobilize resources for engaging in entrepreneurship and innovation (Romero and Valdez, 2016).

The implicit assumption that individual actors have equal access to resources, participation and support within ecosystems does not hold in general (Brush et al., 2019). These discrepancies are even more pronounced in times of crises, as the Covid-19 pandemic has shown, with those positioned at the intersections of social categories (gender, age, ability status, class) being more adversely affected (Martinez Dy and Jayawarna, 2020). Thus, in order to improve ecosystems for women, and other groups located at the margins, more fine-grained analyses of the resource providers, the connectors within ecosystems, as well as the institutional environment embedded within it is necessary (Foss et al., 2019). Contextual factors such as place, culture, social norms, politics, legislations, financial markets and so on, that are in essence ecosystem attributes, have been shown to impact women's entrepreneurial choices and behaviours (Baughn et al., 2006; Carter et al., 2012; DeVita et al., 2014).

Entrepreneurship and innovation are social and relational processes involving multiple actors and occurring in diverse contexts. An explicit recognition of gender, while acknowledging the importance of intersectionality and context (Brush et al., 2019; Marlow and Martinez Dy, 2018; Welter and Baker,

2020), will contribute to our knowledge of the multi-level factors influencing women's entrepreneurship and innovation. It will also provide a more comprehensive and holistic understanding of ecosystems, and how to promote inclusive and sustainable economic growth and societal well-being.

3.   STRUCTURE AND OUTLINE

The book is structured in two parts. Part I, chapters 2–8 explore questions of diversity and innovation in different innovation contexts. The seven contributions present a series of alternative perspectives, focusing primarily on the impact of gender while also raising questions of intersectionality. Part II, chapters 9–14 focus on innovation policies, programmes and initiatives in different ecosystems while addressing gender and diversity. The focus of these six chapters consider the different support initiatives and highlights good practice, as well as the implications and impacts on diverse innovators.

PART I: DIVERSITY AND INNOVATION IN DIFFERENT CONTEXTS

In Chapter 2 *James Bort and Azzurra Meoli* explore the proposition that gender differences in capital markets do exist, and are impacting the outcomes associated with entrepreneurial financing. Focusing on crowdfunding specifically, Bort and Meoli find that this model is more democratic and reduces the advantages held by male entrepreneurs that are commonly experienced in more traditional finance markets. In advancing a conceptual model, they propose an agenda for future empirical research to explore the differences in the equity of explicitly prosocial crowdfunding contexts. The chapter concludes by reflecting on implications for practice, as well as the opportunities and challenges facing women founders pursuing innovative new ventures.

There have been many attempts at explaining the gender disparity in entrepreneurship from economic and policy perspectives. In Chapter 3 *Cecelia Dotzler and M. Gloria González-Morales* draw on concepts from organizational psychology, feminism, leadership, and entrepreneurship studies to explain the lack of representation of women pursuing entrepreneurial and innovative endeavours. The chapter proposes the need for a more relational culture in STEM, and includes a call to action with recommendations to address the under-representation of diverse groups of entrepreneurs and innovators.

Chapter 4 by *Heather Griffiths, Simonetta Manfredi, Alexis Still and Charikleia Tzanakou* focuses on the under-representation of women as founders of university spin-offs in the UK. The conceptual framework focuses on institutional and structural barriers that universities need to address if they are to change this situation which appears to be related to gender stereotypes within academic STEM subjects and gender bias in business and investment communities. The ambiguity in some universities about the value of academic entrepreneurship provides the context for the study. The chapter highlights the intersecting inequalities, in this case around age and ethnicity, that exacerbate this situation and concludes with a series of recommendations.

Focused on the Swedish context, Chapter 5 by *Besrat Tesfaye and Christina Wainikka* draws attention to the obstacles encountered by women entrepreneurs in technology-based enterprises. It explores how their experiences of invention, innovation and entrepreneurship are affected by the male-dominated industry context. The chapter supports the insights into backgrounds, characteristics and experiences of women entrepreneurs, with primary data being based on interviews with members of the Swedish Inventors Association. The issue of intersectionality is highlighted through the personal profiles of women entrepreneurs, as well as the nature of their inventions.

Exploring the gender-specific challenges facing women entrepreneurs, Chapter 6 by *Victoria Tonks and Helen Lawton Smith* adopts the expanded 5M 'gender aware' framework for women's entrepreneurship, to understand whether and how gender is an inhibitor to innovation activities. The expanded framework builds on the traditional 3Ms that is, Money, Management and Market factors, to allow for the consideration of 'Macro' (e.g. legal status of women, gender equality) and 'Meso' (e.g. motherhood, family responsibility) factors in its analysis. Based on the empirical context of the Democratic Republic of Congo (DRC), the chapter explores the intersectional nature of barriers facing women entrepreneurs, and how these can be overcome to enhance entrepreneurial activity. The chapter argues that the pursuit of equality and social recognition can further fuel women entrepreneurs' ambitions and ensure increased participation in the innovation space.

Chapter 7 by *Silvia Cervia* advances a theoretical framework based on the relational theory of gender, focusing on innovation in the healthcare sector. In exploring an experience-based co-design (EBCD) in the healthcare setting, the chapter examines how services are able to address and satisfy unmet social needs. In critiquing the concept of gendered social innovation the discussion introduces the notion of gendering social innovation to better understand how social innovation centred on social relations can positively impact the equity and social justice of outcomes.

The final chapter of the section focuses on diversity and inclusion in the UK context, specifically with regard to women-led SMEs' innovation activities. Using an intersectional lens, Chapter 8 by *Beldina Owalla, Tim Vorley and Elvis Nyanzu* focuses on analysing how gender, ethnicity and place intersect to impact SMEs' engagement in innovation, and provide recommendations on how policy initiatives can support under-represented founders' participation in business innovation. The intersectional approach adopted allows the authors to emphasize the agentic processes and wider structural forces that often impact a social group's positioning and influences their ability to access or mobilize resources. In conclusion, the chapter highlights the fragmented nature of current support, while acknowledging the complexities and interconnectedness of ecosystems. It also recommends a more holistic approach to achieving inclusive economic growth.

PART II: INNOVATION POLICIES, INITIATIVES AND ECOSYSTEMS

Exploring the potential and actual bias in narrow artificial intelligence (AI) systems, *Vidhula Venugopal and Vishal Rituraj* thematically analyse the AI policies of 21 countries across Europe, Asia-Pacific, Middle East and Americas in Chapter 9. Given that bias may be related to that of the programmer or data from existing structures, the chapter argues that innovation policy, particularly with regard to AI should focus on minimizing, if not eliminating bias and discrimination based on gender by anticipating developments in technology where bias may creep in. The chapter concludes by recommending best practices to ensure greater inclusion and fairness in the use of AI.

The focus of Chapter 10 concerns how affirmative action can exacerbate exclusion, and further marginalize women innovators and entrepreneurs. *Katindi Sivi* draws on a case study of Kenya to understand how affirmative entrepreneurship and innovation policies and programmes have resulted in heightened gender unemployment and underemployment profiles. The chapter also explores the question of intersectionality, with respect to age, ethnicity, religion, social status and level of education. The discussion concludes by highlighting the need to consider the unintended consequences of affirmative action policies. It also serves as a crucial reminder to ensure that policy programmes and outcomes are continually monitored and evaluated in order to assess whether they are achieving their intended aims.

The third chapter in this section explores the concept of 'gendered innovation' in the development of scientific research and technological innovation. Based on feminist Science and Technology Studies (STS) perspectives, Chapter 11 by *Ilenia Picardi* argues for a co-evolutionary notion of innovation, that is, 'sociotechnical change', within which individual and collective actors, standards, technological devices, scientific knowledge, skills and knowledge come together in specific associations. Specifically, the chapter investigates the theoretical models of innovation adopted (sometimes implicitly) in policies and projects aimed at promoting gendered innovation and responsible research. Picardi examines how gender informs the technoscientific governance of researchers and innovation, and reciprocally, how technoscientific governance informs the concept of gender and gendered practices among scientific and research institutions. The chapter concludes by underlining the relevance of an ontological model to present a new focus on the *sociomateriality* of gender innovations.

The focus of Chapter 12 by *Allan Villegas-Mateos and Rosa Morales* is on the impact of business institutional context on women's innovative entrepreneurship in emerging and Latin American countries. The analytical theme is that of institutional voids – in other words where women lack access to resources, support and ability to participate compared to their male counterparts. The chapter uses data drawn from the World Bank database index of ease of doing business. The chapter also highlights intersectionality through the different contexts which the analysis considers, with respect to the profile of female opportunity-driven entrepreneurs (as women entrepreneurs and as innovators) and differing institutional arrangements.

A conceptual analysis of the salient informal institutional structures impacting women innovation in sub-Saharan Africa is presented in Chapter 13. The chapter by *Priscilla Otuo, Cynthia Forson, Afua Owusu-Kwarteng and Anthony N-Yelkabong* employs legitimacy theory to understand ways in which gendered norms, attitudes and value shape and mediate African women entrepreneurs' innovation behaviour with respect to their motivation, innovation processes and innovation outcomes. Intersectionality underpins the analysis as the authors take a multi-layered perspective seeking to identify moderating effects of informal structures in the societal context, setting and situated activity (institutional) and self (individual) levels of social action.

Lastly, Chapter 14, *Wendy Cukier, Guang Ying Mo and Jodi-Ann Francis* place intersectionality at the heart of their analysis. The chapter adopts an intersectional lens in order to contribute to a better understanding of the complex, multi-level factors affecting women's involvement in innovation. The context and focus of the chapter are the complexities of innovation ecosystems in Canada. They analyse the macro-, meso- and micro-levels and the interactions between them. The policy agenda relates to how current conceptualizations and support for innovation and entrepreneurship exclude women. The chapter concludes with recommendations of actions to be taken to support the development of more inclusive ecosystems.

In the final chapter, as editors, we offer some reflections on the contributions in this edited collection. As well as providing commentary on the big issues raised by the contributors and what this means for the future of gender, diversity and innovation research and practice, we identify directions for further research. Clearly with the importance of these issues now increasingly recognized among innovation agencies and governments around the world, there remains an ongoing need to ensure that gender and diversity, and their complex intersections, continue to be addressed. It is only in this way that society will realize the potential of all innovators regardless of their diverse backgrounds.

REFERENCES

Ahl, H. (2006), "Why research on women entrepreneurs needs new directions", *Entrepreneurship Theory and Practice*, Vol. 30 No. 5, pp. 595–621.

Ahl, H. (2007), "Sex business in the toy store: A narrative analysis of a teaching case", *Journal of Business Venturing*, Vol. 22 No. 5, pp. 673–693.

Ahl, H. and Nelson, T. (2015), "How policy positions women entrepreneurs: A comparative analysis of state discourse in Sweden and the United States", *Journal of Business Venturing*, Vol. 30 No. 2, pp. 273–291.

Alsos, G.A., Ljunggren, E. and Hytti, U. (2013), "Gender and innovation: State of the art and a research agenda", *International Journal of Gender and Entrepreneurship*, Vol. 5 No. 3, pp. 236–256.

Atewologun, D. (2018), "Intersectionality theory and practice", *Oxford Research Encyclopedia of Business and Management*, Oxford University Press, https://doi .org/10.1093/acrefore/9780190224851.013.48.

Baughn, C.C., Chua, B.-L. and Neupert, K.E. (2006), "The normative context for women's participation in entrepreneurship: A multicountry study", *Entrepreneurship: Theory and Practice*, Vol. 30 No. 5, pp. 687–708.

Blake, M.K. and Hanson, S. (2005), "Rethinking innovation: Context and gender", *Environment and Planning A: Economy and Space*, Vol. 37 No. 4, pp. 681–701.

Botella, C., Rueda, S., López-Iñesta, E. and Marzal, P. (2019), "Gender diversity in STEM disciplines: A multiple factor problem", *Entropy: An International and Interdisciplinary Journal of Entropy and Information Studies*, Vol. 21 No. 1, p. 30.

Bouncken, R.B. (2004), "Cultural diversity in entrepreneurial teams: Findings of new ventures in Germany", *Creativity and Innovation Management*, Vol. 13 No. 4, pp. 240–253.

Bruni, A., Gherardi, S. and Poggio, B. (2004), "Doing gender, doing entrepreneurship: An ethnographic account of intertwined practices", *Gender, Work and Organization*, Vol. 11 No. 4, pp. 406–429.

Brush, C., Edelman, L.F., Manolova, T. and Welter, F. (2019), "A gendered look at entrepreneurship ecosystems", *Small Business Economics*, Vol. 53 No. 2, pp. 393–408.

Brush, C.G., de Bruin, A. and Welter, F. (2009), "A gender-aware framework for women's entrepreneurship", *International Journal of Gender and Entrepreneurship*, Vol. 1 No. 1, pp. 8–24.

Carter, S., Marlow, S. and Bennett, D. (2012), "Gender and entrepreneurship", *Enterprise and Small Business: Principles, Practice and Policy*, pp. 218–231.

Carter, S., Mwaura, S., Ram, M., Trehan, K. and Jones, T. (2015), "Barriers to ethnic minority and women's enterprise: Existing evidence, policy tensions and unsettled questions", *International Small Business Journal*, Vol. 33 No. 1, pp. 49–69.

Coleman, S., Henry, C., Orser, B., Foss, L. and Welter, F. (2019), "Policy support for women entrepreneurs' access to financial capital: Evidence from Canada, Germany, Ireland, Norway, and the United States", *Journal of Small Business Management*, Vol. 57 No. S2, pp. 296–322.

Dai, Y., Byun, G. and Ding, F. (2019), "The direct and indirect impact of gender diversity in new venture teams on innovation performance", *Entrepreneurship: Theory and Practice*, Vol. 43 No. 3, pp. 505–528.

Davis, K. (2008), "Intersectionality as buzzword: A sociology of science perspective on what makes a feminist theory successful", *Feminist Theory*, Vol. 9 No. 1, pp. 67–85.

Delmar, F. and Holmquist, C. (2004), "Women's entrepreneurship: Issues and policies ", *2nd OECD Conference of Ministers Responsible for Small and Medium-Sized Enterprises (SMEs) Istanbul, Turkey 3–5 June 2004*.

DeVita, L., Mari, M. and Poggesi, S. (2014), "Women entrepreneurs in and from developing countries: Evidences from the literature", *European Management Journal*, Vol. 32 No. 3, pp. 451–460.

Díaz-García, C., González-Moreno, A. and Sáez-Martínez, F.J. (2013), "Gender diversity within R & D teams: Its impact on radicalness of innovation", *Innovation: Management, Policy and Practice*, Vol. 15 No. 2, pp. 149–160.

Etzkowitz, H., Smith, H.L., Henry, C. and Poulovassilis, A. (2020), "Introduction: Pipeline break", *Gender, Science and Innovation*, Cheltenham, UK and Northampton, MA, USA: Edward Elgar Publishing.

Fischer, E.M., Reuber, A.R. and Dyke, L.S. (1993), "A theoretical overview and extension of research on sex, gender, and entrepreneurship", *Journal of Business Venturing*, Vol. 8 No. 2, pp. 151–168.

Foss, L., Henry, C., Ahl, H. and Mikalsen, G.H. (2019), "Women's entrepreneurship policy research: A 30-year review of the evidence", *Small Business Economics*, Vol. 53 No. 2, pp. 409–429.

Gatewood, E.J., Shaver, K.G. and Gartner, W.B. (1995), "A longitudinal study of cognitive factors influencing start-up behaviors and success at venture creation", *Journal of Business Venturing*, Vol. 10 No. 5, pp. 371–391.

Gorbacheva, E., Beekhuyzen, J., vom Brocke, J. and Becker, J. (2019), "Directions for research on gender imbalance in the IT profession", *European Journal of Information Systems*, Vol. 28 No. 1, pp. 43–67.

Hardey, M. (2019), "Women's leadership and gendered experiences in tech cities", *Gender in Management*, Vol. 34 No. 3, pp. 188–199.

Henry, C., Foss, L. and Ahl, H. (2015), "Gender and entrepreneurship research: A review of methodological approaches", *International Small Business Journal*, https://doi.org/10.1177/0266242614549779.

Henry, C., Orser, B., Coleman, S. and Foss, L. (2017), "Women's entrepreneurship policy: A 13 nation cross-country comparison", *International Journal of Gender and Entrepreneurship*, Vol. 9 No. 3, pp. 206–228.

Jennings, J.E. and Brush, C.G. (2013), "Research on women entrepreneurs: Challenges to (and from) the broader entrepreneurship literature?", *The Academy of Management Annals*, Vol. 7 No. 1, pp. 663–715.

Kimmel, M. (2008), *The Gendered Society*, third edition, New York: Oxford University Press.

Knight, M. (2016), "Race-ing, classing and gendering racialized women's participation in entrepreneurship", *Gender, Work & Organization*, Vol. 23 No. 3, pp. 310–327.

Kuschel, K., Ettl, K., Díaz-García, C. and Alsos, G.A. (2020), "Stemming the gender gap in STEM entrepreneurship – insights into women's entrepreneurship in science, technology, engineering and mathematics", *International Entrepreneurship and Management Journal*, Vol. 16 No. 1, pp. 1–15.

Lee, H. and Pollitzer, E. (2016), *Gender in Science and Innovation as Component of Inclusive Socioeconomic Growth*, London: Portia Limited.

Leslie, L.M. (2019), "Diversity initiative effectiveness: A typological theory of unintended consequences", *Academy of Management Review*, Vol. 44 No. 3, pp. 538–563.

Lindberg, M., Forsberg, L. and Karlberg, H. (2015), "Gendered social innovation: A theoretical lens for analysing structural transformation in organisations and society", *International Journal of Social Entrepreneurship and Innovation*, Vol. 3 No. 6, pp. 472–483.

Ljunggren, E. and Kolvereid, L. (1996), "New business formation: Does gender make a difference?", *Women in Management Review*, Vol. 11 No. 4, pp. 3–12.

Lo, C., Sun, H. and Law, K. (2012), "Comparing the entrepreneurial intention between female and male engineering students", *JWEE*, No. 1–2, pp. 28–51.

Marlow, S. (2014), "Exploring future research agendas in the field of gender and entrepreneurship", *International Journal of Gender and Entrepreneurship*, Vol. 6 No. 2, pp. 102–120.

Marlow, S. and Martinez Dy, A. (2018), "Annual review article: Is it time to rethink the gender agenda in entrepreneurship research?", *International Small Business Journal*, Vol. 36 No. 1, pp. 3–22.

Marlow, S. and McAdam, M. (2012), "Analyzing the influence of gender upon high-technology venturing within the context of business incubation", *Entrepreneurship: Theory and Practice*, Vol. 36 No. 4, pp. 655–676.

Martinez Dy, A. and Jayawarna, D. (2020), "Bios, mythoi and women entrepreneurs: A Wynterian analysis of the intersectional impacts of the COVID-19 pandemic on self-employed women and women-owned businesses", *International Small Business Journal*, Vol. 38 No. 5, pp. 391–403.

Nilsson, P. (1997), "Business counselling services directed towards female entrepreneurs: Some legitimacy dilemmas", *Entrepreneurship and Regional Development*, Vol. 9 No. 3, pp. 239–258.

OECD. (2017), *The Pursuit of Gender Equality*, https://doi.org/10.1787/9789264281318 -en.

OECD. (2019), *The Missing Entrepreneurs 2019*, https://doi.org/10.1787/3ed84801 -en.

Pecis, L. (2016), "Doing and undoing gender in innovation: Femininities and masculinities in innovation processes", *Human Relations*, Vol. 69 No. 11, pp. 2117–2140.

Pettersson, K. and Lindberg, M. (2013), "Paradoxical spaces of feminist resistance: Mapping the margin to the masculinist innovation discourse", *International Journal of Gender and Entrepreneurship*, Vol. 5 No. 3, pp. 323–341.

Poggesi, S., Mari, M. and De Vita, L. (2016), "What's new in female entrepreneurship research? Answers from the literature", *International Entrepreneurship and Management Journal*, Vol. 12 No. 3, pp. 735–764.

Roberson, Q.M. (2006), "Disentangling the meanings of diversity and inclusion in organizations", *Group & Organization Management*, Vol. 31 No. 2, pp. 212–236.

Romero, M. and Valdez, Z. (2016), "Introduction to the special issue: Intersectionality and entrepreneurship", *Ethnic and Racial Studies*, Vol. 39 No. 9, pp. 1553–1565.

Samuels, G.M. and Ross-Sheriff, F. (2008), "Identity, oppression, and power: Feminisms and intersectionality theory", *Affilia: Journal of Women and Social Work*, Vol. 23 No. 1, pp. 5–9.

Sexton, D.L. and Bowman-Upton, N. (1990), "Female and male entrepreneurs: Psychological characteristics and their role in gender-related discrimination", *Journal of Business Venturing*, Vol. 5 No. 1, pp. 29–36.

Smith, R. (2010), "Masculinity, doxa and the institutionalisation of entrepreneurial iden-tity in the novel *Cityboy*", *International Journal of Gender and Entrepreneurship*, Vol. 2 No. 1, pp. 27–48.

Verheul, I. and Thurik, R. (2001), "Start-up capital: 'Does gender matter?'", *Small Business Economics*, Vol. 16 No. 4, pp. 329–346.

Vitores, A. and Gil-Juárez, A. (2016), "The trouble with 'women in computing': A critical examination of the deployment of research on the gender gap in computer science", *Journal of Gender Studies*, Vol. 25 No. 6, pp. 666–680.

Vorley, T., Lawton Smith, H., Coogan, T., Owalla, B. and Wing, K. (2020), *Supporting Diversity and Inclusion in Innovation*. Policy Brief, Innovate UK, Supporting Diversity and Inclusion in Innovation report – GOV.UK (www.gov.uk).

Walters, J. and McNeely, C.L. (2010), "Recasting Title IX: Addressing gender equity in the science, technology, engineering, and mathematics professoriate", *The Review of Policy Research*, Vol. 27 No. 3, pp. 317–332.

Welter, F. and Baker, T. (2020), "Moving contexts onto new roads: Clues from other disciplines", *Entrepreneurship: Theory and Practice*, Vol. 45 No. 5, pp. 1154–1175.

Wilson, F., Kickul, J. and Marlino, D. (2007), "Gender, entrepreneurial self-efficacy, and entrepreneurial career intentions: Implications for entrepreneurship education", *Entrepreneurship: Theory and Practice*, Vol. 31 No. 3, pp. 387–406.

PART I

Diversity and innovation in different contexts

2. Gender and innovation strategy in crowdfunding

James Bort and Azzurra Meoli

1. INTRODUCTION

Crowdfunding is now understood as a distinct and foundational aspect of entrepreneurial finance (Pollack et al., 2019) and is an increasingly important financing source for nascent ventures (Block et al., 2018). More specifically, crowdfunding aids the development of new innovative businesses at their earliest stage, alleviating the financial challenges commonly faced by entrepreneurs (Schwienbacher & Larralde, 2010). As crowdfunding platforms continue to grow and evolve, they allow a wide range of potential investors an unprecedented opportunity to participate in early-stage innovations directly. Crowdfunding offers a world-wide audience (commonly referred to as 'backers') as it is conducted virtually through Internet-based platforms. As such, crowdfunding alleviates traditional barriers like the geography (Sorenson et al., 2016) and social connections (Colombo et al., 2015) of the entrepreneurs. Further, backers on crowdfunding platforms tend to use community logic rather than the market-based logic often employed by professional investors (Vismara, 2019). Community logic emphasizes a commitment to values, trust, and a sense of group membership. Market-based logic instead places pecuniary outcomes center stage. In sum, crowdfunding has the potential to be a democratizing force in financing risky, but innovative ideas that might be shunned by other types of finance (Mollick & Robb, 2016).

The nature of crowdfunding is unique; thus, the theoretical assumptions of traditional methods of entrepreneurial finance might not hold in this context (Drover et al., 2017). Two such paradoxes have recently emerged in crowdfunding literature. First, research on traditional entrepreneurial finance suggests that male entrepreneurs have an edge. Not only are female entrepreneurs drastically underrepresented (Brush et al., 2018), but even displays of femininity can impair success (Balachandra et al., 2019). However, the very recent studies centered on gender in crowdfunding show a more democratic funding process. Thirty-five percent of project leaders on the Kickstarter platform are women, and female founders proposing technological projects are more likely to succeed than men (Greenberg & Mollick, 2017). Moreover, studies highlight that gender not only influences the outcomes of a campaign but will also influence the way the entrepreneur approaches the campaign (Gafni et al., 2019; Moss et al., 2019). Critically, the advantages held by male entrepreneurs in traditional finance dissipate in the crowdfunding context – and potentially even work against them (Johnson et al., 2018).

Second, numerous studies in entrepreneurial finance highlight the positive role of sources of intellectual property, such as patents, in attracting external finance. Signaling a patent reduces information asymmetry between investors and potential entrepreneurs, and acts as an attractive quality signal to prospective external investors (Hsu & Ziedonis, 2013). However, recent evidence on crowdfunding suggests a negative signaling role of intellectual property in accessing funds on crowdfunding platforms (Meoli et al., 2019). Crowdfunding investors are the earliest possible adopters of innovations, directly participating in the development process (Stanko & Henard, 2017) and view engagement as an important attribute of the campaigns they support (Song & Tian, 2020). It follows that these investors would instead prefer open innovation strategies in which they can directly participate. For example, projects in the open-source software movement typically offer to make their source code open to the general public with a non-restrictive license. This software can then be modified freely, and the lifecycle of the project is typically driven by the community interested in the software, rather than solely the corporation who originally developed the product (Lerner & Tirole, 2002).

Taken together, we suggest that crowdfunding is a highly relevant context to glean insights into the relationship between gender and innovation strategies and propose that female entrepreneurs who pursue innovation strategies that are more open in the crowdfunding context will have optimal outcomes. In particular, the community logic affecting the crowdfunding dynamics is in line with open innovation strategies as they have a social orientation. Females on crowdfunding seem to be more inclined and likely to build a community for the project development, both in terms of project financing and support. To test this proposition, we leverage automated web-harvesting techniques and statistical matching techniques (cf. Meoli et al., 2019) to construct a large and representative sample of rewards-based crowdfunding projects signaling their innovation strategy.

This chapter proceeds as follows. First, we review the recent literature concerning female crowdfunding entrepreneurs (e.g., *creators*) and contrast those findings to those found in traditional entrepreneurial finance. Next, we examine the nature of innovations in crowdfunding and how these innovations are perceived by crowdfunding investors (e.g., *backers*). We then build our core proposition, which is then supported by our large sample of crowdfunding data. Last, we outline an agenda for future empirical research and conclude with a discussion on the practical application of this work, highlighting the opportunities that lie ahead for female founders pursuing innovative new ventures.

2.   CROWDFUNDING AND THE FEMALE CREATOR

There is a growing interest among scholars investigating female entrepreneurs' access to external capital (e.g., Alsos et al., 2017; Jennings & Brush, 2017). Several studies offer empirical evidence showing a substantial gender gap in terms of financial resources acquisition. In comparison, women seem to face several setbacks. First, differences exist in terms of financial ambitions (Jennings & Brush, 2017) and as a result, female entrepreneurs tend to obtain a comparatively lower amount of financial resources (e.g., Alsos et al., 2017; Fairlie & Robb, 2009; Verheul & Thurik, 2001). Next, in terms of the method used to finance the venture, research notes that women are less likely to receive funds from traditional sources of external finance, such as bank financing and private equity funding (Coleman & Robb, 2012).

Looking specifically at debt financing, women experience more difficulty obtaining loans from the bank: they have to pay higher interest rates than their male counterparts (Coleman, 2000), and provide more collaterals than men when seeking a bank loan (Calcagnini et al., 2015). Remarkable differences are observable with private equity financing as well: less than 3 percent of venture capital backed companies in the United States had a female CEO (Greene et al., 2001). Moreover, the investments in such ventures tend to be for smaller amounts, with women receiving less than 5 percent of venture capital funds distributed annually (Brush et al., 2004). Over the last thirty years, women have made progress in attracting venture capital. The number of businesses managed by women and receiving capital funds almost tripled; still, a significant gap exists between a business run by women and those operated by men (Brush et al., 2018). Last, attributes associated with female entrepreneurs are more likely to lead to creditability problems (Carter & Rosa, 1998) and some level of discrimination (Balachandra et al., 2019; Malmström et al., 2017).

Despite the field's progress on the relationship between gender and finance, much remains unknown (Malmström et al., 2017), including how this relationship plays out in the crowdfunding context (Pollack et al., 2019). Crowdfunding takes four major forms; rewards-based, equity-based, lending-based, and donation-based. In rewards-based crowdfunding, backers act as early customers receiving a reward or a thank-you note for their financial contribution (Mollick, 2014). In equity-based crowdfunding, the investors purchase the equity of new firms or become part of a profit-sharing agreement

(Drover et al., 2017). Finally, as for the lending and donation models, the first regards offering loans for the development of a project taking as compensation the interest payments; the second consists of pure donations, without any expectation from the project (Pelizzon et al., 2016). While all of these different forms of crowdfunding are useful in understanding how the innovation process unfold and the specific relationship between gender and financing, this research will focus on rewards-based crowdfunding.

Crowdfunding scholars argue that this relatively new method of entrepreneurial finance has the potential to democratize access to capital as it lends itself to inclusivity. One key reason is the way project backers in crowdfunding view investment in comparison to professional investors (Vismara, 2019). In crowdfunding, creators mobilize financial resources for the project through a community creation process (Murray et al., 2020). As these communities grow in size, entrepreneurs are more likely to find their 'crowd' – this can instead be an advantage for female entrepreneurs (Greenberg & Mollick, 2017). Murray and colleagues (2020) theorize a three-step process concerning resource acquisition in crowdfunding that provides some important clues of why this might be the case.

First, the entrepreneur must build a community of like-minded individuals to support the project. With this support, comes a degree risk – crowdfunding backers must have faith that the project creator will deliver on their promises. Thus, trust is an important part of launching a community, and evidence highlights that females have an advantage in this context (Johnson et al., 2018). Second, the entrepreneur must engage with the community in a meaningful way. Community engagement can be time-consuming and might not yield direct financial gain. However, efforts spent engaging with the community offer intrinsic rewards, and can be a fulfilling part of the entrepreneurial process (Bort et al., 2021). Further, previous research notes that female entrepreneurs place emphasis on social, rather than economic goals (Hechavarría et al., 2017). Taken together, this suggests that female creators derive more value from the community building process, and therefore engage with it in a more authentic manner. Third, the community must continuously expand to draw in a broader audience. Individuals are drawn to these platforms in part because supporting these projects has the potential to support their own intrinsic needs (Allison et al., 2015). Thus, by fulfilling the first two elements – building a community and then engaging with it, backers searching for interesting projects to support will have something important to be drawn to ultimately leading to growth.

Structurally speaking, female entrepreneurs are better represented in crowdfunding, and are more likely to hit their funding target (Mollick & Robb, 2016). Further, and consistent with the findings of Johnson and colleagues (2018), women on crowdfunding are perceived as more trustworthy than men, facilitating the willingness to provide finance. Perhaps just as important, females are also well represented among the population of backers (Gafni et al., 2019). Greenberg and Mollick (2017) theorize that homophily plays a role in investing decisions; thus, having a large pool of female backers increases the potential size of the communities, and thus the success of the project. It is worth noting that there are nuances in fund-raising success depending on the crowdfunding form (e.g., rewards-based versus equity). Initial evidence on equity crowdfunding shows that female entrepreneurs perform more closely to what is found in traditional methods of finance (Cumming et al., 2019). This is likely due to the different motives of crowd-based equity finance, which we address further as we discuss our theoretical model and outline an agenda for future research.

2.1   The Unique Nature of Innovation Strategy and Crowdfunding

In the realm of entrepreneurial finance, crowdfunding is generally used in the early stage of development, similar to angel investing and venture capital (Block et al., 2018; Mollick & Robb, 2016). In turn, many high-risk, but innovative projects look to the 'crowd' for support as access to traditional finance might not be feasible due to social or geographic constraints. However, there are relevant differences should an entrepreneur pursue this avenue to fund an innovative venture.

First, while crowdfunding is an important vehicle for obtaining financial sources, raising financial resources is not the only benefit from a crowdfunding campaign. Crowdfunding platforms also serve as a tool for entrepreneurs to bring risky, highly innovative products to an eager and supportive audience (e.g., backers) (Lee et al., 2015). Because backers are central to a campaign's success, it is important to understand their role in the market process. Crowdfunding platforms operate under different business models, with the largest consumer-oriented platforms using a rewards-based model. In other words, the investors in these highly innovative new ventures are more likely to be interested in the end product rather than the company itself. As such, the backers of a project play a participatory role in shaping the project's development (Stanko & Henard, 2017).

Next, differences occur in terms of contractual arrangements. Crowdfunding involves many small investments from a large number of amateur investors with who the creator ultimately has no formal contract (e.g., if the creator doesn't deliver, any intellectual property remains with the creator). Professional investors, on the other hand, employ contractual covenants that protect their investments and may stake a claim on any of the firms' assets, including intellectual property (Hornuf & Schwienbacher, 2018). Second, very well supported theoretical mechanisms for evaluating intellectual property differ. Professional investors typically utilize a quality signal (e.g., patents) to reduce information asymmetry as they evaluate potential innovations (cf. Hsu & Ziedonis, 2013). However, recent exploratory evidence suggests this does not seem to apply when analyzing amateur investors participating in crowdfunding. Meoli et al. (2019) found that crowdfunding campaigns that offered a signal that innovation was closed (e.g., patented, patent-pending, or even the desire to obtain a patent) were those campaigns less likely to be fully funded.

Last, there are nuances among crowdfunding models. The equity crowdfunding model differs from the rewards-based model as for the commitment and engagement with the project. In rewards-based crowdfunding, backers are looking for new projects to invest in and contribute to – investors aim to support product development by sharing feedback for future iterations of the products directly with the entrepreneurs who launched the campaign. On the other hand, equity-based crowdfunding investors tend to be professional investors who are less interested in product development and more interested in typical venture outcomes (e.g., financial returns).

Though the studies focusing on the intersection of innovation and crowdfunding remain sparse, research thus far highlight that the true value of the crowdfunding model is less about the initial financial benefits, but instead the number of backers and their involvement in the campaign (Stanko & Henard, 2017). Small-scale investors in early-stage product development are essentially beta-testers. Whereas a large-scale firm would typically employ individuals to test these products, the small-scale crowdfunding investor not only pays to back the project but more importantly is enthusiastically engaged, viewing the opportunity to provide feedback as another perk (Agrawal et al., 2013; Gerber et al., 2012).

As we highlight above, crowdfunding defies some long-held theories on entrepreneurial finance. The presence of a patent, for example, in a project on the platform, might signal to the crowd that the development activities are already completed and might alienate potential backers from the participation they enjoy (Meoli et al., 2019). Backers are on the front lines of innovation, as they not only provide financial support, but can also bring knowledge and ideas that aid the creator's product development. Thus, the innovation strategy can play an important role, not only in the initial success of the campaign but also in sustainability after the campaign ends (Stanko & Henard, 2017). These stark differences in the way innovation is evaluated call for further theoretical refinement, and the differences are likely to be influenced by the creator's gender.

2.2   Innovative Female Project Creators and Innovation Strategy

Highly innovative startups have higher levels of uncertainty and as such, experience higher failure rates (Hyytinen et al., 2015). However, not all innovation strategies are created equal. A closed innovation strategy is based on the view that innovations take place exclusively inside the company, from the idea generation and development, to the marketing activities. On the other side, an open innovation strategy refers to opening oneself or a firm self to external ideas, processes and technologies throughout the innovation process (Chesbrough, 2003). As for the crowdfunding setting, while closed innovation strategies seem to dissuade potential crowdfunding investors from backing a project (Meoli et al., 2019), the same might not hold for projects utilizing an open innovation strategy (Stanko & Henard, 2017). For several reasons, we argue that projects utilizing an open innovation strategy and led by females will have a competitive advantage in the crowdfunding context.

Individuals who are attracted to open innovations are typically drawn to them for philosophical reasons, that is, the ideology of free and open is important (Stewart & Gosain, 2006). Whereas closed innovations provide a tangible benefit to the owner, open innovations provide a tangible benefit to society at large. Ownership is more akin to stewardship in the context of open innovation, where the owner directs the project, and the beneficiaries are essentially unlimited. This advantage has the potential to manifest in two primary ways. First, evidence suggests that crowdfunding backers utilize communal logics rather than market-based logics. Open innovation is by definition a communal effort – groups of individuals volunteer to manage, contribute, and maintain large-scale open projects, with no direct financial incentive to do so (Lerner & Tirole, 2002). An open strategy offers a more robust communal element for backers, who are predisposed to participating in projects (cf. Eiteneyer et al., 2019), to join in. Next, crowdfunding is participatory by its nature. Backers are early adopters of new and innovative technologies and place value on the ability to shape the development of the project. Open innovations allow individuals to contribute to projects with a great deal of freedom as these projects are typically offered with no licensing requirements and source materials are available free of charge. Thus, the combination of a participatory method of finance, along with intrinsic benefits from participation, is likely to be attractive to these individuals.

Second, female crowdfunding entrepreneurs find an advantage in terms of their perceived trustworthiness (Johnson et al., 2018). This is not only important as crowdfunding projects require a degree of faith in the creator's ability to deliver after the campaign ends, but is also important for open innovation. Contributors to open innovations are typically volunteers and offer their work with no expectation of future payment based on their contributions. Project leaders are then stewards of these resources, and trust that they will be good stewards of these efforts is critical (Fleming & Waguespack, 2007). Last, this community of contributors is also an avenue to overcome resource constraints common in early ventures (Baker & Nelson, 2005). Female entrepreneurs generally raise less money (Mollick & Robb, 2016), but they can potentially make up for this with the resources from their communities of low or no cost contributors (Lifshitz-Assaf, 2018). Thus, we offer the following propositions:

Proposition 1: Female creators pursuing innovative projects will have superior funding performance than males.

Proposition 2: Female creators pursuing innovative projects using an open innovation strategy will have superior funding performance.

3.   RESEARCH DESIGN

Our propositions are concerned with both the gender of the founder, and their innovation strategy within the crowdfunding context. Thus, we gathered data from Kickstarter, a rewards-based platform founded in 2009 for funding creative projects in the arts, technology, game and publishing. Project creators build funding pages that offer numerous details pertaining to the project. Included among these are textual narratives that offer various signals about the project, including the project's innovation strategy (Meoli et al., 2019). More specifically, some projects are completely open source, and others guard their intellectual property through the use of a patent. Project creators can also offer personal information about themselves to potential backers, including their gender.

One exemplar project demonstrating a female creator utilizing an open innovation strategy is 'Osloom', an open-source loom utilized to weave fabric. The project successfully met its funding goal, raising US$10,000 from 197 backers. Leveraging a non-restrictive license, creator Margarita Benitez blended her interests in technology and weaving into a project that builds, and encourages a community to flourish, as she highlights in her pitch:

> I believe that in order for a loom such as OSLOOM to have the greatest amount of impact it would need to operate on an open-source platform. Therefore, the software to operate the loom will be GPL (General Public Licensed) and the hardware will be OHL (Open Hardware Licensed). This would allow other individuals or groups to create this loom or to further develop this loom in the form of a derivative loom. (https://www.kickstarter.com/projects/mbenitez/osloom-an-open-source-jacquard -loom-diy-electrom)

3.1   Sample

To test our propositions, we closely replicate the matching approach utilized by Meoli et al. (2019), differing primarily in that gender serves as the treatment effect. The sample consisted of 1,316 crowdfunding projects where gender could be algorithmically identified, collected from Kickstarter.com, and represents the years 2009 to 2018. These projects signaled either a patent or an open innovation in their text descriptions, which was found via the Kickstarter search engine and then harvested via automated tools. The matching technique resulted in a three-to-one (male to female, consistent with representation in crowdfunding) gender matched sample of 888 projects.

4.   RESULTS

Table 2.1   Average treatment effect of gender (matched sample)

		ATE (Success)		*p*
Test	**Gender***	**Male**	**Female**	
Full Matched Sample (N=888)		0.21	0.30	0.010
Closed Innovation (N=609)		0.17	0.25	0.030
Open Innovation (N=279)		0.29	0.47	0.024
	N	**222**	**666**	

Note: * Gender determined algorithmically by the R package Gender (Mullen, 2020).

Table 2.1 displays tests of average treatment effects.[1] First, consistent with general trends in the crowdfunding literature, female creators were more successful at hitting their funding threshold across the sample. This suggests that regardless of innovation strategy, female creators are likely to find an advantage over their male counterparts in a rewards-based crowdfunding context, supporting our first proposition. Next, while both genders face a penalty for a closed innovation strategy, consistent with Meoli et al. (2019), the penalty is less severe for female creators in comparison with males. Around 25 percent of female-led projects found success, while male success was around 17 percent. Last, and most notable – nearly half of the female creators who pursued an open innovation strategy were successful in obtaining their funding threshold, supporting our second proposition.

In sum, the results show substantial economic effects and offer promising support for our propositions. However, our tests are limited to the rewards-based crowdfunding context, focus only on the initial success of the campaign, and only offer a correlation rather than a cause. Next, we suggest ways to fill these important gaps and further extend knowledge of the nexus of innovation, gender, and crowdfunding.

5.   GENDER AND INNOVATION IN CROWDFUNDING: LOOKING AHEAD

The goal of this chapter is to highlight the recent developments regarding gender and innovation in the crowdfunding context. More specifically, we argue that innovation strategy has potential to influence fund-raising performance. Supplemented by the evidence presented, we offer a first step in demonstrating that crowdfunding offers promising opportunities for innovative female entrepreneurs, and that they may have advantages not found in certain traditional entrepreneurial finance settings. However, much remains unknown and important research questions remain.

First, rewards-based crowdfunding has served as the primary context for theoretical development in this bourgeoning phenomenon. While rewards-based platforms are by far the most popular, equity-based crowdfunding platforms continue to grow in popularity as regulation catches up to innovation. However, initial evidence suggests that these platforms have their own nuances (Bapna & Ganco, 2020), and thus require separate empirical exploration. Rewards-based crowdfunding is generally low-stakes in comparison to equity investment and is likely to change investment motivation. While we highlight that open innovation is advantageous to female entrepreneurs in rewards-based models, this might not hold across all crowdfunding models.

Second, the most studied outcome in crowdfunding thus far has been whether the campaign meets its fund-raising goal (Pollack et al., 2019). This outcome is crucial as large crowdfunding platforms typically operate on an all-or-nothing funding model. While we suggest that females pursuing an open innovation strategy are likely to find an advantage for this important outcome, it is also likely that they will flourish after the campaign ends. Communities typically contribute their human capital back to open innovations at a very low, or even no cost to the project itself. In turn, this could be an important source of slack resource, which may then spur future growth (George, 2005), and ultimately lead to more sustainable ventures as backers continue to contribute to the product development after the campaign ends. Thus, longitudinal or ethnographic studies following the development of female-led open innovation projects after they raise their initial funds offer a promising route to answering this question.

Third, a growing number of firms are pursuing social and financial goals simultaneously (Moss et al., 2019) and data show that female entrepreneurs also perform remarkably well within prosocial crowdfunding. Open innovations are inherently prosocial as most elements of the project are offered free of charge for anyone to build upon. However, it remains unknown if explicit social goals, for example, open innovations in food packaging intended to benefit those in the middle of a disaster, would be more attractive than projects that are more consumer-oriented. Therefore, measuring the projects hybridity (cf. Shepherd et al., 2019), and whether that moderates the overall campaign performance – the success of the campaign in terms of money gathered – would be a fruitful avenue to pursue this question.

6.   CONCLUSION

Crowdfunding is one of the most important evolutions of entrepreneurial finance. Its significance spans both theory and practice, as it is now one of the largest sources of capital for aspiring entrepreneurs. Further, crowdfunding is one of the most suitable avenues for innovation, as it draws support from a population of early adopters who often hold an intrinsic interest in seeing a project succeed. As such, biases found elsewhere are less likely to exist and allow virtually any aspiring entrepreneur an audience to pitch their innovative creations.

NOTE

1.   Details on the matching procedure, including criteria and diagnostics, can be obtained directly from authors.

REFERENCES

Agrawal, A., Catalini, C., & Goldfarb, A. (2013). *Some Simple Economics of Crowdfunding* (pp. 63–97) [NBER Chapters]. National Bureau of Economic Research, Inc. https://econpapers.repec.org/bookchap/nbrnberch/12946.htm
Allison, T. H., Davis, B. C., Short, J. C., & Webb, J. W. (2015). Crowdfunding in a Prosocial Microlending Environment: Examining the Role of Intrinsic Versus Extrinsic Cues. *Entrepreneurship Theory and Practice*, *39*(1), 53–73. https://doi.org/10.1111/etap.12108
Alsos, G. A., Isaksen, E. J., & Ljunggren, E. (2017). New Venture Financing and Subsequent Business Growth in Men- and Women-Led Businesses: *Entrepreneurship Theory and Practice*. https://journals.sagepub.com/doi/10.1111/j.1540-6520.2006.00141.x
Baker, T., & Nelson, R. E. (2005). Creating Something from Nothing: Resource Construction through Entrepreneurial Bricolage. *Administrative Science Quarterly*, *50*(3), 329–366. https://doi.org/10.2189/asqu.2005.50.3.329
Balachandra, L., Briggs, T., Eddleston, K., & Brush, C. (2019). Don't Pitch Like a Girl!: How Gender Stereotypes Influence Investor Decisions. *Entrepreneurship Theory and Practice*, *43*(1), 116–137. https://doi.org/10.1177/1042258717728028

Bapna, S., & Ganco, M. (2020). Gender Gaps in Equity Crowdfunding: Evidence from a Randomized Field Experiment. *Management Science*, mnsc.2020.3644. https://doi .org/10.1287/mnsc.2020.3644

Block, J. H., Colombo, M. G., Cumming, D. J., & Vismara, S. (2018). New Players in Entrepreneurial Finance and Why They are There. *Small Business Economics*, *50*(2), 239–250. https://doi.org/10.1007/s11187-016-9826-6

Bort, J., Stephan, U., & Wiklund, J. (2021). The Well-being of Entrepreneurs and Their Stakeholders. In M. Cardon, M. Frese, & M. Gielnik (Eds), *The Psychology of Entrepreneurship: New Perspectives* (pp. 340–356). Routledge.

Brush, C. G., Carter, N. M., Gatewood, E., Greene, P. G., & Hart, M. M. (2004). *Gatekeepers of Venture Growth: A Diana Project Report on the Role and Participation of Women in the Venture Capital Industry*. https://www.hbs.edu/ faculty/Pages/item.aspx?num=15986

Brush, C., Greene, P., Dalachandra, L., & Davis, A. (2018). The Gender Gap in Venture Capital – Progress, Problems, and Perspectives. *Venture Capital*, *20*(2), 115–136. https://doi.org/10.1080/13691066.2017.1349266

Calcagnini, G., Giombini, G., & Lenti, E. (2015). Gender Differences in Bank Loan Access: An Empirical Analysis. *Italian Economic Journal*, *1*(2), 193–217. https:// doi.org/10.1007/s40797-014-0004-1

Carter, S., & Rosa, P. (1998). The Financing of Male- and Female-Owned Businesses. *Entrepreneurship & Regional Development*, *10*(3), 225–242. https://doi.org/10 .1080/08985629800000013

Chesbrough, H. W. (2003). *Open innovation: The new imperative for creating and profiting from technology*. Harvard Business Press.

Coleman, S. M. (2000). Access to Capital and Terms of Credit: A Comparison of Men- and Women-Owned Small Businesses. *Journal of Small Business Management*, *7*(2), 151–174.

Coleman, S., & Robb, A. (2012). Gender-based Firm Performance Differences in the United States: Examining the Roles of Financial Capital and Motivations. In K. D. Hughes, & J. E. Jennings (Eds), *Global Women's Entrepreneurship Research* (Chapter 4). Cheltenham, UK and Northampton, MA, USA: Edward Elgar Publishing. https://www.elgaronline.com/view/edcoll/9781849804622/ 9781849804622.00012.xml

Colombo, M. G., Franzoni, C., & Rossi-Lamastra, C. (2015). Internal Social Capital and the Attraction of Early Contributions in Crowdfunding. *Entrepreneurship Theory and Practice*, *39*(1), 75–100. https://doi.org/10.1111/etap.12118

Cumming, D., Meoli, M., & Vismara, S. (2019). Does Equity Crowdfunding Democratize Entrepreneurial Finance? *Small Business Economics*, *56*(2), 533–522. https://doi.org/10.1007/s11187-019-00188-z

Drover, W., Busenitz, L., Matusik, S., Townsend, D., Anglin, A., & Dushnitsky, G. (2017). A Review and Road Map of Entrepreneurial Equity Financing Research: Venture Capital, Corporate Venture Capital, Angel Investment, Crowdfunding, and Accelerators. *Journal of Management*, *43*(6), 1820–1853. https://doi.org/10.1177/ 0149206317690584

Eiteneyer, N., Bendig, D., & Brettel, M. (2019). Social Capital and the Digital Crowd: Involving Backers to Promote New Product Innovativeness. *Research Policy*, *48*(8), 103744. https://doi.org/10.1016/j.respol.2019.01.017

Fairlie, R., & Robb, A. (2009). Gender Differences in Business Performance: Evidence from the Characteristics of Business Owners Survey. *Small Business Economics*, *33*(4), 375–395.

Fleming, L., & Waguespack, D. M. (2007). Brokerage, Boundary Spanning, and Leadership in Open Innovation Communities. *Organization Science*, *18*(2), 165–180. https://doi.org/10.1287/orsc.1060.0242

Gafni, H., Marom, D., Robb, A., & Sade, O. (2019). Gender Composition in Crowdfunding (Kickstarter). *SSRN Electronic Journal*, 1–64. https://dx.doi.org/10.2139/ssrn.2442954

George, G. (2005). Slack Resources and the Performance of Privately Held Firms. *The Academy of Management Journal*, *48*(4), 661–676. https://doi.org/10.2307/20159685

Gerber, E. M., Hui, J. S., & Kuo, P.-Y. (2012). Crowdfunding: Why People are Motivated to Post and Fund Projects on Crowdfunding Platforms. *Proceedings of the International Workshop on Design, Influence, and Social Technologies: Techniques, Impacts and Ethics*, *2*, 10.

Greenberg, J., & Mollick, E. (2017). Activist Choice Homophily and the Crowdfunding of Female Founders. *Administrative Science Quarterly*, *62*(2), 341–374. https://doi.org/10.1177/0001839216678847

Greene, P. G., Brush, C. G., Hart, M. M., & Saparito, P. (2001). Patterns of Venture Capital Funding: Is Gender a Factor? *Venture Capital*, *3*(1), 63–83. https://doi.org/10.1080/13691060118175

Hechavarría, D. M., Terjesen, S. A., Ingram, A. E., Renko, M., Justo, R., & Elam, A. (2017). Taking Care of Business: The Impact of Culture and Gender on Entrepreneurs' Blended Value Creation Goals. *Small Business Economics*, *48*(1), 225–257. https://doi.org/10.1007/s11187-016-9747-4

Hornuf, L., & Schwienbacher, A. (2018). Market Mechanisms and Funding Dynamics in Equity Crowdfunding. *Journal of Corporate Finance*, *50*, 556–574. https://doi.org/10.1016/j.jcorpfin.2017.08.009

Hsu, D. H., & Ziedonis, R. H. (2013). Resources as Dual Sources of Advantage: Implications for Valuing Entrepreneurial-Firm Patents. *Strategic Management Journal*, *34*(7), 761–781. https://doi.org/10.1002/smj.2037

Hyytinen, A., Pajarinen, M., & Rouvinen, P. (2015). Does Innovativeness Reduce Startup Survival Rates? *Journal of Business Venturing*, *30*(4), 564–581. https://doi.org/10.1016/j.jbusvent.2014.10.001

Jennings, J. E., & Brush, C. G. (2017). Research on Women Entrepreneurs: Challenges to (and from) the Broader Entrepreneurship Literature? *Academy of Management Annals*, *7*(1), 663–715. https://journals.aom.org/doi/abs/10.5465/19416520.2013.782190

Johnson, M. A., Stevenson, R. M., & Letwin, C. R. (2018). A Woman's Place is in the … Startup! Crowdfunder Judgments, Implicit Bias, and the Stereotype Content Model. *Journal of Business Venturing*, *33*(6), 813–831. https://doi.org/10.1016/j.jbusvent.2018.04.003

Lee, C. R., Lee, J. H., & Shin, D. Y. (2015). Factor Analysis of the Motivation on Crowdfunding Participants: An Empirical Study of Funder Centered Reward-type Platform. *Journal of Society for e-Business Studies*, *20*(1), Article 1. http://www.calsec.or.kr/jsebs/index.php/jsebs/article/view/160

Lerner, J., & Tirole, J. (2002). Some Simple Economics of Open Source. *The Journal of Industrial Economics*, *50*(2), 197–234. https://doi.org/10.1111/1467-6451.00174

Lifshitz-Assaf, H. (2018). Dismantling Knowledge Boundaries at NASA: The Critical Role of Professional Identity in Open Innovation. *Administrative Science Quarterly*, *63*(4), 746–782. https://doi.org/10.1177/0001839217747876

Malmström, M., Johansson, J., & Wincent, J. (2017). Gender Stereotypes and Venture Support Decisions: How Governmental Venture Capitalists Socially Construct Entrepreneurs' Potential. *Entrepreneurship Theory and Practice*, *41*(5), 833–860. https://doi.org/10.1111/etap.12275

Meoli, A., Munari, F., & Bort, J. (2019). The Patent Paradox in Crowdfunding: An Empirical Analysis of Kickstarter Data. *Industrial and Corporate Change*, 28(5), 1321–1341. https://doi.org/10.1093/icc/dtz004

Mollick, E. (2014). The Dynamics of Crowdfunding: An Exploratory Study. *Journal of Business Venturing*, 29(1), 1–16. https://doi.org/10.1016/j.jbusvent.2013.06.005

Mollick, E., & Robb, A. (2016). Democratizing Innovation and Capital Access: The Role of Crowdfunding. *California Management Review*, *58*(2), 72–87. https://doi .org/10.1525/cmr.2016.58.2.72

Moss, T. W., Renko, M., & Bort, J. (2019). The Story Behind the Story: Microfoundations of Hybrid Communication by Microenterprises. *Academy of Management Proceedings*, *2019*(1), 13052. https://doi.org/10.5465/AMBPP.2019.196

Mullen, L. (2020). *Gender: Predict Gender from Names Using Historical Data* (0.5.4) [R package version].

Murray, A., Kotha, S., & Fisher, G. (2020). Community-Based Resource Mobilization: How Entrepreneurs Acquire Resources from Distributed Non-Professionals via Crowdfunding. *Organization Science*, orsc.2019.1339. https://doi.org/10.1287/orsc .2019.1339

Pelizzon, L., Riedel, M., & Tasca, P. (2016). Classification of Crowdfunding in the Financial System. In P. Tasca, T. Aste, L. Pelizzon, & N. Perony (Eds), *Banking Beyond Banks and Money: A Guide to Banking Services in the Twenty-First Century* (pp. 5–16). Springer International Publishing. https://doi.org/10.1007/978-3-319 -42448-4_2

Pollack, J. M., Maula, M., Allison, T. H., Renko, M., & Günther, C. C. (2019). Making a Contribution to Entrepreneurship Research by Studying Crowd-Funded Entrepreneurial Opportunities. *Entrepreneurship Theory and Practice*, 1042258719888640. https://doi.org/10.1177/1042258719888640

Schwienbacher, A., & Larralde, B. (2010). Crowdfunding of Small Entrepreneurial Ventures. *SSRN Electronic Journal*. https://doi.org/10.2139/ssrn.1699183

Shepherd, D. A., Williams, T. A., & Zhao, E. Y. (2019). A Framework for Exploring the Degree of Hybridity in Entrepreneurship. *Academy of Management Perspectives*, 22.

Song, Y., & Tian, X. (2020). Managerial Responses and Customer Engagement in Crowdfunding. *Sustainability*, *12*(8), 3389. https://doi.org/10.3390/su12083389

Sorenson, O., Assenova, V., Li, G.-C., Boada, J., & Fleming, L. (2016). Expand Innovation Finance via Crowdfunding. *Science*, *354*(6319), 1526–1528. https://doi .org/10.1126/science.aaf6989

Stanko, M. A., & Henard, D. H. (2017). Toward a Better Understanding of Crowdfunding, Openness and the Consequences for Innovation. *Research Policy*, *46*(4), 784–798. https://doi.org/10.1016/j.respol.2017.02.003

Stewart, K. J., & Gosain, S. (2006). The Impact of Ideology on Effectiveness in Open Source Software Development Teams. *MIS Quarterly*, *30*(2), 291–314. https://doi .org/10.2307/25148732

Verheul, I., & Thurik, R. (2001). Start-Up Capital: 'Does Gender Matter?' *Small Business Economics*, *16*(4), 329–345.

Vismara, S. (2019). Sustainability in Equity Crowdfunding. *Technological Forecasting and Social Change*, *141*, 98–106. https://doi.org/10.1016/j.techfore.2018.07.014

3. A gendered multi-level model of STEM entrepreneurship

Cecelia Dotzler and M. Gloria González-Morales

1. INTRODUCTION

The aim of this chapter is to explore the lack of representation of women entrepreneurs in the fields of Science, Technology, Engineering, and Math (STEM) (Global Entrepreneurship Monitor, 2013) and explain it using factors related to the individual actors involved (e.g., entrepreneurs, investors, mentors) and the fact that they are embedded in organizational contexts and cultures. In this chapter we describe a multi-level understanding of STEM entrepreneurship as gendered. We first discuss the individual level psychological processes at play in the STEM entrepreneurship ecosystem such as the social identity of STEM entrepreneurs and the social categorization of STEM entrepreneurs by stakeholders. We then discuss the contextual level at which STEM entrepreneurship takes place that can be described as a masculinity contest culture (Berdahl et al., 2018), which places a low value on relational practices. This review elucidates the, often overlooked, role of culture, rooted in assumptions that require more diverse values such as relational and communal practices (Fletcher, 1998) to foster a sense of belonging for women STEM entrepreneurs. We close the chapter with practical contributions to aid investors and women STEM entrepreneurs to succeed in their respective investments and ventures.

2. LITERATURE REVIEW

2.1 The Individual Level: Identity

We pull from social identity theory to better understand the identity formation challenges of women who are entrepreneurs in STEM fields. Social identity theory (Tajfel, 1974) explains the ways in which we create a sense of belonging to the social world by organizing people into groups using three main cognitive processes: social identity, categorization and comparison. In this section we will focus on the first two: *Social identity* refers to a person identifying with one group because of similarities to members of that group and dissimilarities to members of nongroup members (e.g., a person identifies as a scientist). *Social categorization* refers to the process of placing other people into categories or groups that are alike but dissimilar to other groups (e.g., this young woman is not a scientist because she does not look like most scientists, who are middle-aged men).

2.1.1   Social identity development of women in STEM entrepreneurship

The first step in understanding the gender disparity in STEM entrepreneurship is to look at the forces that encourage or impede the development of a *STEM entrepreneurial identity* as an important antecedent to entering the fields of STEM and developing a STEM entrepreneurial endeavor. According to Bandura and Walters' Social Learning Theory (1977) learning occurs in an individual's environment through the observation of others: having a role model to observe and emulate is needed for an individual to engage in identity development. For women in STEM entrepreneurship, there are far fewer potential role models to observe and emulate (an issue of numbers), and the role models that are available to women in STEM entrepreneurship are high performers that are difficult to relate to (an issue of quality). A recent research study evaluated an entrepreneurship sensitization campaign for young women in France aimed at increasing women entrepreneur role models in the media (Byrne, Fattoum, & Diaz Garcia, 2019). According to this study, the entrepreneurial role models displayed by the media were "superwoman-like" women who were strongly individualistic, distanced themselves from traditional feminine behaviors, separated themselves from their domestic lives, did not believe that entrepreneurship was gendered, and tempered their masculine behaviors. This display of a woman entrepreneur does not portray a relatable or attainable persona for most women – only the highest achieving women would even consider aspiring to be an entrepreneur based on these role models. The study points to the lack of relatable women entrepreneurial role models for young women to look up to and identify with as a challenge for women's entrepreneurial identity formation.

Because most STEM entrepreneurs are men, young men have an abundance of role models to observe, emulate, and learn from that cover a wide swathe of relatable and achievable behaviors. This first step of developing a STEM entrepreneurial identity is easier for men, even for those without the required potential, as suggested by a study by Cimpian, Kim, and McDermott (2020). They analyzed a seven-year longitudinal dataset (HSLS:09) of 5,960 US students from ninth grade (2009–2010) until their first years of college (2016–2017). They found that men with very low STEM achievement scores

(1st percentile of a STEM achievement composite including high-school GPAs and SAT scores) were choosing math-intensive PECS (physics, engineering, and computer science) majors just as often as women at the 80th percentile of STEM achievement. Their study suggests that men are drawn to and retained in the fields of STEM independently of their STEM achievement potential, while only high achieving women are. This is likely due to the strong association that exists tying men to the fields of STEM, or rather the *social categorization* of men as the most representative of STEM individuals. Cimpian, Kim, and McDermott (2020) conclude that the imbalanced gender distribution "... may be perpetuated by male-favoring cultures that disproportionately attract low-achieving men to the field" (p. 1319). Therefore, it is not just a problem of lack of representation. We propose that gender role congruity becomes an additional interactive factor that thwarts women's STEM entrepreneur identity development in comparison to their male counterparts.

2.1.2 Femininity and gender role congruity

Not only do fewer women start entrepreneurial endeavors (Brush et al., 2019), but for women operating in high technology incubators, stereotypically gendered expectations reinforce masculine norms for entrepreneurial behavior (Marlow & McAdam, 2012). This phenomenon has been explained in relation to the gender disparity in organizational positions using *role congruity theory* (Eagly & Karau, 2002) and the notion that women and men are prescribed differing societal roles. Men are expected to be agentic and strong; women are expected to be communal and warm. Current historic and societal standards prescribe the role expectations of an entrepreneur (e.g., competitive, risk averse, agentic) as gendered and related to masculine role traits, and role congruity theory can be applied to explain the gender disparity and the double bind of women entrepreneurs. Because the role of an entrepreneur is incongruent with the feminine gender role, women cannot be perceived as entrepreneurial (agentic) and feminine (communal) at the same time. For a woman to identify as an entrepreneur, she must overcome the barriers imposed by the misalignment of entrepreneurial and gender role expectations in our societal and historical context, and enact a combination of feminine (i.e., nurture, emotion, passivity, and attractiveness) and masculine (i.e., economic and emotional independence, assertiveness, rationality, and autonomy) behaviors.

Lewis (2014) identifies four *entrepreneurial femininities* derived from previous entrepreneurship literature to reflect how women strategically choose available masculine and feminine behaviors to reconcile the conflicting gender and entrepreneurial roles: the *entrepreneur*, reflects individualized behaviors, *mumpreneur* reflects maternal behaviors, *women entrepreneur* reflects relational behaviors, and *nonpreneur* reflects excessively feminine behaviors negating the entrepreneurial identity. Given the culture in which STEM entrepreneurship takes place (addressed in the next section), we believe that women in this arena are most likely to adopt the *entrepreneur* femininity as it is based on the individualized femininity that requires a high level of achievement, a disassociation from the feminine, and the denial of gender imbalances in the field. This form of entrepreneurial femininity is the most widely accepted by actors in the entrepreneurial space and sets women in STEM entrepreneurship up for the most success, but it is the most difficult to enact. According to Stead (2017), this form of entrepreneurial femininity requires that women conceal their femininity, devaluing the characteristics that are associated with women and overvaluing the characteristics associated with men, in order to fit the prescribed role of an entrepreneur. The hiding of femininity not only requires additional emotional labor that depletes women's resources (Grandey & Melloy, 2017; Hofstee et al., 2020), but also supports the social categorization processes by stakeholders that further weaken the association between STEM entrepreneurial identity and femininity.

2.1.3   Social categorization of women by stakeholders

To illustrate how other stakeholders (i.e., mentors, investors) play a role in women's STEM entrepreneurship identity development through social cate-gorization, we refer to a study conducted by Moss-Racusin et al. (2012). They asked science faculty to rate applications to a research assistant position by John or Jennifer; other than their names, the applications were identical. The faculty members *categorized* John as more qualified and as a better fit for STEM than Jennifer, and therefore deemed him as more worthy of pay and mentoring. This social categorization process biases STEM student's self-efficacy and identity development – if women do not receive mentoring and support from faculty, they are less motivated and have fewer resources to stay and develop in the field. This is reflected in the lack of gender parity in STEM, which begins in the early stages and leaks the pipeline of career advancement: women hold a disproportionately low number of STEM degrees, women make up half of the workforce in the US and account for less than 25% of STEM jobs, and women with a STEM degree are less likely than their male counterparts to hold a STEM job (Beede et al., 2011).

The process of social categorization can be also explained through the idea of *implicit leadership theory*, a leading theory in the field of leadership studies (Offermann, Kennedy, & Wirtz, 1994). This theory postulates that a person will evaluate a leader based on their own implicit opinions about how they value leadership. As an example, if I value highly ethical behaviors, I will identify as leaders those who exhibit these ethical behaviors, but I will not a person who does not exhibit these ethical behaviors. Applying this concept to the field of entrepreneurship, an *implicit entrepreneurship theory* explains the social categorization process of other agents involved in entrepreneurial ventures. Professional investors have an existing implicit entrepreneurship theory that positions individuals that exhibit agentic behaviors as the proto-typical and ideal entrepreneur. Therefore, it is harder for them to categorize women, or individuals exhibiting more communal behaviors, as entrepreneurs. This is problematic because the key role of professional investors in the venture process is to select entrepreneurial endeavors for development and advancement, and when an investor cannot view or categorize a woman as entrepreneurial, many pursuits are overlooked. Investors will see women as entrepreneurs when their implicit entrepreneurial theory aligns with a more diversified and global understanding that includes gendered characteristics and practices.

A study published in 2014 by Brooks et al. supports this notion of biased implicit entrepreneurship theories causing investors to view women as less desirable startup founders than men. The aptly titled study "Investors prefer entrepreneurial ventures pitched by attractive men" found that investors were more likely to deem participants' pitch ideas as more viable for investment when the pitches were presented by attractive men, even though the pitch content was identical from men and women founders (Brooks et al., 2014). Another study published in 2019 by Balachandra et al. found that investors did not necessarily prefer founders who were men, but rather investors were more likely to deem a startup pitch viable when it was presented by founders who did not display feminine-stereotyped behaviors such as warmth, sensitive-ness, expressiveness, and emotiveness. Kanze et al. (2018) conducted a study looking at the types of questions asked of men and women entrepreneurs at a TechCrunch conference pitch competition to uncover if there were nuances in the types of questions asked by the expert investors. The analysis of the scripts of the investor questions and founder responses found a statistically significant difference in the way men and women founders were questioned during the pitch competition. Male founders were asked questions that allowed them to use promotive language and speak to the positive benefits of their ideas, while female founders were asked questions that forced them to use prohibitive language that defended their ideas. The use of the different types of founder "voice" has differing effects on audience, and, in the case of a pitch competition, forced the women founders to speak to the more negative aspects of their startup ideas.

In all three studies, representations of entrepreneurial success were cat-egorized through men and/or masculine behaviors, and the investors acted accordingly, disproportionately leaving women out of the entrepreneurial game. No matter how much a woman identifies as a STEM entrepreneur, if the main actors and stakeholders do not *categorize* her as a STEM entrepreneur, she will be excluded and not supported in her entrepreneurial endeavor. As displayed by these studies, the stakeholder's categorization processes are affected by biases that portray men as the representation of the exemplar, hindering women's advancement in STEM and entrepreneurship. The effects of the lack of recognition of women entrepreneurs are a hindrance to overall entrepreneurial success, as studies have shown a positive relationship between the gender diversity of new venture teams and innovation performance of new ventures (Dai, Byun, & Ding, 2019), which is indicative of firm performance (Rogers, 2010). Fitting into the existing implicit entrepreneurship theories held by investors and other stakeholders, is a first step to belong in the entrepreneurial field; and developing a strong sense of belonging is crucial to remain motivated and resilient in the face of a context of exclusion.

2.1.4   Entrepreneurial belonging

Stead (2017) discusses entrepreneurial belonging as the combined factors of acceptance, identity, recognition, and inclusion, and proposes five primary ways in which women develop entrepreneurial belonging: by proxy (i.e., connecting with an existing player in the entrepreneurial space, likely a man), concealment (i.e., hiding or downplaying feminine characteristics), modeling the norm (i.e., copying a man), tempered disruption (i.e. a female being the leader of the business to female clients – disrupting the gendered norm of leadership but tempering it with the female audience), and identity-switching (i.e., enacting more masculine behaviors). For women to belong, they can enact masculine behaviors, conceal their feminine characteristics and model the masculine norm, but this requires additional emotional labor and impedes the representation of realistic role models for young women.

We note that a sense of belonging is not the same as women just "fitting in" to the existing entrepreneurial space. We must create systems in which women are able to develop a sense of belonging in the STEM entrepreneurial sphere without the reliance on proxies or switching to the masculine ideal. We propose that even when an individual identifies as a STEM entrepreneur, they still must be socially categorized as a STEM entrepreneur by members of the entrepreneurial ecosystem. And even when a woman is socially categorized as a STEM entrepreneur by individuals in the entrepreneurial ecosystem, she will need to mobilize resources to remain and thrive as a legitimate member of that ecosystem that tends to exclude women over time. As noted by Huang et al. (2020), remaining in an ecosystem that is designed for exclusion of women is not easy. Women are just as productive as men in STEM publication productivity year by year, but they drop out of the STEM career trajectory earlier and more frequently than men. If women truly belonged in the STEM entrepreneurial space, they would be far more likely to remain and continue to produce.

In this section we have discussed the role of representation and role congruity in the development of women STEM entrepreneurial identities, and the importance of the social categorization processes by other actors of the system. The development of identity and categorization infuses diversity into the system, but this diversity should lead to true belonging (Stead, 2017). We propose that true belonging cannot happen without a culture of the STEM entrepreneurial sphere (e.g., business schools, incubators, investment firms, etc.) that welcomes women, deconstructs the masculinity contest culture in which STEM entrepreneurship lies, and provides room for relational practice. We expand on these concepts in the next section and have included Figure 3.1 as a graphical representation of our proposed framework.

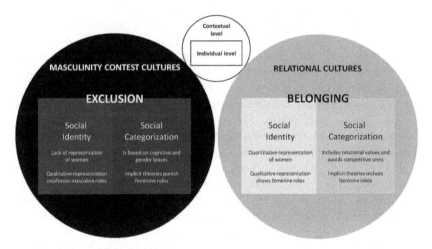

Figure 3.1   Proposed multi-level framework

2.2   The Contextual Level: Culture

The next layer of our framework is around the context and culture in which STEM entrepreneurship lies. We propose that *fixing the women* (Schiebinger, 2008; Fox, 2017) to increase their STEM entrepreneurial efforts is not only unfair, but shortsighted. We borrow two organizational constructs that identify the higher-level levers that need to be pulled to solve the gender disparity in the STEM entrepreneurship problem: Masculinity Contest Culture (MCC) and Relational Practice (RP).

Before we dive into the key concepts of MCC and RP, we propose that the STEM entrepreneurial culture emerges in three distinct contexts throughout the three entrepreneurial lifecycle stages: idea formation, incubation, and maintenance/development. The idea formation stage takes place in business school classes about entrepreneurship and in STEM academia. The incubation stage takes place in startup incubators and accelerators, in academic STEM

technology transfer offices, and in professional investor offices. The mainte-
nance and development stage takes place in Venture Capital offices, startup
conferences, and more developed startup networks. It is important to keep
these stages and context in mind as we explore the emergence and mainte-
nance of MCCs and the devaluation of RP in the entrepreneurial ecosystem
(Ozkazanc-Pan & Clark Muntean, 2021).

2.2.1   Masculinity contest culture

The MCC is characterized by a work culture that encourages a hyper competitive environment (*'winner-takes-all competition'*), where the winners are those
who endorse stereotypical toxic masculinity through ruthlessness, stamina,
and emotional toughness (Berdahl et al., 2018). A context defined by MCC
creates toxic work environments and poor individual and organizational outcomes. One of the main tenants of the MCC is that masculinity is precarious,
meaning it is difficult to achieve and easy to lose (Vandello & Bosson, 2013).
For this reason, men and women operating in an MCC are forced to constantly
compete for masculinity status. Masculinity is proven not only through acts of
masculinity, but also through devaluing acts of femininity. Masculinity also
shows up through men's prescribed duty to be the household breadwinner, and
because of this expectation, securing resources like wealth is another way for
men to perform masculinity in the workplace.

It has been argued that MCCs are most prevalent in industries where
the potential for winning extreme resources or the potential risk for losing
resources is relatively high (Ely & Meyerson, 2010). Additionally, hierarchical
structures set the stage for MCCs as men compete for increased role responsibility. Lastly, external pressures such as competition or high risk of failure are
also likely to lead a culture toward a masculinity contest. In becoming aware
of the existence of MCC in the field of entrepreneurship, one wonders if this
type of culture accounts for a sizeable portion of the high failure rate (90%)
of entrepreneurial endeavors (Patel, 2015) for men and women. Recognizing
the existence of MCC in both the STEM and entrepreneurial fields can explain
lower representation of women in these fields: women have a more difficult
time succeeding in work environments with an MCC because not only do they
have to fit in, but they must also compete for masculinity status while being
commonly relegated to support roles (Williams, Berdahl & Vandello, 2016).
STEM entrepreneurial ecosystems have an ecosystem identity (Ozkazanc-Pan
& Clark Muntean, 2021) that supports the MCC. In identifying that the field
of STEM entrepreneurship is embedded in an MCC, we next develop the argument that STEM entrepreneurial endeavors will be more successful when all
actors enact and place value on less competitive and more communal practices,
such as relational practice.

2.2.2 Relational practice

Relational Theory was introduced by Jordan et al. (1991) and Miller (1976) as an alternative theory to the more mainstream masculine theories of growth that are present in today's workplace. Relational theory argues that growth comes out of the characteristics of connection, interdependence, and collectivity and through interactions characterized by mutual empathy and mutual empowerment, where both parties exercise vulnerability, expect to grow, and feel a responsibility toward the growth of the other. The strengths that are required to enact relationality are empathy, vulnerability, emotion expression, ability to participate in the development of another, and the expectation that growth will occur through the relational practice (RP). We argue that RP, which is characterized by a way of working that is rooted in a relational or feminine belief system, is a much-needed framework in STEM entrepreneurship.

In her study of IT engineers, Fletcher (1998) found that women engineers enacted RP behaviors organized in four broad categories: preserving the life and well-being of the project, mutual empowerment of self and another, achieving goals, and creating teams. Although it would be difficult to argue that these RPs would not lead to greater outcomes and experiences, according to Fletcher (1998), RPs were neither discussed nor valued within the organization, and rather were "disappeared" and invalidated by the engineering organizational culture in which they operated. The RPs were devalued and de-skilled, and employees in the organization made the behaviors and actions "not work," so they were not acknowledged or rewarded. These RPs were disappeared by three main mechanisms: misattributing the intention of the RP (assuming the RP was done unintentionally), not providing a strong language to acknowledge the RP as work and not something other than work (referring to the RP as "other"), and gendering the RPs by associating them with femininity and motherhood (acknowledging the RP as nurturing or feminine).

In her work with RP in the nursing profession, DeFrino (2009) discussed the ways in which the nursing profession allows for a culture where power and value lie in performing RPs, though the RPs are still disappeared in the greater medical (STEM) model. DeFrino posits that it is in the performing of RPs where nurses achieve more positive patient and organizational outcomes. Similarly, a study conducted by Phillips and Austin (2009) found that for female physicians, spending more time with patients and listening more intently (i.e., performing RPs) was beneficial to patients.

We propose that instead of trying to mold women to fit the existing MCC of STEM entrepreneurship, we follow the research evidence (Fletcher, 1998; DeFrino, 2009; Phillips & Austin, 2009) that suggests encouraging those in the STEM entrepreneurial space to address and value RPs as skills and effective methods of achieving desired work outcomes.

In order to promote RPs and provide a context in which they are valued, participants in the field of STEM entrepreneurship must correctly attribute the intention of the RP to the actor enacting the practice (e.g., commend or reward a founder for intentionally empathetically teaching, or creating a team), they must provide a strong language and reward system that acknowledges the value of RP (e.g., name RPs in review and feedback sessions with founders and incorporate them into the cultural jargon), and avoid associating RP with femininity and motherhood (e.g., focus on both men and women in RP acknowledgement).

3.   CALL TO ACTION

Taking the multi-level framework into consideration, we subscribe to the notion that the solution for the gender disparity in STEM entrepreneurship is not to *fix the women* (Schiebinger, 2008; Fox, 2017), but rather to develop awareness and initiatives that create a more welcoming and open space for women to belong and thrive. We should rather *fix the system* by focusing resources on developing ways in which leaders and actors can re-shape cultures to be more encouraging of women's entry, thriving, and belonging in these fields. We encourage STEM and entrepreneurial players to avoid the "call to fix the women" or adjust the ways in which women in STEM and entrepreneurship operate. Women are whole and complete as they are, and exclusion is a byproduct of an MCC associated with STEM and entrepreneurship. For these reasons, we focus our call to action on the actions required from influential individuals, leaders, and organizations connected to the STEM and entrepreneurial ecosystems in which this gender disparity lies, and not from women themselves. We must help shape the culture in which STEM entrepreneurship is no longer based on fragile and toxic masculinity by including and valuing RP. This will also encourage men to display RP behaviors, thereby enhancing their leadership and team performance (citation).

3.1   Call for Relational Practice in Stem Entrepreneurship

Many efforts have been made to foster the social identification of women as STEM professionals and entrepreneurs (e.g., Women You Should Know, Girls Who Code, etc.) and to foster the social categorization of women in STEM by other actors (e.g., VIDS training, Moss-Racusin et al., 2018). However, these efforts are thwarted if enacted in an MCC of agency, competition and individualism. Change must be catalyzed through cultural change. For individual initiatives to flourish they should be planted in the right soil, which is why we call for efforts to promote RPs and culture in STEM entrepreneurship.

Table 3.1   *Actionable items to develop RP culture using Kotter's stages of change*

Stage Description	Messaging/Philosophy	Implementation examples
1. Create a sense of urgency	Entrepreneurial identity is individualistic and needs to move toward collectivist.	Introducing to new entrepreneurs the idea that the entrepreneurial ecosystem is a network of resources that will help you succeed, so collaboration is a value to enhance.
	Supporting other entrepreneurs and agents is a key to success.	Keep strong bridges because repeat entrepreneurs are more successful.
	Entrepreneurship happens within the entrepreneurial ecosystem and competition makes resources scarcer.	Reiterate that the entrepreneur is not alone in the wild, but a part of the system and needs to establish symbiotic relationships with the other actors to survive.
2. Form a guiding coalition	Create a team of passionate and informed investors, STEM professionals, and organizational leaders to implement the RP culture change.	Use co-working spaces to connect with different businesses, other entrepreneurs; create mutually beneficial relationships now or in the future, involve people with diverse identities.
3. Develop a vision	Harness the long-term orientation that is required of STEM research and apply this to entrepreneurship.	Develop organizational target goals aimed at keeping women in STEM fields and entrepreneurship longer.
	Relational practice is mutual and reciprocal and requires involvement of entire ecosystem.	Use symbols to communicate vision and new RP culture.

Stage Description	Messaging/Philosophy	Implementation examples
4. Communicate the vision	Encourage a culture of Cooperation vs. Competition.	Use RP language in entrepreneurial and STEM mission and values statements, performance management systems, and investor training programs. Instead of using a language of competition, RP uses:
	Set and communicate collectivist goals to help all entrepreneurs move away from having to prove their masculinity/power in entrepreneurial spaces.	*Preserving the project by shouldering* (i.e., taking on tasks outside of role responsibilities) *connecting* (i.e., connecting the project to the people and needed resources) and *rescuing* (i.e., calling attention to problems).
	Define entrepreneurial success in RP terms and not the existing win/win, cutthroat competition.	*Mutual empowering* by enabling others' achievements and contributions to the project, including empathic teaching and protective connecting.
		Achieving using relational skills to enhance one's own effectiveness and growth through reconnecting, reflecting, and relational asking.
		Creating and nurturing teams by attending to the individual and the collective.
5. Empower others to enact the vision	Encourage leaders and all agents in the ecosystem to model humility.	Develop norms and practices with clear rationale to allow vulnerability.
	Relational practice can be instrumental in developing social capital.	Implement the ecological belonging intervention in all STEM and entrepreneurship contexts (Binning, 2020).
6. Celebrate wins	Understand that wins are not just profit-driven or productivity, a win is creating a sense of belonging for all and retention of diversity.	Publicly reward managers for D&I retention through awards and incentives.
7. Sustain acceleration of the vision	Create relative goals as opposed to absolute goals.	Name the relational practice's intention and strategy.

Stage Description	Messaging/Philosophy	Implementation examples
8. Institutionalize the change	Reframe success and goals avoiding masculinity contest discourses (Ely & Meyerson 2010).	Develop training programs for founders and scientists that directly address the complexities of gender bias in organizations (Rawski & Workman-Stark, 2018) and the benefits of RPs.
	Define competence in a way that is aligned with task completion and not with traditionally masculine behaviors.	Setup reward and incentive systems for founders and scientists that encourage and promote RPs and belonging for diverse individuals.
	Encourage a learning orientation toward work and avoid the fixed mindset about gender in STEM and entrepreneurship fields.	Create incentives for STEM investors to enlarge and enrich their implicit entrepreneurship theories to include communal behaviors and RP.
		Develop career paths that sustain women in STEM (Huang et al., 2020) and use internal committees for retaining women in STEM.

Many case studies suggest that one of the reasons for startup failure is around interpersonal facets of the founding team members such as personality type, complementary and heterogenous skillsets, and openness to mentorship (Kalyanasundaram, 2018). We propose that facilitating a more relational culture in STEM founder teams would not only provide more opportunities for women, but at the same time, the use and value of RPs would have positive outcomes both at the individual and organizational level. Not only would this foster a more inclusive industry but also a more efficient and successful one for all. RPs are highly important in aiding an entrepreneurial endeavor to move forward, grow, and flourish. We also suggest that women use RPs to gain power and influence in their STEM entrepreneurship endeavors.

Kotter (1996) proposed the Stages of Change model with eight distinct stages of change that are all necessary in order to successfully implement a change that will have lasting power: (1) creating a sense of urgency, (2) forming a guiding coalition, (3) developing a vision for the future, (4) communicating the vision, (5) empowering others to enact the vision, (6) celebrate wins along the way, (7) build upon the change, and (8) integrate the change into the culture. This model has been widely used in organizational change initiatives across cultures and industries since its inception. We use it as a framework to propose the initiatives outlined in Table 3.1, which combine philosophical shifts and tangible programs, that serve to encourage relational practice culture and support women STEM entrepreneurs.

4.   CONCLUSION

At the heart of the debate around the gender disparity in STEM fields and entrepreneurship lies a tension between the notion of *fixing the women*, where women try to mold to the existing structures in place in order to succeed, and *fixing the system*, where we recognize that the current structures are set up in a way that makes it unlikely for women to succeed. It is important that entrepreneurial organizations and contexts create space for women and RPs to flourish and be rewarded. Valuing RP in STEM entrepreneurship contexts can weaken the power of MCCs, so that women can be better set up for success, and the field of STEM entrepreneurship can thrive.

The value of this chapter lies in proposing a framework and language that explain the factors that exclude women from the STEM entrepreneurial ecosystem. Exclusion works through limiting the entry and success of women through social identity and categorization processes embedded and built upon a context of masculinity ideals. These ideals are centered around a hyper competitive environment and stereotypical toxic masculinity in which women are condemned to fail. The proposed solutions to create a sense of belonging for women into the STEM entrepreneurial ecosystem are based on theoretically sound organizational culture change models that can guide the implementation of evidence-based practices.

REFERENCES

Balachandra, L., Briggs, T., Eddleston, K. and Brush, C., 2019. Don't pitch like a girl!: How gender stereotypes influence investor decisions. *Entrepreneurship Theory and Practice, 43*(1), pp.116–137.

Bandura, A. and Walters, R.H., 1977. *Social learning theory* (Vol. 1). Englewood Cliffs, NJ: Prentice Hall.

Beede, D.N., Julian, T.A., Langdon, D., McKittrick, G., Khan, B. and Doms, M.E., 2011. Women in STEM: A gender gap to innovation. *Economics and Statistics Administration* Issue Brief (04-11).

Berdahl, J.L., Cooper, M., Glick, P., Livingston, R.W. and Williams, J.C., 2018. Work as a masculinity contest. *Journal of Social Issues, 74*(3), pp.422–448.

Binning, K.R., Kaufmann, N., McGreevy, E.M., Fotuhi, O., Chen, S., Marshman, E., Kalender, Z.Y., Limeri, L., Betancur, L. and Singh, C., 2020. Changing social contexts to foster equity in college science courses: An ecological-belonging intervention. *Psychological Science, 31*(9), pp.1059–1070.

Brooks, A.W., Huang, L., Kearney, S.W. and Murray, F.E., 2014. Investors prefer entrepreneurial ventures pitched by attractive men. *Proceedings of the National Academy of Sciences,* 111 (12), pp.4427–4431.

Brush, C., Edelman, L.F., Manolova, T. and Welter, F., 2019. A gendered look at entrepreneurship ecosystems. *Small Business Economics, 53*(2), pp.393–408.

Byrne, J., Fattoum, S. and Diaz Garcia, M.C., 2019. Role models and women entrepreneurs: Entrepreneurial superwoman has her say. *Journal of Small Business Management, 57*(1), pp.154–184.

Cimpian, J.R., Kim, T.H. and McDermott, Z.T., 2020. Understanding persistent gender gaps in STEM. *Science, 368*(6497), pp.1317–1319.

Dai, Y., Byun, G. and Ding, F., 2019. The direct and indirect impact of gender diversity in new venture teams on innovation performance. *Entrepreneurship Theory and Practice, 43*(3), pp.505–528.

DeFrino, D.T., 2009. A theory of the relational work of nurses. *Research and Theory for Nursing Practice, 23*(4), p.294.

Eagly, A.H. and Karau, S.J., 2002. Role congruity theory of prejudice toward women leaders. *Psychological Review, 109*(3), p.573.

Ely, R.J. and Meyerson, D.E., 2010. An organizational approach to undoing gender: The unlikely case of offshore oil platforms. *Research in Organizational Behavior, 30*, pp.3–34.

Fletcher, J.K., 1998. Relational practice: A feminist reconstruction of work. *Journal of Management Inquiry, 7*(2), pp.163–186.

Fox, C., 2017. *Stop fixing women: why building fairer workplaces is everyone's business.* Sydney NSW: NewSouth Publishing.

Global Entrepreneurship Monitor, 2013. Global Entrepreneurship Monitor 2012 women's report. *Donna J. Kelley, Candida G. Brush, Patricia G. Greene, Yana Litovsky and Global Entrepreneurship Research Association (GERA).*

Grandey, A.A. and Melloy, R.C., 2017. The state of the heart: Emotional labor as emotion regulation reviewed and revised. *Journal of Occupational Health Psychology, 22*(3), p.407.

Hofstee, G., Jansen, P.G.W., De Lange, A.H., Spisak, B.R. and Swinkels, M. 2020. The cognitive costs of managing emotions: A systematic review of the impact of emotional requirements on cognitive performance. *Work & Stress.* Advance online publication. https://doi-org.ccl.idm.oclc.org/10.1080/02678373.2020.1832608

Huang, J., Gates, A.J., Sinatra, R. and Barabási, A.L., 2020. Historical comparison of gender inequality in scientific careers across countries and disciplines. *Proceedings of the National Academy of Sciences, 117*(9), pp.4609–4616.

Jordan, J.V., Kaplan, A.G., Stiver, I.P., Surrey, J.L. and Miller, J.B., 1991. *Women's growth in connection: Writings from the Stone Center.* Guilford Press.

Kalyanasundaram, G., 2018. Why do startups fail? A case study based empirical analysis in Bangalore. *Asian Journal of Innovation and Policy, 7*(1), pp.79–102.

Kanze, D., Huang, L., Conley, M.A. and Higgins, E.T., 2018. We ask men to win and women not to lose: Closing the gender gap in startup funding. *Academy of Management Journal, 61*(2), pp.586–614.

Kotter, J.P., 1996. *Leading change.* Harvard Business School Press.

Lewis, P., 2014. Postfeminism, femininities and organization studies: Exploring a new agenda. *Organization Studies, 35*(12), pp.1845–1866.

Marlow, S. and McAdam, M., 2012. Analyzing the influence of gender upon high-technology venturing within the context of business incubation. *Entrepreneurship Theory and Practice, 36*(4), pp.655–676.

Miller, J.B., 1976. *Toward a new psychology of women.* Beacon Press.

Moss-Racusin, C.A., Dovidio, J.F., Brescoll, V.L., Graham, M.J. and Handelsman, J., 2012. Science faculty's subtle gender biases favor male students. *Proceedings of the National Academy of Sciences, 109*(41), pp.16474–16479.

Moss-Racusin, C.A., Pietri, E.S., Hennes, E.P., Dovidio, J.F., Brescoll, V.L., Roussos, G. and Handelsman, J., 2018. Reducing STEM gender bias with VIDS (video interventions for diversity in STEM). *Journal of Experimental Psychology*: Applied, *24*(2), p.236.

Offermann, L.R., Kennedy Jr, J.K. and Wirtz, P.W., 1994. Implicit leadership theories: Content, structure, and generalizability. *The Leadership Quarterly, 5*(1), pp.43–58.

Ozkazanc-Pan, B. and Clark Muntean, S., 2021. *Entrepreneurial ecosystems: A gender perspective*, Cambridge University Press.

Patel, N. 2015. 90% of startups fail: Here's what you need to know about the 10%. *Forbes* https://www.forbes.com/sites/neilpatel/2015/01/16/90-of-startups-will-fail -heres-what-you-need-to-know-about-the-10/#6b092c246679

Phillips, S.P. and Austin, E.B., 2009. The feminization of medicine and population health. *Jama, 301*(8), pp.863–864.

Rawski, S.L. and Workman-Stark, A.L., 2018. Masculinity contest cultures in policing organizations and recommendations for training interventions. *Journal of Social Issues, 74*(3), pp.607–627.

Rogers, E.M., 2010. *Diffusion of innovations.* Simon & Schuster.

Schiebinger, L. 2008. Gendered innovations in science, health, and technology. *Wiley Online* Library.

Stead, V., 2017. Belonging and women entrepreneurs: Women's navigation of gendered assumptions in entrepreneurial practice. *International Small Business Journal, 35*(1), pp.61–77.

Tajfel, H., 1974. Social identity and intergroup behaviour. *Information (International Social* Science Council), *13*(2), pp.65–93.

Vandello, J.A. and Bosson, J.K., 2013. Hard won and easily lost: A review and synthesis of theory and research on precarious manhood. *Psychology of Men & Masculinity*, *14*(2), p.101.

Williams, J.C., Berdahl, J.L. and Vandello, J.A., 2016. Beyond work–life "integration". *Annual Review of Psychology*, 67, pp.515–539.

4. Increasing women's representation as founders of university spinout companies: a case for action

Heather Griffiths, Simonetta Manfredi, Alexis Still and Charikleia Tzanakou

1. INTRODUCTION

University spinouts have been perceived as increasingly significant contributors towards economic growth and development at regional and national levels (Guerrero et al., 2015; Shane, 2005; Vincett, 2010). University spinouts are 'based on the exploitation of new processes, products or services arising from the knowledge gained and the results obtained in the university itself' (Miranda et al., 2018, p.1008). According to the UK Higher Education Statistical Agency (HESA, 2017), spinouts are defined as registered companies created to exploit intellectual property (IP) that has originated from within a university or a research institute. These companies are usually created by academics within their normal contract of employment and research duties supported by their institution who retain a stake in the company's equity. Thus, spinouts and commercialisation of research are becoming an increasingly important part of academic careers especially, although not exclusively, for those academics working in STEM disciplines.

Too few women researchers are leading spinout companies. Globally, women only represent 14% of inventors listed in patent applications and within the EU, the ratio of women to men among inventors is 9 per 100 (De Kleijn et al., 2020; Elsevier, 2017). In the UK, only 13% of active university spinouts are founded by women (Griffiths and Humbert, 2019). The underrepresentation of women in university spinouts and academic entrepreneurship does not only prevent the utilisation of an untapped source of talent driving regional and national economic development but can also limit the quality and societal relevance of the produced knowledge technology and/or innovation (EC, 2020).

Existing literature has investigated challenges for women academic entrepreneurs but they are often framed as individual problems (Miranda et al.,

2018; also Oftedal et al., 2018; Zalevski and Swiszczowski, 2009) rather than structural barriers. This chapter examines the experiences of women and men spinout founders in the UK higher education landscape focusing particularly on the challenges of time and work–life balance, access to relatable role models and funding, and finally gender bias as structural challenges. Thus, this chapter provides key insights to higher education institutions in the UK and beyond in terms of fostering an inclusive and more enabling environment for academic spinouts and entrepreneurship.

This chapter starts by outlining the problem and reviewing the main themes from extant literature. This is followed by a brief explanation of the methodology and a presentation of the key findings from this research. It concludes with some reflections on the research findings and some recommendations to improve women's representation in spinout leadership.

2. WOMEN'S UNDERREPRESENTATION IN ACADEMIC ENTREPRENEURSHIP

2.1 The Higher Education and Spinout Landscape in the UK: Setting the Context

Encouraging and understanding women's engagement in spinout companies is of strategic importance to the UK's new Industrial Strategy which aims to increase investment in science, research and innovation and to support new businesses and growth. It has been estimated that addressing women's representation in entrepreneurship more widely could boost the UK economy by £250 billion, which is the equivalent to 11.8% of the UK's yearly GDP (Rose, 2019, p.6).

It is difficult to establish the extent of the underrepresentation of women researchers as founders of spinout companies in the UK, as there is no official publicly available data. The UK Higher Education Business and Community Interaction (HEBCI) survey, which provides information on spinout activities, does not report on the gender of founders or any other equality characteristic. At present, a private company called Beauhurst[1] is the only source where comprehensive data can be found which relates to women's representation as founders as well as information about their companies, such as their size, type of investments and stage of development. As part of our project, we purchased data from Beauhurst and undertook comprehensive analysis, which revealed that in 2019 only 13% of active university spinouts in the UK were founded by women (Griffiths and Humbert, 2019). These findings are consistent with previous studies that highlighted the paucity of women researchers' involvement with academic entrepreneurial activities and spinouts in particular (see for example Hewitt-Dundas, 2015; Jarboe et al., 2018; Lawton Smith et al., 2017;

Pennington Manches, 2017; Rosa and Dawson, 2006). These studies show that little progress has been made in this area in terms of achieving a better gender balance.

The limited number of women spinout founders cannot be entirely attributed to their overall underrepresentation of women in STEM subjects and professorial roles (Rosa and Dawson, 2006). In the UK, women's representation in academic staff varies across STEM fields ranging from electrical, electronic, computer engineering (15.9%), physics (19.7%), and chemistry (29.1%) to more reasonable levels in biosciences (46.2%). However, only 22.6% of women occupy professorial posts in STEM subjects (Advance HE, 2020; Guyan et al., 2019). Academic entrepreneurship seems to also reflect the wider UK entrepreneurial landscape that, as highlighted by the Rose Review of Female Entrepreneurs (Rose, 2019),[2] is highly male dominated.

Griffiths and Humbert (2019) also revealed that the spinouts landscape is highly polarised, not just in terms of gender but also in terms of geography and institutions' research intensity. Half of spinout companies are created in the so-called 'golden triangle' of UK cities where the elite universities of Cambridge, Oxford and London are located. Moreover, 70% of spinout companies originate from research-intensive Higher Education Institutions (HEIs) in the elite Russell Group.[3] Unsurprisingly, universities with a higher number of spinouts also had a higher proportion of women compared to the national average of 13%. These were Imperial College with 22% of women founders, the University of Oxford 18% and the University of Cambridge 17%. The institution with the highest proportion of women's representation as founders is the non-Russell Group university, Royal College of Art (RCA) with 12 of their 28 spinouts having a woman founder, translating into 43% of their spinouts being founded by a woman or mixed gender team (ibid., p.20). The RCA is a unique case as they are the only institution known to include student developed IP within their spinout classification (Beauhurst, 2021) and design-led innovation is embedded in the institution's heritage, and continues to be a core part of the teaching and research culture. Although this analysis of the UK spinouts data provides a comprehensive overview, it is an ad hoc study undertaken as part of a specific project and it does not address the problem about the lack of publicly available data to benchmark and monitor women's participation in spinout leadership. However, the polarisation it exposes suggests a need for more focus on the challenges to spinout creation from a structural perspective.

This institutional polarisation with gender implication might be further amplified with the introduction of the Knowledge Exchange Framework (KEF),[4] which has brought into focus commercialisation of research and university spinout companies. The need for addressing gender imbalances in spinout leadership seems to have gone under the radar of equality-driven initiatives within the higher education sector, for example Athena SWAN and the Public Sector Equality Duty (Equality Act 2010) that requires institutions to place equality considerations at the core of all their policies and practices. A lack of proactive structural interventions in research and innovation has also been highlighted by a review undertaken by Advance HE (2019) on Equality, Diversity and Inclusion (EDI). This has identified 'a gap in relation to EDI interventions in other areas of the R&I [research and innovation] landscape' and in particular 'work related to innovation' (p.6) which provides the environment for spinout activities.

2.2 University Spinouts in the Literature – a Gender Perspective

As highlighted by Hayter et al. (2018) in their extensive review of literature on spinout companies, academic entrepreneurship is often seen as a male dominated enterprise, which reflects how entrepreneurship is more widely perceived. There is a small but growing body of literature that looks at the underrepresentation of women researchers in academic entrepreneurial activities, including spinouts.

Reflecting wider trends in gender and entrepreneurship research, much of the existing literature on women academic entrepreneurs frames barriers as individual problems, such as women's lack of entrepreneurial intention (see Miranda et al., 2018; also Oftedal et al., 2018; Zalevski and Swiszczowski, 2009); their reduced social capital (Murray and Graham, 2007; Parker et al., 2017; Rosa and Dawson, 2006); or lack of business experience (DeTienne and Chandler, 2007; Ding et al., 2006; Rosa and Dawson, 2006; Zalevski and Swiszczowski, 2009). Several of these same studies also identify structural barriers that may affect women researchers more than men, such as exclusion from the 'boys club' (Murray and Graham, 2007) or insufficient support, information, or encouragement from institutions and TTOs (Rosa and Dawson, 2006; Zalevski and Swiszczowski, 2009; see also Sinell et al., 2018). More specifically women academic entrepreneurs have fewer role models (Sinell et al., 2018; Zalevski and Swiszczowski, 2009) and less time available to dedicate to commercialisation than men academics (Rosa and Dawson, 2006; Parker et al., 2017; Sinell et al., 2018.) For women, these challenges are set against a backdrop of a male-dominated investment space (Jarboe et al., 2018; Malmström et al., 2018; Teare and Desmond, 2016) where women's innovation receives less funding than men's (Amatucci and Sohl, 2004; Minniti, 2009) and women's spinout companies receive less than 10% of the total available investment (Pennington Manches, 2017). What emerges from all of these studies is the need for locating the problem within institutions and focusing on structural barriers that exclude women, especially in STEM disciplines, from engaging in spinout leadership. Thus, this chapter contributes towards highlighting the structural barriers that women spinout founders face in the UK higher education landscape.

To analyse these challenges and barriers, our findings are interpreted using Sturm's 'second generation bias' (2001, p.460) theory. Second generation bias is described as:

> social practices and patterns of interaction among groups within the workplace that, over time, exclude non dominant groups. Exclusion is frequently difficult to trace directly to intentional, discrete actions of particular actors, and may sometimes be visible only in the aggregate. Structures of decision-making, opportunity, and power fail to surface these patterns of exclusion, and themselves produce differential access and opportunities.

Often these practices and patterns of interaction are disguised as being gender neutral but they are heavily gendered and pose almost invisible barriers difficult to pin-point. However, as argued by Sturm (ibid.) it is essential to define the problem in order to design and implement effective remedies that can tackle second generation bias. By analysing interview data through the lens of gender, this study helps us to better understand what these established practices and patterns of interaction may look like in the spinouts ecosystem[5] and how they affect women's access to opportunities for academic entrepreneurship and business leadership.

3.   RESEARCH METHODOLOGY

This study is based on qualitative data from 35 interviews undertaken with spinout founders within the science, technology, engineering and mathematics (STEM) fields. The sample comprised of 20 women and 15 men who had spun out their research from institutions across the UK. The sample size was designed to ensure we could explore a breadth of experiences with contextually rich accounts (Bowen, 2008) whilst ensuring that common and environmental themes emerge that are meaningful across the cohort (Alasuutari, 1995; Seale, 1999).

The age range of the sample was 28 to 77 years old, with women being on average 45 years old and men 46 years old. Only 31% of interviewees were senior academics (professor or associate professor) when they spun out their research, challenging the common perception amongst research participants and the wider academic community that academic entrepreneurship is the preserve of older, more established academics (Hayter et al., 2018). Interestingly though, men were overrepresented in this group as only four women were in senior positions at the time of spinning out compared to seven men. Similarly, eight women (40%) founded their spinouts when they were early career researchers (ECRs) compared to only three men (20%).

Over three quarters (77%) of founders were employed by Russell Group universities at the point of spinning out, which is similar to the national average of 70% (Griffiths and Humbert, 2019). Despite efforts to include underrepresented groups in the sample, the majority of participants were white and disclosed no disabilities or other protected characteristics. This means that our research has limited capacity to explore other forms of diversity within the spinouts ecosystem but the study has highlighted some intersectional issues that would benefit from a deeper focus in further research.

Interviews were conducted between January 2019 and October 2019 with the majority (n = 39) conducted over the phone the remainder held face-to-face. Interviews were audio recorded and transcribed verbatim. Several members of the research team coded the first ten transcripts to ensure continuity and develop a mutually agreed coding framework drawing on key themes from the literature and interview guide. The final framework incorporated the most frequent and significant themes (Charmaz, 2006) and was structured around the chronology of the spinout journey.

4.   FINDINGS

Women and men often reported very similar challenges across their spinout journeys but when analysed through the lens of gender the way they experienced these challenges differed. Thematic analysis of the interview data showed that these differences were most pronounced in the areas of time and work–life balance, access to role models and funding, and experience of gender bias and discrimination. In this section, we follow these themes using quotes from the interviews to give a voice to our participants. Although the sample included women and men founders, the majority of the quotes are from women as it is their experience we wish to highlight in this chapter.

4.1   Time and Work–life Balance

A major challenge identified by many participants was having sufficient time to devote to the development of a spinout company with all the other demands of an academic role. Participants' accounts highlighted a tension between the 'publish or perish culture' of academia and their pursuit of academic entrepreneurship. Their narratives suggested that universities may be at best ambivalent as to how they view these activities. Several interviewees commented about the lack of proper recognition of commercial activities by universities in academic promotion criteria, as illustrated by the quote from this man founder:

> [The university] does not recognise this kind of thing in terms of promotion, so even if you are making hundreds of millions of products the university doesn't recognise that at all. [Interviewee 17, Man founder]

This lack of formal recognition by institutions is also reflected in the participants' responses on how they divided their time between managing their spinout and maintaining their existing academic responsibilities. It transpired that individuals had very little or no support from their institutions about how to best manage their time so had to find their own way to 'make it work' often at a personal cost. The following responses were typical of how participant's felt about their time management and work–life balance:

> You have to make it work which is not helpful and people ask me and I wish I could give a better answer as to how one does it. [Interviewee 36, Woman]
> How do I manage my time? Badly is probably the answer [...] I've got a full teaching commitment, dissertation students, PhD students, other research activities, course admin, industry, outreach activities, all the usual stuff [...] you're just having to squeeze it in where you can. [Interviewee 15, Man]

Others relied on the understanding of their line managers and colleagues as reported by this woman founder:

> I consider myself very fortunate because my line manager and his line manager are very supportive of what I do. To be honest, they probably cut me some slack in the university [...] I'm very lucky that I have had colleagues around me, who aren't being obstructive and that is not universal, and I know people in other parts of the university, who have had more obstructive line managers or colleagues. [Interviewee 4, Woman]

The lack of formal time allocation within workload planning for commercialisation activities impacts negatively on individuals' work–life balance and places those with caring responsibilities at a greater disadvantage. When specifically asked about this, several men founders praised their partners for doing all the childcare and acknowledged that without this help they would probably not have been able to establish their spinouts. On the contrary, several of the women founders with children talked about their struggle to combine the two, like this woman founder who said:

> The balance between family and business, that's another challenge [...] Sometimes the balance is there, sometimes the balance is not there, but being aware that the balance should be there I think is already a step forward. [Interviewee 32, Woman]

Others instead mentioned devising strategies which suited their needs, such as the following:

> I try and really schedule my time so I have four days where I am really focused on work and three days when I am more focused on the children or at least in their waking hours, and maybe do a bit of extra work […] but not so it affects them, just try to get a good balance. [Interviewee 28, Woman]

For many founders, managing their time was about balance and for these women that included actively making time for family. Many founders, but particularly those with young children, relied on support from family to help them maintain this balance. Some women who successfully founded a spinout company eventually opted to work full-time for the business and left academia altogether resulting in a loss of talent to the Higher Education sector. A lack of formal recognition of academic entrepreneurship at an institutional level means that the availability of time is clearly a significant barrier to spinning out. This is likely to deter many women from pursuing spinout leadership, but also men who wish to have greater involvement with childcare and those with other caring responsibilities or life priorities.

4.2   Access to Role Models and Funding

Most participants spoke about the importance of having good mentors who could guide them through the business development process, something that the majority of scientists would not have experience of. Several interviewees valued the support received from their mentors. However, most mentors from the business community tended to be older (white) men and some women felt that this generational gap was unhelpful, as highlighted by the following experiences:

> The mentor I was assigned to was male and I liked him, but he was very old school … He was like a different generation and he treated me like a bit of a silly daughter. [Interviewee 1, Woman]
> We didn't have the commercial experience […] so we had this series of what we used to call blind dates where we'd meet mostly retired gentlemen in pubs, who were trying to help us, none of whom was of any use whatsoever. [Interviewee 12, Woman]

Some women spoke about the lack of relatable mentors or role models, which for them meant other women who had recently been through a similar experience. They wanted someone like themselves to inspire and guide them and ideally offer emotional as well as practical support. As Ahl and Marlow (2012, p.544) identify, women rarely feature within the 'mindset or image of what an entrepreneur is or should be' and more women mentors and visible role models would change perceptions not only of women spinout founders but also of women in STEM. Consequently, seeing women as STEM leaders and spinout founders may also help to attract more women to study these disciplines and pursue careers in the sciences and challenge the patterns of interaction that create second generation bias (Sturm, 2001) for women across their spinout journeys.

An interesting observation was made by a woman founder who saw a connection between the ability to win large grants from research funding councils and the creation of the conditions to become an academic entrepreneur. She pointed out that:

> If you become an entrepreneur, you have to have good standing in the university. You only have good standing in the university if you are bringing in money. [Interviewee 23, Woman]

She went on to explain that securing large grants gives credibility in the eyes of an institution and this would make it easier for an individual academic being offered support and resources to commercialise their research. Although this represents the view of just one participant, it is a point worth considering especially as an analysis undertaken by UKRI (2020, p.3) shows that women principal investigators receive less money than men principal investigators across all funding councils. This suggests that it may be problematic for women to secure the amount of funding that would put them in 'good standing' with their university and provide them with the resources to dedicate more time to their research.

Securing funding and investment was a challenge for all founders but especially those who were relying on money from Venture Capitalists (VC). Investment from VCs would typically be sought once the company has reached a certain level of maturity, especially as VCs tend to look for quick returns on their investments within a period of about five or six years. For women founders however, it seems that securing funding may present an additional challenge, as the investment community is highly male dominated and possibly biased against women founders. When talking about her experience of engaging with the investor community, one woman founder said:

> It is very male dominated. I was a female professor and professors in the science world are also male dominated, but I was not prepared for the extent of that within that sector. Getting used to walking into a roomful of [...] generally older men in suits. [Interviewee 23, Woman]

Women often feel 'othered' in male dominated sectors (Powell and Sang, 2015) through differential treatment. This was demonstrated in one of the accounts of a woman founder who described a rather uncomfortable experience with an all-male panel of investors. She felt that she was not being taken seriously and this knocked her confidence to the point that she almost gave up on developing her company:

> The first question one of the guys on the panel asked me was, 'Why are you even here?' […] One of the guys said to me, 'Nobody is ever going to buy a single one of these', and I said to him, 'You don't understand', people are already buying them and they are being used across the world. It was like they couldn't hear me […] I came away from it I thought, I just don't know if I want to put myself through this. [Interviewee 1, Woman]
> Another woman founder commented that 'it is harder for women to raise money from the old boys' club' [Interviewee 12, Woman].

Although not all women felt they experienced gender bias during the investment process, many of them identified the sector as being dominated by men and on many occasions they were one of only a small number of women in the room. As a consequence, these extracts offer examples of what Sturm (2001, p.460) refers to as the 'intentional, discrete actions' within second generation bias that accumulate over time to create exclusion and 'produce differential access and opportunities'. Some founders commented that things were slowly changing and that in recent years they have seen more women in the investment community but that progress remained slow. Although firm conclusions cannot be drawn from these experiences reported by a small sample of women founders, if we consider them within the context of a series of recent studies on gender bias in investment (Malmström et al., 2018; Rose, 2019) the lack of women in this space is problematic for women as academic entrepreneurs and business leaders.

4.3   Gender Bias and Discrimination

Almost all women in the sample felt that their gender had not detrimentally impacted their academic or entrepreneurial experience, however, there were several accounts of gender bias, discrimination and stereotypes from women of all ages and backgrounds, even if they did not recognise it as such for themselves. Here we argue that these instances of gender bias create an 'accumulated disadvantage' (Valiant, 1999) for women that, as Sturm (2001, p.460) identifies, become visible 'only in the aggregate'.

Women founders in our sample are used to working in highly male-dominated environments and, as one of them said, '[I have] always been in STEM, always been in the minority rather than the majority so I've kind of got used to that' [Interviewee 32, Woman]. As the minority, women in STEM have become stereotyped, particularly about the way they look and behave. This is exemplified by the experience of one woman who, as she was having her photo taken for an article in the press, was asked by the journalist to make changes to her appearance to fit a stereotypical and unfeminine image of a woman scientist:

> I had my hair down [...] I was wearing lipstick and a nice top and they literally said to me [...]'Could you please put laser goggles on and could you tie up your hair and do you have like a jumper and could you wipe off your lipstick? [...] We want to purposefully show that there are females in science, but also let's make you fit the stereotype so that people believe you are a scientist. [Interviewee 12, Woman]

Some stereotypes were more sinister in the way they portrayed women, such as the insinuation that women 'sleep their way to the top'. As this younger woman founder explains, this experience is ubiquitous amongst her female peers in innovation and entrepreneurship:

> There were fourteen of us, and there were five women, and we were discussing about how women are perceived in business, and we did a straw poll of all the [members] and said put your hand up if you've been accused of sleeping with somebody to get to your position of CEO. Every single woman put their hand up. [Interviewee 3, Woman]

Being used to 'always being in the minority' probably explains why these women have not reported specific incidents of stereotyping or discrimination that are typical of second generation bias (Sturm, 2001). They have become resilient to these comments over time but for many women academic entrepreneurs, overcoming gender stereotypes creates an additional challenge.

Some of the accounts from this study hinted at possible additional disadvantage caused by the intersection between gender and other protected characteristics like age and ethnicity. Although this study sample was too small to properly investigate these issues, it has flagged up some possible intersectional issues that may warrant further investigation. The intersection of gender and age emerged more prominently especially as several women in our sample were rather young when they founded their companies. For example, among participants who talked about their experience of patenting, young women seem to find this process particularly challenging, as typified by this extract from an interview with a 28-year-old founder who started her company as a postdoc:

> It was something of an uphill struggle to get to the point of filing a patent. Once I was able to convince those who held the purse strings that it should [be patented], things got a lot better. [Interviewee 4, Woman]

Lack of support from university Technology Transfer Offices (TTOs) combined with difficulties to convince institutions to fund their patents suggest that the gender compounded with age raised issues around lack of credibility that possibly acted as an additional barrier for younger women.

Age and gender were also raised as issues within the context of networking and mentoring relationships. A woman founder pointed out that networking with potential investors, who tend to be part of a highly male dominated community, could be uncomfortable for younger women:

> If you are in a sea of men and they tell you, 'You must network', and your pitch to a sea of men is essentially to proposition them for money, there are basic things which are pejorative to women because essentially is like prostitution on some level. Not really that but it has some undercurrents to that. [Interviewee 23, Woman]

On the theme of networking, seen as playing an important function to facilitate connections with the business domain, it was also highlighted that the common practice of networking events taking place in the evening and over a glass of wine might be problematic for women with care responsibilities. A woman founder challenged the current practices of evening networking by saying:

> Why couldn't it be over afternoon tea? Why does networking always have to be in the evening to begin with, over wine and beer? [Interviewee 23, Woman]

She thought that if more women get involved in these networks they could bring about change and lead to different ways of socialising. Changing patterns of socialisation would be more inclusive for women but also for individuals from different cultural backgrounds. It can be seen how networking could be even more problematic for example for a Muslim female scientist.

Although firm conclusions cannot be drawn from our limited sample, these insights highlight the dynamics of intersectionality and how these can potentially double disadvantage and create additional barriers for women.

5.   DISCUSSION AND CONCLUSIONS

Our founders describe a spinout journey full of challenges and new experiences. They would often return to their motivation to find the determination and resilience needed to persevere through these challenges, but none of them regretted taking this leap into the unknown. Yet we can also see here a pattern of 'accumulated disadvantage' (Valiant, 1999) for women founders, impacting the way they access opportunities and explore different career paths. This disadvantage is further amplified by intersectional issues, for example between age and gender, creating additional challenges for some women.

Much of this disadvantage can be attributed to 'second generation bias' where 'social practices and patterns of interaction' (Sturm, 2001) gradually create an environment that privileges the majority and excludes minorities. In

the context of academic entrepreneurship, many of these practices and interactions take place at the institutional level and are embedded in a culture that
promotes masculine norms. One example of this is the expectation at many
institutions that running a spinout company will be done in the academic's
own time. This follows a discourse within some institutions, and across the
wider academy, that academic entrepreneurship is a less legitimate pursuit
of knowledge than more traditional forms of research. This is reflected in the
responses of many founders who said they were not given any formal time
allocation for this work, creating a significant challenge for those who wanted
to maintain a sustainable work–life balance, especially for those with caring
responsibilities. In our sample, it was women with young children who were
most vocal about this and in many cases, these women left academia altogether
to focus on their businesses resulting in a loss of talent in the higher education
sector. To try and retain these women and help many other founders better
manage their time, HEIs can challenge their own cultural practices, such
as recognising academic entrepreneurship as a valuable part of knowledge
exchange and support researchers to integrate commercialisation activities
within their existing workload.

Whilst changes at the institutional level are welcome, second generation
gender bias is still an issue within the wider innovation landscape and will
remain so whilst it continues to be dominated by men. Many of the examples
above show how subtle second generation gender bias can be, such as young
women struggling to assert their credentials during the patenting process or
their business idea being belittled by a male investor panel. More worryingly,
there is also evidence of more blatant discrimination as our women founders
described being stereotyped about their appearance or lack of ability and
sexuality. As long as women are the minority in both STEM research and the
business community, they will continue to face these subtle, or in some cases
not so subtle, instances of gender bias. Thus, it is crucial that HEIs and those
in the wider innovation ecosystem work together to ensure women are more
visible in these spaces. It is recommended that they seek out more women
entrepreneurs to act as role models and mentors, especially at events designed
to support academic entrepreneurship; ensure more women and other under-
represented minorities feature on investment panels and at all levels; create and
promote funding opportunities that support diversity in research, entrepreneurship and commercialisation; and perhaps most importantly, be reflective of
their own practices and interactions, such as the persistent reliance on evening
networking events with drinks.

Such actions create additional challenges for those working in HEI innovation spaces but in turn may enable more women and minorities to access
academic entrepreneurship opportunities and create successful businesses.
As with many EDI interventions, beneficiaries extend beyond women and

minorities to the wider community of (potential) entrepreneurs who might share similar challenges and would benefit from additional support from their institution and others in their network. As the higher education sector leans ever further towards impact and knowledge exchange, it has a responsibility to ensure all academics have the opportunity to engage in this directional shift and shape this largely uncharted territory in an inclusive way to ensure a more level playing field from the very beginning.

NOTES

1. Beauhurst is a private organisation that tracks high-growth companies in the UK, including all companies that have spun out from an academic institution. Data are collected from a variety of publicly available and licenced sources, including the national registrar of UK businesses, media articles and press releases, company websites, LinkedIn and from large public bodies such as Innovate UK. Beauhurst's data on university spinouts was acquired when they bought out the company Spinouts UK in 2018, which has tracked the progress of UK spinouts and their fundraising activity since 2011.
2. The Rose Review of Female Entrepreneurs is an independent review commissioned by the UK government's Treasury department and conducted by Alison Rose, Deputy CEO at NatWest Holdings and CEO of Commercial & Private Banking.
3. The Russell Group is a self-selected group of UK universities that formed in 1994 and is currently made up of 24 institutions, including Oxford, Cambridge and several London colleges. The group has a reputation for representing the 'best' and most 'research intensive' universities in the UK but this proclamation regularly comes under scrutiny (see for example, Boliver, 2015).
4. The Knowledge Exchange Framework is one of three assessment criteria introduced by the UK government to monitor and benchmark activity within the HE sector. The KEF assesses an institution's knowledge exchange outputs and sits alongside the Research Excellence Framework (REF) and Teaching Excellence Framework (TEF).
5. In the context of university spinouts, the innovation ecosystem can be defined as 'the strategic and collective actions of various [internal and external] organizational components [...] in order to maximize both the entrepreneurial and innovative contributions of universities' (Adapted from Hayter, 2016).

REFERENCES

Advance HE (2019) 'Equality and higher education: staff statistical report 2019'. https://www.advance-he.ac.uk/knowledge-hub/equality-higher-education-statistical -report-2019 (Accessed 12 November 2020).

Advance HE (2020) 'Equality and higher education: staff statistical report 2020'. https://www.advance-he.ac.uk/knowledge-hub/equality-higher-education-statistical -report-2020. (Accessed 11 November 2020).

Ahl, H., and Marlow, S. (2012) Exploring the Dynamics of Gender, Feminism and Entrepreneurship: Advancing Debate to Escape a Dead End? *Organization*, 19(5), pp.543–562.

Alasuutari, P. (1995) *Researching Culture: Qualitative Method and Cultural Studies*. London and Sage Publications.

Amatucci, F.M. and Sohl, J.E. (2004) Women Entrepreneurs Securing Business Angel Financing: Tales from the Field. *Venture Capital*, 6(2/3), pp.181–196.

Beauhurst (2021) 'Spotlight on Spinouts: UK Academic Spinout Trends'. https://www .beauhurst.com/research/spinouts-spotlight/ (Accessed 27 January 2021).

Boliver, V. (2015) Are there Distinctive Clusters of Higher and Lower Status Universities in the UK? *Oxford Review of Education*, 41(5), pp.608–627.

Bowen, G.A. (2008) Naturalistic Inquiry and the Saturation Concept: A Research Note. *Qualitative Research*, 8(1), pp.137–152.

Charmaz, K. (2006) *Constructing Grounded Theory*. London and Thousand Oaks, CA: Sage Publications.

De Kleijn, M., Jayabalasingham, B., Falk-Krzesinski, H.J., Collins, T., Kuiper-Hoyng, L., Cingolani, I., Zhang, J., Roberge, G. et al. (2020) *The Researcher Journey Through a Gender Lens: An Examination of Research Participation, Career Progression and Perceptions Across the Globe*. Amsterdam: Elsevier. www.elsevier .com/gender-report (Accessed 23 February 2021).

DeTienne, D.R. and Chandler, G.N. (2007) The Role of Gender in Opportunity Identification. *Entrepreneurship Theory and Practice*, 31(3), pp.365–386.

Ding, W.W., Murray, F. and Stuart, T.E. (2006) Gender Differences in Patenting in the Academic Life Sciences. *Science*, 313, pp.665–667.

Elsevier (2017) *Gender in the Global Research Landscape: Analysis of Research Performance Through a Gender Lens Across 20 Years, 12 Geographies, and 27 Subject Areas*. Amsterdam: Elsevier. https://www.elsevier.com/connect/gender -report (Accessed 23 February 2021).

European Commission (EC) (2020) *Gendered Innovations 2: How Inclusive Analysis Contributes to Research and Innovation*. Luxembourg: Publications Office of the European Union.

Griffiths, H. and Humbert, A.L. (2019) Gender and University Spinouts in the UK: Geography, Governance and Growth, Oxford: Oxford Brookes University Centre for Diversity Policy Research and Practice.

Guerrero, M., Cunningham, J.A. and Urbano, D. (2015) Economic Impact of Entrepreneurial Universities' Activities: An Exploratory Study of the United Kingdom. *Research Policy*, 44(3), 748–764. https://doi.org/10.1016/j.respol.2014 .10.008

Guyan, K., Douglas, F. and Oloyede, D. (2019) Inclusion in Research and Innovation: UK Review. https://www.ukri.org/files/final-edi-review-uk/ (Accessed 15 January 2020).

Hayter, C.S. (2016) A Trajectory of Early-Stage Spinoff Success: The Role of Knowledge Intermediaries Within an Entrepreneurial University Ecosystem. *Small Business Economics*, 47(3), pp.633–656.

Hayter, C.S., Nelson, A.J., Zayed, S. and O'Connor, A. (2018) Conceptualising Academic Entrepreneurship Ecosystems: A Review Analysis and Extension of the Literature. *Journal of Technology Transfer*, 43, pp.1039–1082.

HESA (2017) HE-BCI Record 2016/17 – General Guidance on Table 4: Intellectual Property (IP). https://www.hesa.ac.uk/collection/c16032/hebci_b_table 4 (Accessed 12 November 2020).

Hewitt-Dundas, N. (2015) Enterprise Research Centre: Profiling UK University Spin-Outs. https://www.enterpriseresearch.ac.uk/wp-content/uploads/2015/07/ERC -ResPap35-M.-Hewitt-Dundas.pdf (Accessed 14 March 2019).

Jarboe, N., Grisoni, L. and Manfredi, S. (2018) University Spinouts: Exploring Women's Participation – A Discussion Paper. https://www.brookes.ac.uk/ uploadedfiles/faculty_of_business/gender_and_university_spinouts/site_assets/ documents/university%20spinouts.pdf (Accessed 11 November 2020).

Lawton Smith, H., Etzkowitz, H., Meschitti, V. and Poulovassilis, A. (2017) Female Academic Entrepreneurship and Commercialisation: Reviewing the Evidence and Identifying the Challenges. In Henry, C., Nelson, T. and Lewis, K. (Eds), *The Routledge Companion to Global Female Entrepreneurship* (pp.78–92). London: Routledge.

Malmström, M., Voitkane, A., Johansson, J. and Wincent, J. (2018) When Stereotypical Gender Notions See the Light of Day, Will they Burst? Venture Capitalists' Gender Construction Versus Venturing Performance Facts. *Journal of Business Venturing Insights*, 9, pp.32–28.

Minniti, M. (2009) *Gender Issues in Entrepreneurship*. Boston: Now Publishing.

Miranda, F.J., Chamorro-Mera, A. and Rubio, S. (2018) Re-thinking University Spin-off: A Critical Literature Review and a Research Agenda. *The Journal of Technology Transfer*, 43(4), 1007–1038.

Murray, F. and Graham, L. (2007) Buying Science and Selling Science: Gender Differences in the Market for Commercial Science. *Industrial and Corporate Change*, 16(4), pp.657–689.

Oftedal, E.M., Iakovleva, T.A. and Foss, L. (2018) University Context Matter: An Institutional Perspective on Entrepreneurial Intentions of Students. *Education + Training*, 60(7/8), pp.873–890.

Parker, M., Hayter, C.S., Lynch, L. and Mohammed, R. (2017) Barriers to Academic Entrepreneurship Among Women: A Review of the Constituent Literatures. In Link, A.N. (Ed.), *Gender and Entrepreneurial Activity* (pp.117–150). Cheltenham, UK and Northampton, MA, USA: Edward Elgar Publishing.

Penningtons Manches (2017) Academic Spinouts: A Report on the Funding of UK Spinouts 2016–2017. https://www.penningtons. co.uk/media/1314304/ academicspinouts-a-report-on-the-funding-of-ukspinouts-2016-2017.pdf (Accessed 1 February 2020).

Powell, A. and Sang, K.J. (2015) Everyday Experiences of Sexism in Male-Dominated Professions: A Bourdieusian Perspective. *Sociology*, 49(5), pp.919–936.

Rosa, P. and Dawson, A. (2006) Gender and the Commercialisation of University Science: Academic Founders of Spinout Companies. *Entrepreneurship and Regional Development*, 18(4), pp.341–366.

Rose, A. (2019) The Alison Rose Review of Female Entrepreneurship. https:// natwestbusinesshub.com/content/rosereview (Accessed 11 November 2020).

Seale, C. (1999) Quality in Qualitative Research. *Qualitative Inquiry*, 5(4), pp.465–478.

Shane, S. (2005) Government Policies to Encourage Economic Development Through Entrepreneurship: The Case of Technology Transfer. In Shane, S. (Ed.), *Economic Development Through Entrepreneurship: Government, University, and Business Linkages* (pp.33–46). Cheltenham, UK and Northampton, MA, USA: Edward Elgar Publishing.

Sinell, A., Müller-Wieland, R. and Muschner, A. (2018) Gender-Specific Constraints on Academic Entrepreneurship and Engagement in Knowledge and Technology Transfer. *Technology Innovation Management Review*, 8(2), pp.15–26.

Sturm, S. (2001) Second Generation Employment Discrimination: A Structural Approach. *Columbia Law Review*, 101, pp.458–568.
Teare, G. and Desmond, N. (2016) The First Comprehensive Study on Women in Venture Capital and Their Impact on Female Founders. *Tech Crunch*, https://techcrunch.com/2016/04/19/the-first-comprehensive-study-on-women-in-venture-capital/ (Accessed 1 February 2019).
UKRI (2020) Diversity Results for UKRI Funding Data: 2014–15 to 2018–19. https://www.ukri.org/wp-content/uploads/2020/10/UKRI-020920-DiversityResultsForUKRIFundingData2014-19.pdf (Accessed 13 November 2020).
Valiant, V. (1999) *Why So Slow? Advancement of Women*. Cambridge, MA: MIT Press.
Vincett, P.S., (2010) The Economic Impacts of Academic Spin-Off Companies, and Their Implications for Public Policy. *Research Policy* 39, pp.736–747.
Zalevski, A. and Swiszczowski, L. (2009) Gender and Attitudes to Enterprise: Survey of UK Doctorate Students in Science, Engineering and Technology. *Equal Opportunities International*, 28(1), pp.65–79.

5. Women entrepreneurs in new technology-based businesses in Sweden: experiences as inventors, innovators, and entrepreneurs

Besrat Tesfaye and Christina Wainikka

1.   INTRODUCTION

There is a growing concern about women's participation in technological innovation and entrepreneurship. Although women contribute to all innovation endeavors in all fields, they remain highly under-represented in terms of access, participation, and being rewarded for those endeavors. The case of Sweden makes a useful illustration. Sweden is among the top ten world innovation leaders, measured in number of patents, but there is a persistent gender gap in all areas of the intellectual endeavors underlying technological innovation. Only 5 of the 100 "high-profiled" Swedish innovations over the last three centuries are attributed to women inventors (Sandström, 2014). In more recent years, a small but positive development has been observed, although change is happening at a very slow pace. A special report on women's participation in patent applications to the Swedish Intellectual Property Office (PRV, 2019), for example, shows that approximately 14 percent of all the patent applications submitted included at least one woman and a mere 4 percent of the patents were granted to women-only teams. The level of women's participation in the formation of new technology-based firms (NTBF) is even lower. During the years 2000–2017, the share of NTBF with at least one woman in the team was only 10 percent (European Commission, 2020). The gender gap in women's participation in intellectual endeavors is also evident when considered in view of the participation of women in traditionally male-dominated areas such as engineering. A report from the Swedish Higher Education Authority (UKÄ, 2020) shows that the number of women graduates has been increasing during the past ten years. In 2010/2011 the number of women graduates constituted 28 percent. In 2018/2019 the number of women graduates increased to 35 percent of all engineering graduates. A closer look at differences between the various schools of engineering shows that most women graduate from "soft" sub-fields such as Industrial Organization.

Although the existence of a gender gap is not contested, its measurements are not clear and precise. All inventions may not be patentable or patented, and all patents may not lead to the startup of NTBFs. Yet patents are used as a measure of inventiveness or innovativeness and often as proxy for the innovation itself. Likewise, entrepreneurship (NTBF) is used as an indicator of the level of commercialization of innovations. Taken together as process, however, invention, innovation, and entrepreneurship can be helpful in understanding gender-disadvantage and shed light on the low participation of women in technological innovations. This study departs from a process view of invention, innovation, and entrepreneurship and assumes these to be different phases of innovative entrepreneurship. Invention can be defined as a novel (patentable) solution resulting from a combination of existing knowledge. Innovation is the introduction of these new combinations (an invention) to the market (Utterback, 1971; Schumpeter, 1934).

The gender gap in innovative entrepreneurship is not specific to Sweden. It is universal, persisting across nations, regions, industries, technologies, and enterprises (Ejermo and Jung, 2014; Frietsch et al., 2008; Thévenon et al., 2012; WIPO, 2020). Women hold fewer intellectual property rights (IPRs), particularly patents, and are less likely to convert their inventions into economic opportunities by establishing new technology-based businesses (Dautzenberg, 2012; Frietsch et al., 2008; Thévenon et al., 2012; WIPO, 2020). In its annual report on patent statistics for 2019, the World Intellectual Property Organization (WIPO) stated that women were named in only 18.7 percent of all international patent applications. Patents with women inventors are less likely to be cited and kept enforceable for long (Jensen et al., 2018). Moreover, their participation in patent applications was largely confined to biotechnology, pharmaceuticals, and organic chemistry. Perhaps more striking is the large deficit of women in the startup and ownership of new technology-based firms (European Commission, 2020; 2008). In the European Union, only 5–15 percent of new technology-based firms were owned by women only. The corresponding figure for the US is 5–6 percent (Coleman and Robb, 2009).

NTBF are of particular interest since these presumably introduce new products, services, processes, organizing methods, etcetera, to the market, and are therefore considered the core of an innovative economy (BarNir, 2012). NTBF contribute to the conversion of innovative ideas into economic opportunities, create jobs, and improve productivity (Zapata et al., 2017). However, the formation and successful startup of NTBF is closely intertwined with patents and the patent system. They need to be considered as an essential part of a study of the participation of women in the new technology development. A patent awards the inventor/patentee an exclusive right to own and exploit the new technology temporally (normally for a maximum of 20 years) for a given fee. By providing protection of investments in commercializing inventions, patents play a vital role in the formation and success of NTBF. In addition to temporary protection, patents benefit entrepreneurs by signaling expertise, quality, and the legitimacy of their innovations (Graham et al., 2009). These are factors that can give entrepreneurs leverage in the financing of their businesses, marketing of their new products and services, in licensing their patents, and in negotiations. Moreover, patents play a key role in the acquisition of financing for NTBF. Women hold fewer patents and are thus hindered in their efforts to capitalize on their inventions by starting a NTBF.

Whereas the existence/persistence of a gender gap in innovative entrepreneurship is well documented, very little is known about why the gap exists. Our study addresses this issue by exploring the experiences of women in inventing, patenting and commercializing their products in a highly male-dominated setting. The objective is to gain insight into the influence of gender on the performance of women as innovative entrepreneurs. We do so by studying the various obstacles women meet on their journey, from invention to innovation and entrepreneurship, using a feminist intersectional framework of analysis. We highlight intersectionality through the personal profiles of women entrepreneurs as well as their inventions. Some personal variables such as ethnicity and religion have not been considered, since the cases are homogeneous (the same ethnicity and religion as the national majority).

The remaining parts of this chapter are organized as follows. In the next section, a brief review of literature is presented. This is followed by a description of research design and method. The last section describes and analyzes the case study. In concluding the chapter, the results of the study are summarized and discussed with a view to future research.

2.   LITERATURE ON GENDER AND INNOVATIVE ENTREPRENEURSHIP

The literature review begins with an overview of the concepts of innovation, entrepreneurship and NTBF. These are concepts that together constitute innovative entrepreneurship. Innovative entrepreneurship takes place in an institutionalized socio-economic setting embedded in gendered values, norms, and traditions. The second part of the literature review, therefore, focuses on the impact of gender on innovative entrepreneurship. We summarize mainstream research on the mechanisms of gender disadvantage and how these affect the participation and performance of women in innovative entrepreneurship. However, gender disadvantages are not equally distributed. Women occupy diverse socio-economic positions and are impacted in various degrees and intensities. The final part of the literature review attempts to capture this diversity and the intersectional character of gender disadvantage. The concept of intersectionality and its application as an analytical tool in studying gender disadvantage is discussed.

Innovation and entrepreneurship are two closely related areas, sometimes regarded as two sides of the same coin. However, the level of attention given to gender in innovation as compared to in entrepreneurship research is quite different. Whereas the individual entrepreneur is central and gender occupies a strong position in mainstream entrepreneurship research, the individual is neglected and gender is almost invisible in innovation (Alsos et al., 2013; Brännback et al., 2012; Marlow, 2013; Poutanen and Kovalainen, 2013). Schumpeter (1934) defines innovation as the introduction of a new combination of existing resources, for example, a new product, a new process or a new source of material. According to this view, innovations are introduced to the market (commercialized) by an entrepreneur, who can be defined as a function rather than an individual. People are thus invisible, the role of the innovator/ entrepreneur under-communicated. Although a large body of mainstream entrepreneurship research has adopted the Schumpeterian view of innovation, the individual now occupies a focal position. Schumpeter distinguishes between inventions and innovations: a common definition of a patentable invention is a technology that is novel, unique, and has impact on the technological future (Dahlin and Behrens, 2005). For practical purposes, we consider inventions that are patented and introduced on the market as innovations. In this context, patents are assumed as proxy for innovations.

The field of entrepreneurship has expanded rapidly during the past 30 years and there is a growing body of literature. However, there is no consensus on the definition of the concept of entrepreneurship (Gartner, 1985). There is a wide variety of definitions in the literature, for example as opportunity recognition (Kirzner, 1997; Shane and Venkataraman, 2000), new business creation (Garner, 1985; Shapero and Sokol, 1982), and business growth (Davidsson et al., 2006). The concept of an entrepreneur, too, is multifaceted. It may refer to an individual, a group of individuals, or an organization who introduces an innovation on the market (Schumpeter, 1934); it may be an alert individual who recognizes opportunities (Kirzner, 1997), an individual with a higher need for achievement (McClelland, 1961), and so on. An entrepreneur in this study refers to the individual/s who has/have founded and operate/s a new technology-based business. Innovative entrepreneurs are those who create a new business in order to commercialize their patented inventions. We depart from a process view of entrepreneurship in our analysis of the journey, focusing on the gender barriers women face in their efforts to generate novel ideas and convert these into commercial opportunities such as patents and/or NTBF.

There is a growing body of literature exploring the influence of gender upon women's entrepreneurial propensity and their experiences of new business creation. The impact of gendered assumptions and institutional biases on women's entrepreneurship is recognized (Marlow, 2013). Nevertheless, a large body of this literature has been criticized for treating women like a homogeneous category, thus neglecting how various factors intersect to situate women in differing socio-economic positions (Ahl, 2006; Carter et al., 2003; Henry et al., 2016; Marlow, 2013; Swail and Marlow, 2018). Marlow (2013, p.103), for example, states that "the focus has been almost exclusively upon women's experiences of business ownership generally articulated as explorations of female entrepreneurship." This being the case, attributes such as gender, race, and class, which are also embedded in the institutional biases that critically influence women's access and experiences of entrepreneurship (ibid.), are neglected. Against the backdrop of this criticism, there has emerged a shift of focus in literature towards the broader socio-economic gender disadvantages that determine the entrepreneurial intentions, behaviors, and experiences of women.

A small proportion of this literature focuses NTBF (Alsos et al., 2013; Kuschel and Lepeley, 2016; Marlow and Swail, 2014; Nählinder et al., 2015; Neergaard et al., 2006; Ozkazanc-Pan, 2014; Poutanen and Kovalainen, 2013; Whittington and Smith-Doerr, 2005). Some of this literature ascribes the low proportion of women in innovation to the bias of the concept towards technological products and thereby an exclusion of services (Nählinder et al., 2015). Others refer to a mix of individual, organizational and institutional gender disadvantages. Zapata et al. (2017), have identified age, education, work experience, role models, and self-efficacy as individual factors with significant influence on women's involvement in innovative entrepreneurship. Whittington and Smith-Doerr (2005), for example, indicate that the involvement of women decreases as the level of commercialization of the technology increases. They suggest that personal, structural, and organizational filtering processes are behind the low proportion of female inventor-entrepreneurs. Neergaard et al. (2006) found that women entrepreneurs in male-dominated industries were considered as higher-risk creditors, since financial institutions believe that women are less able to cope with high competition. Our study departs from this emerging intersectional understanding of gender disadvantages. Intersectionality can be a useful analytical framework in exploring the critical influence of the various dimensions of social inequality on women's experience of innovation and entrepreneurship.

Intersectionality is the notion that the various systems of oppression interact in multiple and complex ways that, when taken together, may determine how people respond to their social environments or are responded to by others. Intersectional gender analysis has been widely adopted by feminist theorists

(Garry, 2011), but is still emergent in the areas of innovation and entrepreneurship (Martinez Dy and Agwunobi, 2019). A review of the extant literature shows a flexible use of the framework. Williams-Forson and Wilkerson (2011), for example, adopted an intersectional framework of analysis to explore the influence of gendered, raced, and classed business sectors, while Swail and Marlow (2018) use the framework to analyze the impact of gender on entrepreneurial legitimacy in the context of nascent entrepreneurship. Martinez Dy and Agwunobi (2019) explore access to resources, and Martinez Dy et al. (2017) focus on women's experiences of digital enterprising. Poutanen and Kovalainen (2013) apply intersectionality in their study of the gendering of invention processes.

Intersectional analysis of gender in the context of innovative entrepreneurship is still in emergence. However, it is evident that the intersectional framework can be a useful tool in analyzing the interplay between individual and institutional impairments on women's entrepreneurship. Institutions, formal and informal, lay the ground for all interactions and transactions between actors. As North (1991) expresses it, institutions are the rules of the game. However, the playground (institution) is not gender neutral and it is important to explore various institutional mechanisms that appear to filter out women entrepreneurs. Extant literature provides ample evidence of the gender gap and has identified a multiplicity of factors that may filter out women during the innovative entrepreneurship journey. Very little is known about how these factors manifest themselves at the various phases of the innovative entrepreneur process and impact the participation and performance of women. Our study contributes with insights from women with personal experiences of the process of innovative entrepreneurship. But first, a short presentation of our methodology.

3.　　METHODOLOGY

The overarching question in this study is why women are under-represented in innovative entrepreneurship, the focus being on gender disadvantages women experience in the various phases of the process of innovative entrepreneurship. The aim is to identify the various gender disadvantages experienced by women and analyze how these impact on the participation and performance of women in innovative entrepreneurship. The research strategy is a multiple case study (Eisenhardt, 1989; Yin, 2016). The case study method is a well-established strategy that has been widely applied in entrepreneurship and small business research (Martinez Dy et al., 2017; Poutanen and Kovalainen, 2013). By employing a qualitative approach, we were able to make in-depth interviews that enabled us to get insight into the entrepreneurs' perceptions, experiences, and reflections. This approach was particularly useful in understanding the way in which individual and institutional factors interact and shape the behaviors and experiences of women. Seven female entrepreneurs were selected among members of the Gothenburg Inventors Association (GUF)[1] for inclusion in the study. As a rule, members of GUF are independent (private) inventors, as opposed to employees or business owners. Therefore, our sample is selected from a population of independent, female inventors-entrepreneurs that are members of GUF.

Prior to conducting the case interviews, we had discussions with two experts with personal experiences of innovative entrepreneurship and are directors of Inventor Associations. They are also advisors/coaches/mentors in the areas of Intellectual Property Rights (IPR) and new business creation. They have broad experiences from the work of various inventor's associations. The expert interviews have been an important source of knowledge regarding the overall structure of the Swedish system of innovation (regulations, resources, support systems, etc.) and personal experiences gained through counseling and other types of support for female innovative entrepreneurs. The interviews are not presented separately, but are integrated in different parts of the case study, for example in the development of the interview guide.

The case studies were conducted in a series of steps. First, an introductory letter was sent to the Swedish Inventors Association with information about the study and request for contacts. This resulted in responses from two different regional associations, one with the least and the other with the highest number of female members. Following preliminary discussions, the chairs of the two regional associations were provided with a letter containing detailed selection criteria and request for participation in the study to be distributed to their female members. The primary criteria was that the female member had at least one patent and had, or was in the processes of, commercializing the invention/s. Since patents can be commercialized in different ways, the second criteria was that the member had an established business or was in the process of starting up a new enterprise. Seven members from the regional office in Gothenburg, Southern Sweden, responded that they were interested in participating in the study. The only female member in the second Inventors Association was unable to participate in the study. An interview guide was prepared, encompassing a set of themes and prompts to steer the conversation in a similar manner, and the interviews were conducted using the media platform TEAMS. The conversations were also recorded on TEAMS. Moreover, interviews were conducted in Swedish, with the length of each interview being 60 minutes. Additional data were collected through archives, websites, company reports, and the like.

The following section discusses the main themes that emerged from the data in the seven cases. These are organized under three subsections. First, the attributes of the case entrepreneurs is presented and discussed. This is followed by a discussion of the experiences of gendered institutions by the entrepreneurs. We use excerpts from the interviews in support of our arguments and then summarize and comment on the results.

4.   THE CASE ENTREPRENEURS (E1–E7) AND THEIR PATENTS

The demographic attributes that influence the entrepreneurs' opportunities and experiences, as well as their patents and motives for patenting, are summarized in Table 5.1. The case entrepreneurs are between 31 and 76 years of age; they are highly educated and have experiences working in different industries. Their inventions are not directly connected to their fields of education or experiences in their working lives. The inventions also tend to concentrate to the areas of medical technology. They live and work in and around the city of Gothenburg, which explains their membership in Gothenburg Inventors Association. This region of Sweden is highly dynamic,[2] having some of the best educational facilities, but also some of the largest innovative industrial companies.

The women had different family backgrounds. Some had an entrepreneurial background, having grown up with parents that were either entrepreneurs or had creative jobs such as artists or music teachers. There were differences, too, as to how they operated their businesses. Some women worked together with other family members, while others had founded their companies by themselves.

The study shows that primarily three demographic attributes influence (positively and negatively) the experiences of innovative entrepreneurs: their age, education, and career background.

Age: In terms of age, three generations are "represented." Each generation carries a unique set of knowledge and experiences that shape their perception of gender, career path, self-efficacy as inventors and entrepreneurs, their networking ability, and so on (Zapata et al., 2017). The older generation emphasizes the role of upbringing and family background. One stated that "women are fostered to be docile." A second one reasoned in a similar vein, observing that "women are raised to please men." An older respondent pointed out that women had a tendency to be withdrawn, "a woman may sit with her hat in her hand, thinking, "I shouldn't." The same respondent also described that this was not always the case with the younger women. She indicated that there is a difference between generations, pointing out that age in itself is a factor, and implying that there is an age-based discrimination. Younger women, she said, are more often promoted, and older women are seen as "difficult." Another respondent mentioned that women her age were more withdrawn, as younger women were more "sure of themselves and had more drive." However, yet another respondent pointed out that younger women may be promoted almost "for show," rather than as capable individuals.

Table 5.1   *Demographic attributes of the inventor-entrepreneurs*

Attribute/ Case	Age	Education	Career background	Place of residence	Patent/ Industry	Motive for invention
E1	57 years	Master in Marine Biology	CEO Project, Inventor-Entrepreneur, Project manager in industry	Gothenburg	patent, medical technology	To solve a problem experienced in a workplace
E2	61 years	Psychologist, Designer	Inventor-Entrepreneur, Prior experience of work in marketing, design in co-owned firms	Malmö	patents, medical technology	To solve a self-experienced problem
E3	42 years	Ph.D. candidate – Design of medical devices	CEO, Inventor-Entrepreneur Industry R&D, Engineering and design work	Borås	patents, medical technology	Involvement in R&D project to develop a new solution to a problem experienced by many in her surroundings
E4	31 years	Engineer (Physics)	CEO, Inventor-Entrepreneur, Project leadership, design in industry	Gothenburg	patents, musical instruments	To solve a problem experienced by a partner
E5	52 years	Technical gymnasium (high school)	CEO, Inventor-Entrepreneur Project leadership, R&D in industry	Gothenburg	patents, health and hygiene	Part of her expertise as a professional product developer
E6	76 years	Professional education	CEO, Inventor-Entrepreneur	Gothenburg	patents, medical technology	To solve a self-experienced problem
E7	69 years	Professional education (post-gymnasium)	Inventor-Entrepreneur, Business advisor, Educator	Gothenburg	patent, health and hygiene	To solve a self-experienced problem

The age at which women engage in innovation activities influences their resource endowments (including social capital) and their interactions with institutions positively/negatively. In general, younger women emphasize their upbringing less. One respondent explained that she was not aware of any critical differences between herself and her male counterparts. "I really do not feel that I was raised differently than the boys and am not sure that I am disadvantaged." At the same time, she pointed out that her husband was actively involved in her work and that the process had been a shared experience. But she also mentioned that being an entrepreneur was a way for her to combine work with her family life, especially since she had experienced a burn-out in the past.

Education: The cases have formal education in varying fields, but generally at post-gymnasium levels. However, as academic institutions/fields have embedded gender biases, few women access the more highly privileged fields of education. Among the cases, only one entrepreneur had a degree in the fields of STEM (science, technology, engineering and mathematics), which are normally upheld as harbingers of new technology and carry a lot of privileges in this context. Educational background influences career paths, the nature and status of the career, as well as the skills and experiences gained over time.

Career background: Career background is important as a learning ground, a source of knowledge, a way of accruing skills such as problem-solving, a platform for networks and social capital, as well as income. Career backgrounds critically influence the window of opportunities for entrepreneurship. Women constitute approximately 50 percent of the labor market in Sweden. A majority of them work within health and social care, education, and in the public sector. One of the women had started her innovation journey at a large corporation, which let her be part of innovative teams. Initially, they were uninterested in her merits, but she was able to prove her skills and gain respect as an inventor. That knowledge and experience has now come to serve for her entrepreneurial endeavors. One of the women had a background as a researcher and therefore had access to some of the support systems at her university.

Women are highly under-represented in male-dominated industries such as engineering and information technology. This skewed labor distribution applies to both paid work and entrepreneurship, since people start businesses within the industries in which they have previously worked. Five of the cases mentioned workplace experiences as the initial trigger of their journey. A respondent described that she was working in a large corporation and was given the opportunity to work in different innovative projects. That gave her the possibility to grow. Some other respondents noted that women's inventions may face biases due to the fact that women's competence is neglected. The concentration of the patents in the areas of health and hygiene and medical technology is indicative of the women entrepreneurs' previous career.

These three personal characteristics represent a very small part of the multiplicity of individual attributes that influence the socio-economic position of women. However, taken together, these three personal attributes illustrate the gendered institutions that women are raised, educated, and work in, and how this impacts their opportunities for entrepreneurship. It is important to understand the institutional mechanisms that steer the path of women's fields of education and career, in order to get insight into the under-representation of women in innovative entrepreneurship.

4.1 Motives Behind their First Patented Inventions

The cases have many similarities, but also differ in terms of their patenting behavior.

Patenting behavior: The cases had applied for one or more patents. As a rule, they had a national patent although some had applied for international patents. Commonly, they owned national patents. Patents are just one of several IPRs. Depending on the nature of the innovation, it may be suitable to combine patents with other rights. Some had also applied for trademark protection, since that is useful especially for consumer products. In one case, the entrepreneur had applied for protection for a utility model in Germany, as there is no protection for utility models in Swedish law. As a consequence, protection of utility models is almost unknown in Sweden. However, it can be useful in situations where a patent protection is not an option. One of the cases had an innovation that consisted not only of a technical solution, but also a design. She had applied for a patent as well as design protection. Whether a first patent triggers more patents appears to be related to the commercial output and potential of the technology in the specific industry. An emerging technology in an industry appears to encourage further investments in patents. A successful licensing of the first patent also appears to lead to continued efforts to patent and related IPR.

Motives for patenting: The cases had very different motives for patenting. The exclusive right that comes with patenting was a dominant motive. It was also pointed out that a patent could be a useful way to assert oneself as a female inventor/innovator and entrepreneur. Yet another reason for patenting was to attract financiers and investors. At the same time, the case entrepreneurs said that patenting could be very useful, but that it could also be the most expensive "paper" ever. In most cases, the decision to patent is triggered by some external event such as advice or a comment from a seed-financer, a colleague or a counselor. The motives are often an afterthought.

Triggering events for invention and patenting: The initial trigger to invent is normally a self-experienced event. A case entrepreneur recounts that her idea can be traced to a visit to her dental hygienist: "After the treatment, my face was completely covered with some kind of powder. It didn't feel nice at all." She decided to solve the problem after having discussed it with the dental hygienist. The result is the invention of a new facial protection device during dental treatment that is available on the market; some of us have probably used it sometime. As evidenced in Table 5.1, a self-experienced problem (whether in the private sphere or at work) is the main trigger for engaging in inventive activities. A variation of the self-experienced trigger is a problem faced by someone close to the entrepreneur. One of the respondents recalled that her husband had wanted to develop a new version of an instrument that he uses: "I got involved in order to realize his ideas." These "everyday" problem-driven inventions that appear to be common among the cases seldom represent institutional norms of the "new", that is, state-of-the-art technologies, and thus risk being belittled and underrated.

4.2   Gendered Institutions

The two expert interviews, which were later confirmed by the case entrepreneurs, pointed out that, for example, the support system for innovation is dominated by men. The Swedish system of innovation – which includes a wide variety of actors, the patent offices, and government agencies, provide seed financing, startup capital, law agencies, advisory services, and professional associations – is critical to innovative entrepreneurship. The cases, particularly the older generation, describe the world of innovate entrepreneurship as male-dominated, a place where there are no female entrepreneurs to look up to, a place where there is no place for women. The two directors of Inventor Associations that were interviewed as experts have described many cases where the institutional mechanisms filter out highly competent and innovative women entrepreneurs. One of the cases, for instance, commented that as a woman it is easy to "drown in the system." Others exemplify situations in which their competence as women was ignored or questioned. One case, for example, recounted a situation where she had participated in several meetings and long discussions to locate a competent male, despite the fact that the participants were aware that she had the same competence as that which was being sought. The women experience institutional biases even within their professional associations, where they expect to access various resources, such as mentors. Therefore, they have started separate meetings and structures for women only, so that female members have a forum for discussing their innovations without having men present. All the cases relate difficulties in accessing all types of financing, for example, seed capital, innovation support, or startup capital or a credit account.

Taken together, the stories of the case entrepreneurs touch upon several interrelated norms and biases that women experience in their interaction with institutions: systemic gender bias. In male-dominated areas such as entrepreneurship, institutions are structured along norms of masculinity; subsequently, women and their ideas are evaluated according to these criteria. As a result, women entrepreneurs are filtered out of the system. Likewise, female stereotypes are embedded in the fabric of the institutions. These female stereotypes position women in preconceived roles and spaces. The case in which the woman's competence was ignored is a good example of how female stereotypes determine what women can, would, and should do. Systemic gender biases are cemented in the structures of institutions. This makes their influences subtle and difficult to articulate. But we only need to take a cursory look at the statistics on entrepreneurship to understand the impact of systemic gender biases on women. In a sense, women are practically weeded out of the world of innovative entrepreneurship. In general, the many hours of conversation with the women entrepreneurs in our study support the experiences expressed by one case entrepreneur: "We are not seen, heard or appreciated." In the following, we summarize the interaction between individual and institutional obstacles, and the impact on the performance of women's innovative entrepreneurship.

5.   SUMMARY AND CONCLUSIONS

We have identified three individual characteristics that appear to have a critical influence on their position in innovative entrepreneurship. Moreover, we have detected a number of institutional mechanisms, including norms of masculinity and female stereotypes – systemic gender bias – that impede women's participation in innovative entrepreneurship. Figure 5.1 summarizes our findings and the impact of the interaction of these influences on women entrepreneurship.

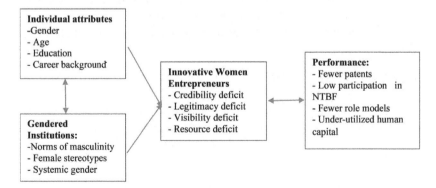

Figure 5.1   Influences on women's participation in innovation and entrepreneurship

Figure 5.1 shows that the interaction of individual and institutional factors places women in a position where their credibility, legitimacy and visibility as innovative-entrepreneurs is undermined. Moreover, a deficit in one aspect, for example, credibility, contributes to a deficit in legitimacy, and visibility, or vice versa. This condition critically influences the opportunities for women to successfully engage in innovative entrepreneurship. The individual entrepreneur is central in decisions for financing an innovative-entrepreneurial venture; the lack of credible women examples – that is, visibility – further undermines their presence and contributions. As a consequence, women entrepreneurs may appear more vulnerable, and more of a risk to invest in, a situation that further limits their access to financial resources and, in general, their performance. Lower performance, of course, negatively impacts the credibility of innovative women entrepreneurs. Essentially, what we are describing is a kind of a vicious circle. It is not entirely wrong to conclude that gendered institutions place innovative women entrepreneurs in an impossible socio-economic position.

We do not expect that symbolic policies and sporadic investments in innovative women entrepreneurship would solve the type of gender disadvantages discussed. We do, however, believe that more research is required in order to understand core issues. Much of the research in this area looks at specific phases of a long process, for example, patenting or business startup; our research is an attempt to draw attention to the whole process, from invention to entrepreneurship. But our research is limited to a small number of cases and needs to be expanded. For example, while we recognize that race and class is a factor, we have not looked at the situations of female innovative entrepreneurs with non-European backgrounds, and would encourage others to do so. We have considered difference in class, but have not been able to observe significant differences. To conclude, it is important to understand this complex and intertwined process, and we join the call for research on the concept and measurements of innovation as proposed by, for example, Nählinder et al. (2015).

ACKNOWLEDGMENT

We gratefully acknowledge the financial support of the Foundation for Baltic and East European Studies (Östersjöstiftelsen, Stockholm).

NOTES

1.   GUF is an independent spin-off from the Swedish Inventors Association (SUF) which is a national network for established and potential inventors, innovators, and enterprises. GUF has 300 members and the largest representation of

women inventor-entrepreneurs in the country. The objective of the Inventors Associations is to support inventors in their efforts to convert their innovations into business opportunities.

2. https://ec.europa.eu/info/research-and-innovation/funding/funding-opp ortunities/prizes/icapital/icapital2018_en.

REFERENCES

Ahl, H. (2006), 'Why research on women entrepreneurs needs new directions'. *Entrepreneurship, Theory and Practice*, 30 (5), 595–621.

Alsos, G.A., Ljunggren, E. and Hytti, U. (2013), 'Gender and innovation: State of the art and a research agenda'. *International Journal of Gender and Entrepreneurship*, 5 (3), 236–256.

BarNir, A. (2012), 'Starting technologically innovative ventures: Reasons, human capital, and gender'. *Management Decision*, 50 (3), 399–419.

Brännback, M., Berglund, K. and Carsrud, A.L. (2012), 'Understanding the entrepreneur and innovator nexus as basis for the coming of the science of the artificial'. *Research on Entrepreneurship and Small Business Conference*, November 20–23, Lyon, France.

Carter, N.M., Brush, C.G., Greene, P.G., Gatewood, E. and Hart, M.M. (2003), 'Women entrepreneurs who break through to equity financing: The influence of human, social and financial capital'. *Venture Capital*, 5 (1), 1–28.

Coleman, S. and Robb, A. (2009), 'A comparison of new firm financing by gender: Evidence from the Kauffman Firm Survey data'. *Small Business Economics*, 33, 397–411.

Dahlin, K.B. and Behrens, D.M. (2005), 'When is an invention really radical? Defining and measuring technological radicalness'. *Research Policy*, 34, 717–737.

Dautzenberg, K. (2012), 'Gender differences of business owners in technology-based firms'. *International Journal of Gender and Entrepreneurship*, 4 (1), 79–98.

Davidsson, P., Delmar, F. and Wiklund, J. (2006), *Entrepreneurship and the Growth of Firms*. Cheltenham, UK and Northampton, MA, USA: Edward Elgar Publishing.

Eisenhardt, K.M. (1989), 'Building theories from case study research'. *The Academy of Management Review*, 14 (4), 532–550.

Ejermo, O. and Jung, T. (2014), 'Demographic patterns and trends in patenting: Gender, age, and education of inventors'. *Technological Forecasting & Social Change*, 86, 110–124.

European Commission (2008), *Evaluation on policy: Promotion of women innovators and entrepreneurship*, Enterprise and Industry, Directorate General, Brussels.

European Commission (2020), *Science, Research and Innovation Performance of the EU: A fair, green and digital Europe*, SRIP, 1049 Brussels.

Frietsch, R., Haller, I., Vrohlings, M. and Grupp, H. (2008), 'Gender-specific patterns in patenting and publishing, Fraunhofer ISI Discussion Papers'. *Innovation Systems and Policy Analysis*, No. 16, Fraunhofer ISI, Karlsruhe.

Garry, A. (2011), 'Intersectionality, metaphors, and the multiplicity of gender'. *Hypatia*, 26 (4), 826–850.

Gartner, W.B. (1985), 'A conceptual framework for describing the phenomenon of new venture creation'. *Academy of Management Review*, 10 (4), 696–706.

Graham, S.J.H., Merges, R.P., Samuelsona, P. and Sichelman, T.M. (2009), 'High technology entrepreneurs and the patent system: Results of the 2008 Berkeley Patent Survey'. *Berkeley Technology Law Journal*, 24 (4), 1255–1328.

Henry, C., Foss, L. and Ahl, H. (2016), 'Gender and entrepreneurship research: A review of methodological approaches'. *International Small Business Journal*, 34 (3), 217–241.

Jensen, K., Kovács, D. and Sorenson, O. (2018), 'Gender differences in obtaining and maintaining patent rights'. *Nature Biotechnology*, 36, 307–309.

Kirzner, I. (1997), 'Entrepreneurial discovery and the competitive market process: An Austrian approach'. *Journal of Economic Literature*, 35 (1), 60–85.

Kuschel, K. and Lepeley, M.T. (2016), 'Women start-ups in technology: Literature review and research agenda to improve participation'. *International Journal of Entrepreneurship and Small Business*, 27 (2/3), 333–346.

Marlow, S. (2013), 'Exploring future research agendas in the field of gender and entrepreneurship'. *International Journal of Gender and Entrepreneurship*, 6 (2), 102–120.

Marlow, S. and Swail, J. (2014), 'Gender, risk and finance: Why can't a woman be more like a man?' *Entrepreneurship & Regional Development*, 26 (1–2), 80–96.

Martinez Dy, A. and Agwunobi, A.J. (2019), 'Intersectionality and mixed methods for social context in entrepreneurship'. *International Journal of Entrepreneurial Behavior & Research*, 25 (8), 1727–1747.

Martinez Dy, A., Marlow, S. and Martin, L. (2017), 'A web of opportunity or the same old story? Women digital entrepreneurs and intersectionality theory'. *Human Relations*, 70 (3), 286–311.

McClelland, D. (1961), *The Achieving Society*. New York: Van Nostrand-Rheinhold.

Nählinder, J., Tillmar, M. and Wigren, C. (2015), 'Towards a gender-aware understanding of innovation: A three-dimensional route'. *International Journal of Gender and Entrepreneurship*, 7 (1), 66–86.

Neergaard, H., Nielsen, K. and Kjeldsen, J. (2006), 'State of the art of women's entrepreneurship, access to financing and financing strategies in Denmark', in Brush et al. (eds.), *Growth-oriented Women Entrepreneurs and Their Businesses: A Global Research Perspective*. Cheltenham, UK and Northampton, MA, USA: Edward Elgar Publishing, pp. 88–111.

North, D.C. (1991), 'Institutions'. *Journal of Economic Perspectives*, 5 (1), 97–112.

Ozkazanc-Pan, B. (2014), 'Postcolonial feminist analysis of high-technology entrepreneuring'. *International Journal of Entrepreneurial Behaviour & Research*, 20 (2), 155–172.

Poutanen, S. and Kovalainen, A. (2013), 'Gendering innovation process in an industrial plant – revisiting tokenism, gender and innovation'. *International Journal of Gender and Entrepreneurship*, 5 (3), 257–274.

PRV (2019), 'Statistikårsbok 2019', Swedish Intellectual Property Office, Stockholm.

Sandström, C. (2014), 'Var skapades Sveriges 100 främsta innovationer?', Reforminstitutet, Stockholm.

Schumpeter, J.A. (1934), *The Theory of Economic Development: An Inquiry into Profits, Capital, Credit, Interest, and the Business Cycle*. Cambridge, MA: Harvard University Press.

Shane, S. and Venkataraman, S. (2000), 'The promise of entrepreneurship as a field of research'. *Academy of Management Review*, 26 (1), 217–226.

Shapero, A. and Sokol, L. (1982), 'The social dimension of entrepreneurship', in Kent, C.A., Sexton, D.L. and Vesper, K.H. (eds.), *Encyclopedia of Entrepreneurship*, Englewood Cliffs, NJ: Prentice Hall, pp. 72–90.

Swail, J. and Marlow, S. (2018), 'Embrace the masculine; attenuate the feminine – gender, identity work and entrepreneurial legitimation in the nascent context'. *Entrepreneurship & Regional Development*, 30 (1–2), 256–282.

Thévenon, O., Ali, N., Adema, W. and del Pero, A.S. (2012), 'Effects of reducing gender gaps in education and labour force participation on economic growth in the OECD'. *OECD Social, Employment and Migration Working Papers*, No. 138, OECD Publishing.

UKÄ (2020), *Statistisk Analys,* 2020-03-23, Universitets kanslers ämbetet, https://www.uka.se/download/18.4dcfa4c0171537ea94033d3/1587032843135/Statistisk%20analys%20examinerade%202020-04-16.pdf.

Utterback, J.M. (1971), 'The process of technological innovation within the firm'. *The Academy of Management Journal*, 14 (1), 75–88.

Whittington, K.B. and Smith-Doerr, L. (2005), 'Gender and commercial science: Women's patenting in the life sciences'. *Journal of Technology Transfer*, 30, 355–370.

Williams-Forson, P. and Wilkerson, A. (2011), 'Intersectionality and food studies'. *Food, Culture & Society*, 14 (1), 7–28.

WIPO (2020), *World Intellectual Property Indicators 2020*, World Intellectual Property Organization, Geneva, Switzerland.

Yin, K.R. (2016), *Case Study Research and Applications: Design and Methods*. Sixth Edition. London: Sage Publications.

Zapata, G., Fernandez, S., Neira, I. and Rey, L. (2017), 'The role of the entrepreneur in new technology-based firms (NTBFs): An analysis according to context development'. *Regional and Sectoral Economic Studies*, 17 (2), 25–42.

6. Is gender an inhibitor to innovation and entrepreneurial activity in the Democratic Republic of Congo?

Victoria Tonks and Helen Lawton Smith

1. INTRODUCTION

Africa is the world leader for female entrepreneurship (World Bank 2018). In the Democratic Republic of Congo (DRC), however, society creates particular obstacles for female entrepreneurs. While the DRC has considerable potential for economic development with significant mineral deposits, a youthful population of circa 80 million people, plenty of water and land, and borders with several trading partners, for most, doing business in the DRC is challenging. Political cronyism, state corruption and recent conflict have made this vast sub-Saharan country into one of the poorest in the world. The lack of internal infrastructure including poor transport routes and power supply outside of the capital Kinshasa means that most of the population live a rural subsistence lifestyle rather than exploiting these opportunities.

For women wanting to become entrepreneurs, additional barriers are culturally underpinned by the legal system. DRC is a traditional patriarchal society with equality for women only being introduced in law as recently as 2017 when workplace discrimination based on gender was prohibited. A number of legal barriers inhibit entrepreneurship. A significant one is that married women need written consent from their spouse in order to legally register a business or open a bank account.

This chapter is based on a small study of female entrepreneurs in the DRC, exploring gender-specific barriers to entrepreneurship and innovation. The purpose of the study was to explore if given substantial start-up capital rather than micro loans, women would think big. The main empirical contribution of this chapter is to demonstrate that this does work in practice. The chapter makes the argument that, given the right opportunities starting and growing their businesses, women can overcome social barriers and their own inhibitions to operate in the innovation space. Indeed, the pursuit of equality and social recognition helps to fuel their ambition. The corollary of this is that if gender-based barriers can be overcome then there is some hope for better economic development prospects in the DRC.

In reviewing the evidence, the chapter takes into account the cultural, social and legal contexts in the DRC. The analytical framework adopted for understanding whether and how gender is an inhibitor to innovation and entrepreneurial activity in this country, is the expanded "5M" "a gender aware framework for women's entrepreneurship" (Brush at al. 2009). The framework is based on the premise that all entrepreneurship is socially embedded. In the DRC where the role of women is traditionally based in the home, any entrepreneurial activity could perhaps be considered innovative because of its novelty. Hence a second contribution is to reflect on the merits of the 5M framework in such adverse contexts. In particular, as Bastian et al. (2018) point out, studies of female entrepreneurship have tended to over-emphasise macro-level indicators, such as culture and religion and under-emphasise organisational-level variables. There has been a lack of studies that analyse female entrepreneurship within ethnic groups, or studies that acknowledge the complex social, cultural and religious diversity of the region.

The chapter proceeds by setting out the 5M framework and argues for its analytical power and its limitations in this study. It then introduces the gender context of the DRC and the methodology used to examine the interplay between context, gender and entrepreneurial ambition in a sample of women in the DRC. This is followed by analysis and conclusions.

2. THEORETICAL FRAMEWORK

In the model, the traditional 3M micro considerations are: Money, Management and Market. This level focuses on the individual woman entrepreneur – her motives, orientations and self-confidence and explores personal attributes and characteristics (Bastian et al. 2018). Included is whether a woman's motivation to become entrepreneurial is a push or pull factor (Atef and Al-Balushi 2015) or both.

In the Brush et al. (2009) 5M framework two further considerations are added: "Macro" and "Meso". The macro environment is defined as including national level policies, culture, laws and economy (Brush et al. 2009). This includes the legal status of women, gender equality and the economy of the country and how it affects women – in other words, how certain political-cultural institutional contexts can either enable or constrain entrepreneurial success (Zhao and Yang 2021). Meso considerations include gender equality in the home, motherhood, how domestic responsibility affects working women, and the social status of women in their communities. Meso institutions include occupational networks, business associations and industries. Networks are part of the societal context in which women are embedded and how their presence or absence may translate into distinct noneconomic gender differences that present particular challenges to women's enterprise (Brush et al. 2009). They also include such factors as women's management styles, structures and business cultures, besides the performance and survival of women-owned firms (Bastian et al. 2018; Shakeel et al. 2020). Brush et al. (2009) applied the 5M framework to exploring gender differences in an empirical context.

Meso factors or intersectional factors have long been found to be crucial in understanding women's entrepreneurial behaviour (Allen and Truman 1993). This is especially important in developing countries (e.g. Goyal and Yadav 2014; De Vita et al. 2014; Zhao and Yang 2021). For example, traditional caring roles of women as mothers have a bearing on their ability to run a business because of conflicting demands on their time. This has been acknowledged as the main gender barrier for females in business – whether starting and running their own business or working as an employee and often dictates the sectors within which they are employed (Forson and Ozbilgin 2003). Forson and Ozbilgin cite Allen and Truman (1993) who argue that, throughout the world women are most likely to be found in food production, nutrition, health and childcare.

According to Cabrera and Mauricio (2017), a simple explanation of entrepreneurship as a process works adequately in the context of this study. It is a sequence of activities that ends with the development of a business idea that potentially resolves a problem faced by a sector of society by one or more individuals who have relevant competencies. It starts with motivation and then moves on to opportunity identification, resource acquisition and performance. This definition describes the activity of a Congolese fish seller who uses her cooking skills to prepare food to sell at a roadside stall. The problem her simple business solves is the hunger of her passing customers, similarly it describes the business of a Kinshasa shop owner who sells juice and cakes (ÉLAN RDC 2017) to satisfy the thirst and hunger of her customers. These businesses demonstrate the 3M framework considerations of Money, Management and Market where these women are exploiting a local market for refreshments and using their skills in food preparation to generate revenue to enable the continuation of their business and an income for their families.

At a basic level, innovation can be defined as "the specific tool of entrepreneurs, the means by which they exploit change as an opportunity for a different business or a different service". (Drucker 1985, 28). What are the opportunities for innovation in these settings? Food preparation is a natural extension of a domestic activity for many women so expanding this into a retail setting would seem a relatively straightforward pathway for a female entrepreneur even in the DRC. The shop owner in Kinshasa has expanded her business by diversifying into financial services with the addition of a digital financial services terminal on her premises (ÉLAN RDC 2017). Her cake shop on a busy street in the capital city attracts much passing trade and she is able to exploit the fact there are few retail banks in DRC by expanding into the digital banking sector; exploiting new transactional banking technology to offer additional services to existing customers and attracting new ones. This demonstrates innovation in the sense that it is opportunistic by nature as well as exploiting a new way of banking and although the financial technology is not her own development, this business owner recognises the opportunities presented by digital banking innovations to add value to her enterprise.

Central to the 5M framework is finance. It is particularly important in the DRC context as has been found in other African countries. For example, micro finance loans in Kenya helped improve the lot of female entrepreneurs by improving their chances of success with their chosen business (Lock and Lawton Smith 2016). As with the previous examples in Mali and Burkina Faso, the outcomes were alleviation of poverty and improved living standards. The experience of success does not appear to generate ambition for growth, but what is noteworthy is that there was a desire for self-improvement and to resume education (Freedom from Hunger 2018).

3. METHODOLOGY

3.1 The DR Congo Context

While female entrepreneurship in Africa is on the increase, the opportunities for women vary by country. For example, recent research into programmes designed to promote innovative and entrepreneurial business activities amongst women in the DRC. Some of these are sponsored by international governments, global commercial companies and third-sector organisations. The review positions the empirical research within a broader context so as to help identify the key gender-specific barriers to women in business and whether there are particular barriers to women doing business in the DRC and the consequent outcomes.

Intersectional categories such as age, gender and marital status are significant. For example, women marry young in DRC as this offers a measure of protection against a social backdrop described by General John Holmes, the United Nations Under Secretary 2008, as: "the worst place in the world to be a woman or girl ... the levels of brutality and violence against women are almost unimaginable" (Hayes and Perks 2012, 539). This lack of social status for women coupled with their traditional family roles makes it challenging to find and survey female entrepreneurs. The language, security and travel restrictions facing any visitors to this troubled country further compound the barriers to research which in part explains the fact that the Department for International Development (DFID) sponsored Élan project previously cited was limited to the capital Kinshasa and region around it.

3.2   Exploring the Framework: Research Design

The empirical evidence is based on an original study of female entrepreneurship in the DRC undertaken by the first author, which has been recently updated. This explored the nature of barriers and how these can be overcome so that women develop successful enterprises. The research was focused in the South Kivu area of DRC. This is a country where beyond the capital of Kinshasa, the basic infrastructure is poor with limited road, power and communications networks and frequent unrest. Working with two charities we were able to see some of the possibilities and barriers for would-be women entrepreneurs. The area of South Kivu is on the east side of DRC where it borders Rwanda and Burundi, making it easier to access. Two UK based charities Ensemble (Ensemble Pour La Difference 2018) and Congo Action[1] are working in this area to develop projects that support local people, sponsoring income-generating activities to help families move beyond subsistence, and provide means to access healthcare and schooling for their children. The first author approached both these organisations to recruit survey participants as they have local representatives who can meet with and engage with subjects; digital, telephone or postal communications do not have sufficient coverage to allow their use.

There are many facets to entrepreneurial opportunity within DRC and many inhibitors giving rise to a broad range of questions to ask this sample audience. This lends itself to a mixed-method study with a general questionnaire for a large sample of female entrepreneurs and a more in-depth interview style to tease out the finer details from a subset of the sample. We found that there were not sufficient numbers of women to facilitate a larger general study. Congo Action had begun work in the region in 2000, creating a clothing workshop training and business opportunity for local women and micro loans to support smallholders' purchase of livestock. However, at the request of the population they were working with they switched their focus to purchasing building supplies so the people living in the area could build a school for their children. This changed the focus of the charity from small business sponsors and the opportunity to survey their beneficiaries. The Chair of trustees of Congo Action, Martine Le Buzullier, cautioned charities and development agencies alike about projecting a western view of what will be of most benefit for a given population "do not impose well-intentioned but patronising ideas of what help to give".[2] The DRC Community Congo Action works with prioritised education for the next generation over small-scale income smoothing activities.

The first author thus conducted unique research in 2018 working in partnership with the charity Ensemble, which provides business loans: their proposition is different from the micro loans system. Ensemble works with the would-be entrepreneurs to develop a business plan and encourage projects that provide goods and services that are important to the local population, sustainable and provide employment. Ensemble representatives acted as agents for the first author to survey the local women entrepreneurs using face-to-face interviews to explore their experiences of starting a business. Face-to-face interviews were chosen because not all the participants were suitably literate to give written answers to a questionnaire and although the Ensemble agents were removed from the research project and would not potentially probe for fuller answers during questioning, the fact that they were known to the subjects ensured there was a high degree of trust between interviewer and interviewee.

The survey participants, although a sample limited in number, are most varied in their chosen businesses covering textile design and production, power, agriculture and business services. We interviewed four subjects, there was a fifth willing to participate but her location is remote and during the research period it was not possible to travel to meet her. All our subjects are married and mothers and aged between 25 and 49 years of age. (see Appendix 1). The survey questions and application of the 5M framework is presented in Table 6.1.

Table 6.1   Survey question and framework application

Survey Question	Framework topic
What was your motivation for starting a business?	*Market: identifying a need*
	Management: use of knowledge and skill
	Meso: personal motivation, ambition
Why choose funding from Ensemble Pour La Difference?	*Money*
Do you employ staff?	*Management*
How has your company evolved?	*Market*
	Management
Are you planning to expand your company and if so how?	*Market*
	Management
What do you believe are the greatest obstacles facing women wishing to launch their own business in DRC?	*Macro*

4.   FINDINGS: APPLYING THE 5M FRAMEWORK

4.1   Money

Money, or access to start-up capital, is difficult for all in DRC because of its economy. Poverty in DRC is high, remains widespread and pervasive. In 2018, it was estimated that 73% of the Congolese population, equalling 60 million people, lived on less than $1.90 a day (the international poverty rate) (World Bank 2022). For women this is even harder, making money a relevant part of the gender framework. The general availability of banking services for all in DRC is poor and for women even more so with only 3% of female start-ups receiving funding via a bank loan (World Bank 2016). This makes money an important consideration of the 5M gender framework when considering what can support innovative and entrepreneurial ambition of women in DRC.

Investment capital was a key theme with subject C the owner of a fish farm describing the high interest rates offered by DRC retail banks as "crazy" at between 30% and 35%. Comparably the Ensemble loans which charge interest of between 4% and 6% allowed this entrepreneur to establish her business investing in developing the necessary multiple fish pond infrastructure and employing staff to help her whilst still being able to make regular repayments against the loan.

This was a common theme echoed by subject D who has started a cloth design and dyeing business. A business loan from Ensemble has enabled her to build a workshop and employ more staff, helping more women access training, new skills and a livelihood that lifts them outside of traditional rural activities which are essentially subsistence living and gain skills, earn more and support their families and wider community. She describes the traditional lot of women, "Their job is to go to the fields, give birth to and look after the children and if, in the end, the fields have not produced anything these women and their children have nothing to eat and go to bed on an empty stomach."

Projects that provide funding to help those who are self-employed often focus on improving agricultural productivity where the majority of a country's population live and work. This is true of DRC and much of sub-Saharan Africa where over 80% of women work on the land. Projects are often based on or supported by the Gameen Bank micro finance initiatives where the focus is to improve farming methods to increase yields and provide a surplus to trade. Such activity supports improved nutrition and health with access to medicine and it can also support the education of a family's children with the potential to lift the family out of poverty but are unlikely to provide employment outside of the familial group.

The Ensemble loans empowered these women to reach higher and introduce innovation to the DRC entrepreneurial activity, locally produced fresh fish, hydro-electric power, and new methods of cloth production. this would suggest that, if you want to create a significant impact, the investment needs to match the ambition; micro loans create micro improvements, one person or family at a time. Bigger change comes with bolder action.

These women are using access to business capital to demonstrate innovation both by creating businesses that incorporate novel production methods such as a new way of dyeing cloth but also by being ambitious beyond creating something for the benefit of their immediate family. Subject D describes developing a skilled workforce "the art of making cloth, as well as the mixing of colours and how to use their imagination and creativity". For this woman and her team, working is not just about the economic security for themselves and their families, it is also an opportunity for personal development and self-expression.

4.2   Market

The Market theme in the DRC context is limited by the local population's purchasing power which, as we have described, is poor due to the low per capita income. This is compounded by the statistic that one-quarter of the gender gap in profits in the DRC can be explained by the fact that women operate in comparatively less profitable sectors.

In order for a business to succeed, identifying a local need and being able to exploit this is key. In our introduction we reviewed the business of some sole traders, the dried fish seller with her roadside stall and the cake shop trader based in Kinshasa who have clearly identified local passing trade who buy their wares. These are small businesses limited in capacity by the owners' ability to buy the ingredients for and have sufficient time to make the products they sell each day. These follow a business model rooted in an extension of the traditional domestic roles of women.

These are not business activities that could be described as innovative, more an extension and exploitation of a centuries-old home-learned daily chore, tradition is the common thread here, but looking at the nature of businesses that have succeeded in the South Kivu with the support of a business loan from Ensemble perhaps demonstrates that given sufficient encouragement, finance in this case, women will be more creative and innovative as they take a look beyond the traditional markets for their talents of food and care-giving to wider societal needs. In the case of our interview subjects, fresh fish production to compete against poor quality and expensive imports, production of electricity for a community based far from the very limited Congolese power grid and reliant on fossil fuelled generators for their power and a women's business group with the purpose to develop the skills of female entrepreneurs to support their ambition and encourage success in their chosen fields.

The identification of a current market for a commodity such as power is clearly understood and demonstrated by subject A and goes beyond just servicing a need for electricity; she explains the immediate market need for power, "The lack of electric power as the existing SNEL network is unreliable: there are consumers in various places such as hospitals, schools, households, IT centres, cyber cafes." She then draws in the management, meso and macro elements:

> I wanted to diversify local economy by creating production units which could assist the rural woman thus leading to her emergence and empowerment too. To increase her full participation to the development in rural areas through agricultural business (e.g. preservation and transformation of the agricultural produce before putting them on the market).

4.3   Management

The traditional 3M framework gives us the management theme. Entrepreneurial acumen often begins with education both tertiary and professional business skills. Would-be women entrepreneurs in DRC face a significant barrier due to poor literacy and numeracy. There is no universal education provision in DRC and paternalistic norms mean that many girls marry young and motherhood often follows, so even those in education often leave early to start family life and the low incomes of most families means paying for school for their children is often prioritised for the boys. Although a lack of access to education is a common factor for all Congolese children, it is recognised that overcoming this is vitally important to individual advancement and that of the country as a whole. The ambition of education is something existing women entrepreneurs aspire to both for their children and themselves too.

Feedback from the women in our survey gives context to this idea, as subject A explained: "when you cannot read it is difficult to express yourself in front of people." This coupled with a lack of "professional training ... creates an inferiority complex". This idea that literacy supports equality was echoed by subject C stating that "the biggest obstacle is a lack of self-confidence". This desire to develop basic literacy and business skills has created the impetus of subject B's women's business group which she describes as "a business which involves various industries such as agriculture, innovation and technology" and one with ambition, "I am going to work with people who have long-term projects and are able to change their lifestyle and that of those surrounding them." Both subjects C and D describe a lack of job opportunities as part of their motivation to start their own businesses. Subject C told us "I have completed my studies for more than seven years and still had not found a job." Subject D explained "What motivated me to start my company was the conditions I encountered in my first job which did not encourage women to go further, to become a manager in that company." The women have the skills and training but no opportunity to use them to work or progress in the local employment market.

This suggests that Congolese women are not lacking in ambition or motivation, given opportunities they will demonstrate an appetite for hard work and self-advancement. A DFID-backed project called Élan sought to encourage entrepreneurship in DRC to improve wider economic outcomes for the country as a whole. An agriculture-based programme focused on the production of maize in an attempt to encourage subsistence farmers to grow cash crops. DRC has an abundance of rich fertile land and plenty of water so this is a logical development step. Men and women were included in the study, each had the same area of land on which they grew the maize for a local landowner who paid them for their output: the women were found on average to be more productive than their male counterparts, resulting in a greater income from their plots. The benefit was not just worth one season's money – as maize is a perennial crop there was the opportunity to return to the plots the following year when the landowner reemployed a higher proportion of the women. The Élan study looked at how the women used their new income and described "complex entrepreneurial activities to further economic opportunities" (ÉLAN RDC 2017). These included the acquisition of land and building properties to generate rental income and purchase of goods to trade. In addition to diversification of income streams to provide more reliably for themselves and their families, the women also described how they felt "gains in respect" (ÉLAN RDC 2017) from the local community, making social standing an important by-product of their business success. This extends the gender considerations for female entrepreneurs beyond the 3M framework to include female emancipation, which leads us to consider the expanded 5M framework as described by Brush at al. (2009).

4.4   Macro and Meso Considerations

The place of women in Congolese society underpins the gender constraints to their personal development academically, politically and economically. Modern DR Congo is traditionally paternalistic; this is underpinned by its colonialist past. Although now independent of Belgium, the elite ruling class is modelled on colonial leadership with all of the power and most of the significant industries and wealth controlled or owned by a few who are both political and business leaders and almost exclusively male (Dana and Anderson 2007).

While the legal status of women is confused, there have been recent moves by the government of DRC to improve the position of women within society, making some constitutional changes by introducing legislation on gender equality. "The law regarding Women's Rights and Gender Equality" prohibits "discrimination against workers based on gender" (White & Case 2017). These authors find that in spite of this positive intention there are still gender barriers to female business owners because of contradictory legislation within family law. Married women need written consent from their spouse to register a business and open a bank account, both essential for the entrepreneur. "Women experience even lower rates of financial inclusion, in part because men are considered legal heads of household, with married women requiring their husbands' permission to open a bank account" (IFC undated). This suggests that the political leaders of DRC are paying lip service to the notion of gender equality within the workplace and there does not appear to be any state-led financial or practical support mechanism to encourage and support aspiring businesswomen.

The women who are bucking the trend and succeeding in the innovation and entrepreneurship space are doing so with help from overseas-funded economic aid projects such as the DFID Élan and third-sector Ensemble funders. Some of our survey responders underpin this idea that there is little state-led encouragement for women; subject B states that the "Congolese government does nothing to support entrepreneurs and even less if they are women" and subject C describes this as a societal problem "traditions which put women in the background". Subject D did her own research amongst her peers and reports that "After carrying out research and surveying the women in the village whom I worked with many times, they feel they are not treated equally as the men who work in the village." Success factors mention personal emancipation as a driver; subject A describes her motivation to build a Micro Hydro Electric plant thus: "To allow me, a village woman not to be dependent but valued as a producer creating jobs for man and woman.... I wanted to diversify the local economy by creating production units which could assist the rural woman thus leading to her emergence and empowerment too." Despite the societal constraints these women have encountered they appear determined not to let their gender inhibit their opportunities or stifle their innovative ambitions, and their personal entrepreneurial pathways clearly take others with them; they want to influence, empower and benefit the wider community.

Whilst our survey reveals that women see their gender as a barrier to a career and recognition, much of their motivation to work is deeply rooted in meso considerations. Those we spoke to cited family as a great entrepreneurial motivator. Subject C started her fish farm to increase the family income: "there came a time when my husband was no longer able to support our family needs on his own. That's when I decided to breed fish and sell them to earn money and support my needs". She expands on this putting her traditional meso role at the heart of her motivation:

> I am a mother and I am the one preparing food for my children and my husband. I went to the market many times to buy fish and noticed that the Congolese market is full of fish which comes from China or other countries where the traders use preserving agents which can be toxic. Moreover, this fish arrives in the Congo already damaged and often rotten. I felt that the life of my children and that of the whole population were in danger by eating rotten fish full of preservatives.

This suggests that it is both the health and prosperity of her family which are motivators for this women's business. Subject D also talked about the need to feed the family as something that fuelled her ambition, but she, like Subject C, alluded to the safety and prosperity of other women in her local village; the local community and wider population concern these women and support their innovative and entrepreneurial aspirations. This suggests that what are perceived as potential barriers to women in business family obligations in this sample at least are actually the driving force behind these business women. The sample for this original research was small, only four subjects, due to the challenges of identifying female entrepreneurs where there is safe access and having an opportunity to interview them. Ideally a follow-up interview with the original participants would have been desirable but the coronavirus pandemic during 2020/21 prohibited travel to DRC, borders were closed making this impossible. This has also limited the opportunity for the emergence of additional research subjects because of DRC's pandemic-related lockdown.

The first author was able to speak to the CEO of Ensemble, Mike Beeston, who reported that businesses of all those interviewed continue to trade; two have repaid their initial loans and in the case of subject C, the fish farmer has taken out a new loan to expand her operation. The Women's Business Group now has many more members and employs four management staff to support them. The Micro Hydro Electric plant is providing power to seventy-five homes and has capacity to supply up to one hundred and seventy-five more. The cloth-dyeing business has temporarily suspended business due to the coronavirus pandemic; the closure of the borders with neighbouring countries has interrupted both their supply of raw materials and export market for finished products but they plan to resume as soon as they are able. The innovative and resilient spirit of this small cohort of female entrepreneurs demonstrates what can be accomplished despite the obstacles they encounter because of their sex.

5.   CONCLUSIONS

In this chapter we have examined whether gender is an inhibitor to innovation and entrepreneurial activity in the Democratic Republic of Congo using limited published academic resources available and original research by the first author. We have examined the various obstacles facing women in business in DRC using the 5M research framework (Brush et al. 2009) in order to include and consider societal and domestic obstacles which are unique for female entrepreneurs.

It is clear that traditional barriers to innovation and business success are present in this setting; access to affordable business loans is a challenge for all start-ups in DRC with an underdeveloped banking system and very high interest rates. There are additional gender inhibitors for women because of socio-political constraints where legally women's access to banking services are restricted by law, likewise the ability to register a business (White & Case 2017). What we have seen from the published studies and our research is that given access to business funding, women can succeed both in traditional agrarian industries, but also and most notably, will demonstrate strong innovative instincts developing and championing new production methods as shown by our research subjects who started businesses introducing novel cloth-dyeing methods, fresh fish production and clean, sustainable electricity.

Macro and meso considerations from the 5M framework (Brush et al. 2009) revealed gender-based restrictions with the aforementioned family law inequalities putting women at a disadvantage when starting and running a business. These may be legal barriers with spousal permission being a requirement for banking services access and business law (White & Case 2017) but amongst those we surveyed we saw no local evidence of this. All our subjects were married and none stated being a wife or mother a barrier to their entrepreneurial aspirations, indeed the opposite appears to be true with a desire to help their spouse provide for the family and to affect wider community prosperity being significant motivators. There are signs that the Congolese government is recognising the importance of women in business introducing gender equality to the statute book in 2017 (White & Case 2017); however, without changing the existing family law this is problematic.

The Congolese government can do much more to support and encourage their entrepreneurial women by creating an equal society. The immediate removal of legal barriers that inhibit their ambitions and reinforce societal prejudice would be an important step. Establishing equality within Congolese society could encourage greater investment from international aid and development organisations, some of whom could be discouraged from doing so by the patriarchal norms. Recognition of women as equal in society could instil greater ambition in younger children and foster the demand and development of education for girls and all children, which can only be good news for a development in all areas of Congolese society.

Since the first author conducted this research there have been small steps forward to support gender equality in DRC with the election of women to the Kinshasa Assembly. Although making up less than 8% of the Assembly representatives they are highly motivated and determined to improve the lot for women but also that of the wider community.

> Since long ago, we've been ruled by men.... We want women to bring another way of governing, not to make laws for individual benefit, but for the good of the community. (Chantal Mpeme Kinshasa Assembly)

Whilst we believe that gender is an inhibitor to innovation and entrepreneurship for women in the DR Congo, this is against the backdrop of a society struggling with multiple challenges of extreme poverty, lawlessness, and poor infrastructure. The women who are succeeding in business demonstrate ambition, resilience and creativity in order to start and run their businesses.

NOTES

1. http://www.congoaction.co.uk/.
2. Interview with Victoria Tonks May 2018. Congo Action [online] http://www.congoaction.co.uk.

REFERENCES

Allen, S. and Truman, C. (Eds) (1993). *Women in Business: Perspectives on Women Entrepreneurs*. London: Routledge.

Atef, T.M. and Al-Balushi, M. (2015). Entrepreneurship as a means for restructuring employment patterns. *Tourism and Hospitality Research*, 15(2), 73–90.

Bastian, B.L., Sidani, Y.M. and El Amine, Y. (2018). Women entrepreneurship in the Middle East and North Africa. *Gender in Management: An International Journal*, 33(4), 14–29.

Brush, C., de Bruin, A. and Welter, F. (2009). A gender-aware framework for women's entrepreneurship. *International Journal of Gender and Entrepreneurship*, 1(1), 8–24.

Cabrera, E. and Mauricio, D. (2017). Factors affecting the success of women's entrepreneurship: A review of literature. *International Journal of Gender and Entrepreneurship*, 9 (1), 31–65.

Dana, L.P and Anderson, R. (2007). *International Handbook of Research on Indigenous Entrepreneurship*. Cheltenham, UK and Northampton, MA, USA: Edward Elgar Publishing.

De Vita, L., Mari, M. and Poggesi, S. (2014). Women entrepreneurs in and from developing countries: Evidences from the literature. *European Management Journal*, 32 (3), 451–460.

Drucker, P. (1985). *Innovation and Entrepreneurship*. New York: HarperCollins.

ÉLAN RDC. (2017). *Home*. http://www.elanrdc.com/ [Accessed 18 September 2020].

Ensemble Pour La Difference. (2018). *Home*. https://www.ensemblepourladifference.org/ [Accessed 18 September 2020].

Forson, C. and Ozbilgin, M. (2003). Dot-com women entrepreneurs in the UK. *International Journal of Entrepreneurship and Innovation*, 4(1) doi: 10.5367/000000003101299366.

Freedom from Hunger. (2018). *Fatoumata (Burkina Faso)*. https://www.freedomfromhunger.org/ [Accessed 18 September 2020].

Goyal, P. and Yadav, V. (2014). To be or not to be a woman entrepreneur in a developing country? *Psychosociological Issues in Human Resource Management*, 2(2), 68–78.

Hayes, K. and Perks, R. (2012). 'Women in the artisanal and small-scale mining sector of the Democratic Republic of the Congo'. In *High-Value Natural Resources and Peacebuilding*, P. Lujala and S.A. Rustad (Eds). London: Earthscan, Chapter 26.

IFC (undated). Case study: Women entrepreneurs open a path for digital financial services in the Democratic Republic of Congo 10953_Gender_Case_Study_FINCA. pdf (ifc.org).

Lock, R. and Lawton Smith, H. (2016). The impact of female entrepreneurship on economic growth in Kenya. *International Journal of Gender and Entrepreneurship*, 8(1), 90–96. http://dx.doi.org/10.1108/IJGE-11-2015-0040 (viewpoint) ISSN 1756-6266.

Shakeel, M., Yaokuang, L. and Gohar, A. (2020). 'Identifying the entrepreneurial success factors and the performance of women-owned businesses in Pakistan: The moderating role of national culture', SAGE Open. April–June 2020: 1–17 doi: 10.1177/2158244020919520.

White & Case (2017). *Democratic Republic of Congo: Closing the Credit Gap for Women Entrepreneurs*. Closing the credit gap for women entrepreneurs | White & Case LLP (whitecase.com).

World Bank (2016). *What Does It Mean to Be a Woman Entrepreneur in the Democratic Republic of Congo?* http://www.worldbank.org/en/news/feature/2017/01/10/what-does-it-mean-to-be-a-woman-entrepreneur-in-the-democratic-republic-of-congo [Accessed 18 September 2020].

World Bank (2018). *Female Entrepreneurs: the Future of the African Continent*. https://www.worldbank.org/en/news/opinion/2018/11/29/women-entrepreneurs-the-future-of-africa [Accessed 23 June 2021].

World Bank (2022). Democratic Republic of Congo Overview: Development news, research, data | World Bank [Accessed 13 January 2022].

Zhao, E. and Yang, L. (2021). Women hold up half the sky? Informal institutions, entrepreneurial decisions, and gender gap in venture performance. *Entrepreneurship, Theory and Practice*, 5(6), 1431–1462 doi: 10.1177/1042258720980705.

APPENDIX

Table 6A.1   *Research subjects*

Subject	Age	Family	Business
A	49	Married with 7 children aged 12 to 28	Micro Electric Plant
B	26	Married with 1-year-old daughter	Women's Business Group
C	35	Married with 4 children aged 10, 7, 5 and a 1-year-old baby	Fish Farm
D	25	Married with a 1-year-old daughter	Cloth Dyeing Business

7. From *gendered social innovation* to *gendering social innovation* and co-production in healthcare settings

Silvia Cervia

1. INTRODUCTION

This chapter derives its specific approach to analysing social innovation (SI) from a gender perspective by adopting a relational approach to defining a unitarian framework in which SI would become more effective. Some scholars have pointed to SI as a contested concept by taking a relational perspective to analysing SI and its core goal, which is universally identified by its alleged ability to address and satisfy unmet social needs by including marginalized groups in decision-making processes. SI is a contested concept poised between two opposite outcomes: the redefinition of social relations in a more inclusive and equitable way with the aim of addressing and satisfying unmet social needs by including marginalized groups in decision-making processes and the manipulative use of this redefinition as a smokescreen for cuts in public service delivery for the purpose of furthering neoliberalism, which leads to a reduction in public services and the shift of service provision to societal sectors (Ayob, Teasdale and Fagan, 2016; Massey and Johnston-Miller, 2016).

To avoid this risk, the chapter draws on the relational theory of gender theoretical implications to move from *gendered social innovation* to *gendering social innovation* as a more profitable and gender-sensitive framework in which SI can become more effective. As I will argue, this is not a merely terminological issue but a substantial change, as the gender relational perspective has the potential to foster the core goal of SI. By doing so, the chapter proposes moving from a merely conceptual approach to one that holds theory and practice together, as relational theory does, and applying this perspective at the micro-, meso- and macro- levels while keeping in mind that gender is a social construct formed and performed within interactions and institutions according to the well-known argument of 'doing gender' (West and Zimmerman, 1987).

In the relational theory of gender, state regulation and institutions are investigated as being characterized by gender regimes that permeate the way in which states and institutions work as 'bearers of gender relations' and filters of legitimate points of view by influencing the content of public policies (Connell, 2006, p. 436). Historically, the gender inequalities of voice and authority structured into healthcare organizations and institutions have influenced the planning of healthcare, marginalizing women's interests and therefore triggering the women's health movement (Kuhlmann and Annandale, 2010). Relational gender theory – speaking directly to the terrain on which health policy and innovation must work, that is, creative social practice and the gender regimes of institutions (Connell, 2012) – seems the most promising framework for an effective understanding of SI policies and the co-production initiative in the healthcare sector as well as in other specific domains of public initiatives.

In the domain of SI studies, the relational approach claims to provide a 'holistic framework' focused on SI as innovation of social relations, which emphasizes the link between the effect (innovation) and the process, which is innovative itself because it is defined by including marginalized groups in the decision-making process (Moulaert et al., 2013). First, the chapter analyses this framework, which pretends to offer a theory able to face the risk that SI will become a sort of Trojan horse to pave the way for neoliberalism, fostering the diminishing role of governments in guaranteeing basic universal rights (ibid.). The chapter then critically considers the process of applying theoretical thought, first by considering the widespread practice of specifying the meaning of a concept by resorting to another contested concept (co-production) and then by analysing the application method in a healthcare setting (namely, experience-based co-design – EBCD) and its criticisms, which question exactly the EBCD ability to redefine power relations in a more inclusive way (Palmer et al., 2019).

Second, the chapter theorizes *gendering social innovation* as a framework for SI that overcomes the shortcomings of the previous concept of *gendered social innovation*, which is described in the academic literature as a specific kind of SI (Lindberg, Forsberg and Karlberg, 2015). Considering that the criticisms of EBCD that focus on power relations point out the necessity of building upon the recognition process developed by gender and feminist studies, the chapter derives from these recent studies some useful implications for defining an approach to recognition and gender that is sensitive to the other axes of social differentiation (Fraser, 2007). The relational theory of gender and its multidimensional perspective (Connell, 2012) reviews the epistemic warrant of *gendered social innovation* by defining *gendering social innovation* as a useful lens through which complex relations between multiple groups not only within but also across identities and analytic categories, at the intrapersonal, interpersonal and institutional levels, can be used to analyse the effect of specific initiatives and processes from multiple perspectives.

In conclusion, the chapter points to the challenges associated with implementing a gender approach to SI to foster effective co-production that primarily concerns the methods and procedures for recognizing and composing the plurality of expertise, experiences, values and knowledge in the field.

2.   SOCIAL INNOVATION AS AN INNOVATION OF SOCIAL RELATIONS: THEORIZING AND PRACTICING CO-PRODUCTION (IN HEALTHCARE SETTINGS)

In recent years, the concept of SI has acquired increasing relevance in policy-making at national and supranational levels due to its alleged ability to tackle pressing social challenges while ensuring basic universal rights in a more inclusive and equitable way (Moulaert et al., 2013). Despite its success, it remains a contested concept, with multiple and contrasting meanings, which give rise to very different and often opposite practices (Ayob, Teasdale and Fagan, 2016; Marques, Morgan and Richardson, 2018). No systematic analysis of SI theories, characteristics and impact to back its significance has been carried out in the public sector (Howaldt, Domanski and Kaletka, 2016; Andion et al., 2017). This reluctance among social policy researchers has been attributed to its conceptual imprecision (Pol and Ville, 2009; Massey and Johnston-Miller, 2016), but the broad use of this concept as a guideline for policy interventions combined with the lack of consensus regarding the definitions of SI have to be considered carefully, especially in the public sector, as it has been proven to be used by policymakers to disguise 'an agenda of further liberalisation and public service withdrawal' (Baglioni and Sinclair, 2014, p. 410).

More recently, some scholars have attempted to fill this gap by providing a content analysis of the more influential scientific literature, selected by snowball (Marques, Morgan and Richardson, 2018) or bibliometric sampling (Ayob, Teasdale and Fagan, 2016), to provide a more specific conceptualization of SI by suggesting specific types or identifying its meaning as a definitional process. What emerges is the focus on SI as the innovation of social relations, in which the ethical dimension of SI is related to social justice (Moulaert et al., 2013). These literature reviews allow us to identify three constituent factors: (a) SI actively promotes inclusive relationships among individuals, especially those relationships that are (or have been) neglected by previous economic, political, cultural or social processes; (b) SI is explicitly concerned with addressing and satisfying unmet social needs; and (c) SI is often aimed at specific domains, such as education, health or migration (Marques, Morgan and Richardson, 2018).[1]

From this perspective, the SI literature underlines that SI initiatives are context driven (Van Dyck and Van den Broeck, 2013), path-dependent (Howaldt and Schwarz, 2010) and path-building (Van Wijk et al., 2019). The model conceptualizes SI processes as the product of agentic, relational and situated dynamics in three interrelated cycles that operate at the micro, meso and macro levels of analysis (Van Wijk et al., 2019) and require changing the cultural, normative or regulative structures of society, which enhance collective power resources and, in doing so, improves economic and social performance (Hämäläinen and Heiskala, 2007).

Considering SI embeddedness, I move from a merely conceptual approach to one that holds theory and practice together, as relational theory does, to analyse the definitional process of SI as co-creation and co-production in the public sector (Voorberg, Bekkers and Tummers, 2015). For the purposes of public value and market interest, the chapter, like most of the studies devoted to this topic (ibid.), deals primarily with healthcare and health-related services to back the significance and impact of SI initiatives on the three constituent factors mentioned above.

Starting with a theoretical review, it is worth considering, as SI echoes concepts such as the co-creation, co-production and co-design, which emphasize the importance of broad participation through the inclusion of end-users, or citizens, in the design and delivery of goods and services, primarily those that are offered through or with the support of the health authorities. This is the reason why SI initiatives tend to be circumscribed to a specific domain (education or health, for example), tend to rely on community-based initiatives, and are usually the product of specific national welfare regimes (Marques, Morgan and Richardson, 2018). In this process, the public bodies are called upon to play an important role in triggering, supporting and scaling up the SI process because of the collective nature of goods (i.e., health) and services (i.e., healthcare) (Mendes et al., 2012).

It is notable, however, that in defining the meaning of SI through the mentioned concepts such as co-creation/co-production, the cited authors utilize other contested concepts with nuanced contours. Despite an initial rejection based on a theoretical contrast between the co-creation/co-production and collaboration approaches, in which only the second is considered inextricably connected with SI,[2] a systematic review of the evolution of the SI concept and practices identified the collaboration approach as a litmus test that can be used to identify when SI initiatives and their co-creation/co-production are effective (Ayob, Teasdale and Fagan, 2016). Thus, the notion of co-creation overlaps with that of co-production,[3] which presents a higher level of theoretical conceptualization and therefore deserves to be analysed more in depth.

The concept of co-production was introduced by Elinor Ostrom in 1996 to identify 'a process through which inputs from individuals who are not "in" the same organization are transformed into goods and services' (p. 1073). Moving from this first conceptualization, two streams of literature have been developed: the first stream, from public administration, emphasizes the role of co-production to enhance the performance of public administration from a managerial perspective (Alford, 2009), and the second stream, from service management, focuses on the empowerment of citizens as end-users as a key factor to implement publicly desirable outcomes (Bovaird and Loeffler, 2012). More recently, this contrast has been overcome in the meaning proposed by Stephen Osborne and Kirsty Strokosch, who adopt a more comprehensive perspective by moving away from a relational approach (Bassani, Cattaneo and Galizi, 2016), which implies 'the empowerment of the service user within the service production process, as a key arbiter of service quality and performance' (Osborne and Strokosch, 2013, p. S38). This perspective seems to be the theoretical framework in which co-production is utilized in the SI literature mentioned.

Within the broader field of co-production, one method has gained popularity in the health domain and healthcare setting: experience-based co-design (EBCD). Even if it is a relatively young approach – it was developed by Paul Bate and Glenn Robert in collaboration with the NHS Institute for Innovation and Improvement (2006) by combining a user-centred orientation ('experience-based') and collaborative change processes ('co-design') – the approach has gained increasing popularity all over the world (Donetto et al., 2015) and has been used to address a broad range of clinical areas, including emergency medicine, drug and alcohol services, cancer services, paediatric diabetes care and mental health care. The EBCD method was developed by matching several research approaches (participatory action research, user-centred design, learning theories, and a narrative-based approach) to involve patients in improvement efforts on equal terms with healthcare professionals (Bate and Robert, 2006). The EBCD method, which typically takes 9 to 12 months, is divided into six steps: (1) setting up the project; (2) gathering staff experiences through observational fieldwork and in-depth interviews; (3) gathering patient and carer experiences through observation and filmed narrative-based interviews (usually between 10 and 15); (4) bringing staff, patients and carers together in a first co-design event to share their experiences of a service, by using a short movie (not exceeding 20 minutes) taken from the patient narrative as *stimulus*, and identifying priorities for change; (5) sustaining co-design work in small groups formed around those priorities (typically 4–6); and (6) holding a celebration and review event (Donetto et al., 2015).

The success of the EBCD method and the rapid spread of EBCD across the world have just as quickly highlighted its limits, the most relevant of which refers to the EBCD impact on empowerment and power relations (Palmer et al., 2019). The study conducted by Palmer and colleagues underlines that little information exists about the EBCD method and its alleged ability to facilitate empowerment, foster trust and develop autonomy, self-determination and choice, including staff at health services (ibid.). They pointed out the need to redefine the approach by stressing the mechanisms of change and the entities, processes and structures that underpin the redefinition of power relations to evaluate the effectiveness of the 'relational shift' promoted by the EBCD method (ibid.). In doing so, they stressed the role of power asymmetries that 'skew our collective understandings such that the understandings of the more powerful social groups dominate; the task of codesign work is to align symmetries' (ibid., p. 7). Their 'explanatory theoretical model of change' (ibid., p. 1) intends to focus on the relational transitions fostered (or not) by EBCD starting from the recognition process, which is assumed as the basic mechanism enabling the subsequent steps of change (dialogue, cooperation, accountability, mobilization, enactment, creativity and attainment). In defining the recognition mechanism, they refer to Miranda Fricker's (2007) understanding and to her concept of epistemic justice by adopting a normative approach to evaluate the introduced changed mechanism at the epistemic level. The model allows us to evaluate the degree of recognition achieved in terms of voices, experiences and narrative legitimation in a given and specific case, but it remains blind to detecting the mechanisms of the reproduction or transformation of power relations at the interpersonal and institutional levels and is unable to foster change.

By using the concept of recognition in the sense described by Miranda Fricker, the cited authors transpose a critical-analytical concept in a normative way. The following paragraph intends to overcome the normative approach, deepening the meaning of the recognition process from the feminist conception, as in Miranda Fricker's thinking, and seeks to explore its potential in relational terms, in which the structural, ontological and epistemic dimensions are considered strictly interrelated.

3.   FROM GENDERED SOCIAL INNOVATION TO GENDERING SOCIAL INNOVATION AND CO-PRODUCTION

The introduction of the concept of recognition is a useful framework through which EBCD criticisms can be further developed and utilized for the purpose of SI from a gender inclusive perspective. The notion of recognition has a long tradition in political philosophy, in which it has been theorized and analysed together with the concept of redistribution to gain social justice. Very briefly, theorists such as Gitlin (1995) and Rorty (2000) argue that the focus on recognition serves to distract from the real issue of distributive injustice because concentrating on identity exaggerates difference rather than emphasizing commonalities; theorists such as Taylor (1992) and Honneth (2003) argue that ignoring difference and focusing exclusively on redistribution can serve to reinforce injustice by compelling minority groups and identities to comply with the norms of the dominant group. They argue that recognition is crucial to obtaining social justice. In this theoretical struggle, the feminist philosopher Nancy Fraser develops a non-identitarian account of recognition capable of synergizing with redistribution, based on her review of gender theory (2003; 2007).

In Fraser's thought, gender is a broad and capacious conception elaborated to accommodate at least quasi-Marxist, labour-centred understandings of gender to culture and identity-based conceptions that require the deinstitutionalization of androcentric value hierarchies. In doing so, gender emerges as a two-dimensional category:

> It contains both a political-economic face that brings it within the ambit of redistribution and also a cultural-discursive face that brings it simultaneously within the ambit of recognition. Moreover, neither dimension is merely an indirect effect of the other. To be sure, the distributive and recognition dimensions interact with one another. (Fraser, 2007, p. 26)

In Fraser's thought, social justice requires an equal distribution of material resources, but at the same time, it necessitates that institutionalized patterns of cultural value express equal respect and ensure equal opportunity for achieving social esteem. These conditions define the principle of 'parity of participation', which requires social arrangements that permit all (adult) members of society to interact with one another 'as peers'. From this perspective, she redefines the recognition politics in a non-identitarian way. She critiques the demand of recognition in terms of identity politics aimed to repair internal self-dislocation by rejecting demeaning androcentric pictures of femininity in favour of new self-representations of their own making. While recognizing some genuine insights concerning the psychological effect of sexism, Fraser critiques this approach because it tends to reify femininity and to obscure cross-cutting axes of subordination (including 'race', sexuality, ethnicity, nationality and religion). Her alternative proposal is based on social status. 'What requires recognition is not feminine identity but the status of women as full partners in social interaction' (ibid., p. 30). Social interaction, as not simply a by-product of status hierarchy nor wholly a by-product of economic structure, is the *locus* in which misrecognition and maldistribution interact with one another, defining gender as a status differentiation. 'Gender injustices of distribution and recognition are so complexly intertwined that neither can be redressed entirely independently of the other' (ibid., p. 34). This is the reason why, in Fraser's theory, politics of recognition are strictly and inextricably connected with politics of redistribution; moreover, according to Fraser's analysis, misrecognition and maldistribution need to be addressed by the joint use of structural and cultural approaches. For the purpose of the chapter, it is crucial to underline that Fraser's notion of recognition implies a contextual approach in which broader society is involved – including labour markets, sexual relations, family life, the public sphere, and voluntary associations in civil society – and that it is necessary that this process crosses all major axes of social differentiation, not only gender but also 'race', ethnicity, sexuality, religion, and nationality. In Fraser's thinking, the proposed reforms must be evaluated from multiple perspectives, and hence, proponents must consider whether measures aimed at redressing one sort of disparity are likely to end up exacerbating another (ibid.).

I would suggest that Fraser's thought recognition (and gender) is compatible with Connell's theoretical contribution, and understanding gender in relational terms and exploring this link could be useful to operationalize the concept of recognition. Fraser's and Connell's gender theorizing comes from the necessity to overcome the identity/categorical thinking of gender and to match the structuralist with the culturalist approach. They both found this match by adopting a relational approach. I further argue that Connell's work provides a model for the kind of contextual analysis I believe is called for to analyse the effects of EBCD practices or SI initiatives within specific contexts. In considering gender as a relation, Connell underlines that the everyday social practices in which gender is enacted are creative but not random. They occur in a dense and active social tissue of institutions and sites, such as families, companies, governments and neighbourhoods. In doing so, she constrains both the categorical thinking about gender – whether or not it is based on biological essentialism, which persistently underplays diversity within the gender categories and is not useful for conceptualizing the dynamics of gender – and the poststructuralist approach – which is very fruitful as a way of thinking about the role of culture and as a critique of gender essentialism but is unable to properly consider the role of economic processes, organizational life, material interests, or non-discursive forms of power. From the relational perspective, gender 'is a relation', a multidimensional relation, embracing at the same time economic relations, power relations, affective relations and symbolic relations and operating simultaneously at intrapersonal, interpersonal, institutional and society-wide levels (Connell, 2009; Lorber, 1994). It is important to underline the implication of this point: a change in one dimension of gender may happen at a different pace, or even in a different direction, from a change in another dimension (Connell, 2012). Relational theory affects the core of SI interest by promoting the restructuring of social relations in a more equitable way.

Moreover, from the relational perspective, Connell derives some relevant concepts for gendering SI. On the one hand, she introduced the concepts of 'gender order' and 'gender regime' to distinguish between the structural inventory of an entire society and the structural inventory of particular institutions

(Connell, 1987). From this perspective, the public bodies devoted to promoting and fostering the SI initiatives and the EBCD experiences turn out to 'have well defined gender regimes' in which 'the dynamics of gender regimes influence the planning of health care through these institutions' (Connell, 2012, p. 1678). This could be carefully considered and thematized when public bodies promote and implement such a process. Moreover, we have to carefully consider the broad 'gender order' in which public agencies and the EBCD processes are placed. Connell's theory also refers to the relational approach when considering the role of the other axes of social differentiation, such as 'race', ethnicity, sexuality, religion, and nationality, an approach that seems to be perfectly compatible with Fraser's non-identitarian approach. Instead of a categorical approach, she prefers the anti-categorical approach, used by intersectionality scholars to deconstruct systems of categorization, and instead focuses on complex relations between multiple groups not only within but also across identities and analytic categories (McCall, 2005).

By considering SI and gender from a relational perspective, it becomes clear that both refer to social interactions as embedded and context-driven concepts in which misrecognition and maldistribution interact with one other. This is why, when assuming that the recognition process is a crucial factor for promoting an effective EBCD, it is necessary to remember that such initiative is inserted in an organizational/institutional and societal context and interacts with the related gender regime and gender order. Promoting effective inclusiveness requires that the recognition processes operate at all three analytical levels, which are reciprocally interrelated; in so doing, we promote an effective approach to *gendering social innovation* (see Figure 7.1).

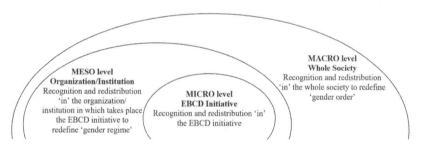

Figure 7.1   Gendering social innovation approach

At this point, it is possible to understand how this approach overcomes the conception of *gendered social innovation*, which has been recently introduced in academic literature as a 'type of social innovation that is based on the normative identification of societal challenges of gender inequality and social needs among women or men as underrepresented or disadvantaged groups in various areas' (Lindberg, Forsberg and Karlberg, 2015, p. 479). Even from these few lines, it becomes evident that *gendered social innovation* adopts a normative approach to identifying the necessary societal challenges and moving from a categorical and identitarian approach to gender entails the risk of reifying femininity/masculinity and its alleged needs and obscuring cross-cutting axes of subordination. These risks can be avoided only by abandoning a normative and categorical approach and instead taking a relational perspective that is capable of considering social interactions as a *locus* in which the different lines of status differentiation take shape and is therefore capable of promoting effective SI.

4.   CONCLUSION

Fully developing the potential of the relational approach to gender and to SI, the chapter defines a new framework, named *gendering social innovation*, which seems to provide the most promising approach to fulfil the promises of SI in terms of redefining social relations in a more inclusive and equitable way to address and satisfy unmet social needs.

First, feminist theories and gender studies have broadly reflected on and debated the dimensions of misrecognition and maldistribution linked to gender and in so doing offer a very fruitful framework for SI, at both the theoretical and methodological levels, in innovating social relations in an inclusive and equitable way, in which the ethical dimension of SI is related to social justice. More specifically, the chapter finds a further point of convergence in the growing importance that the relational approach has taken on in both SI theories and gender studies. By adopting a relational approach, both consider the axes of social differentiation as multidimensional, operating at the micro, meso and macro levels, and interrelated, needing to be understood in their dynamics of reciprocal action and retroaction. This could be encouraging because it does mean that relational power structures do change, but we have to carefully consider that historical change is not all progress.

From this threat derives the specific relevance of the relational approach to co-production in healthcare settings. When defining co-production as collaboration – which implies the empowerment of the service user within the service production process – the relational approach to gender and the related concepts of 'gender regime' and 'gender order' become crucial to consider institutions as not neutral, being bearers of a clearly oriented system of values and norms specifically for gender but also for the other axes of social differentiation. The relational approach makes it necessary to consider the co-production process in its context and in its reciprocal interrelation at the meso and macro levels as these interrelations define the meaning and the outcome of the innovation practices introduced at micro level. Hence, the second claim of the chapter. The statement of SI theories, which underline the fact that no SI initiative is implemented in a *vacuum* – being, as aforementioned, context-driven, path-dependent and path-building – became, in adopting a relational approach to gender, a methodological imperative: any EBCD processes, hopefully integrated by the analysis of the eight mechanisms of change (Palmer et al., 2019), cannot be effective without promoting initiatives throughout the whole of social life. Recognition 'in' the process requires social justice 'in' the institution and 'in' society as a whole. Recognition and redistribution need parity of participation in a multiplicity of interaction arenas, including the EBCD process, the institution in which the EBCD initiative is implemented (in order to redefine its 'gender regime') and in the socio-political arena (in order to modify the 'gender order').

Third, the relational approach to gender allows us to identify the major risk of *gendered social innovation*, as defined in recent literature (Lindberg, Forsberg and Karlberg, 2015). The adoption of a categorial approach to gender remains blind to the other axes of social differentiation, threatening to conflict head-on with efforts to remedy homophobia, racism, religious discrimination, and so on. Lindberg, Forsberg and Karlberg seem to seize a more comprehensive potentiality inherent to the gender approach when they argue, 'these subjects thereto require the use of appropriate measures that will enable the transformative potential to be identified from an inclusive perspective, which is provided by the elaboration of gendered social innovation' (ibid., p. 480). This is an important statement because it thematizes the key feature of the connection between SI studies and the gender approach, which resides in focusing on inclusiveness (recognition) and restructuring the power relations (redistribution) as a primary issue for both. To be effective, this statement needs to abandon the categorical and identitarian thinking of gender and instead adopt a relation approach. In doing so, *gendering social innovation* could explain its universal value, not as a universal measure but as a critical and analytical perspective for detecting power dynamics as multidimensional and reciprocally interrelated.

In the framework defined above, *gendering social innovation* is a movement aimed at fertilizing SI studies with a gender perspective by adopting a relational approach. The chapter does not conclude or complete such studies but rather offers a new framework through which to deepen the different theoretical and methodological issues questioned in the SI literature and consider the risk that SI initiatives could foster new power relations that are more unfair and exclusive.

NOTES

1. The focus on social aims or about improving social welfare is used from some scholars as the distinguishing element of SI (Borzaga and Bodini, 2012; Cajaiba-Santana, 2014; Graddy-Reed and Feldman, 2015).
2. From the co-creation perspective, the core attentional is at the improvement in the product (without any consideration for equity); from the collaboration approach, the concepts of accountability and responsiveness come into play, contributing to the 'publicness' of the public sector and improving its legitimacy (Newman and Clarke, 2009).
3. For a more comprehensive analysis of co-creation and co-production as synonymous when referring to citizens' active participation in delivering and designing the services they receive, see Brandsen, Steen and Verschuere (2018).

REFERENCES

Alford, J. (2009), *Engaging Public Sector Clients: From Service Delivery to Co-production*, London: Palgrave Macmillan.

Andion, C., Ronconi, L., Moraes, R.L., Gonsalves, A.K.R. and Serafim, L.B.D.S. (2017), 'Civil society and social innovation in the public sphere: a pragmatic perspective', *Brazilian Journal of Public Administration*, **51** (3), 369–387.

Ayob, N., Teasdale, S. and Fagan, K. (2016), 'How social innovation "came to be": Tracing the evolution of a contested concept', *Journal of Social Policy*, **45** (4), 635–653.

Baglioni, S. and Sinclair, S. (2014), 'Introduction: Social innovation and social policy', *Social Policy and Society*, **13** (3), 409–410.

Bassani, G., Cattaneo, C. and Galizi, G. (2016), 'Co-production in action: The case of an Italian residential care home', in Mariagrazia Fugini, Enrico Bracci and Mariafrancesca Sicilia (eds), *Co-production in the Public Sector: Experiences and Challenges*, Heidelberg: Springer, pp. 59–76.

Bate, P. and Robert, G. (2006), 'Experience-based design: From redesigning the system around the patient to co-designing services with the patient', *Quality & Safety in Health Care*, **15** (5), 307–310.

Borzaga, C. and Bodini, R. (2012), *What to make of social innovation? Towards a framework for policy development*, Euricse Working Paper, N.036.

Bovaird, T. and LoeffLer, E. (2012), 'From engagement to co-production: The contribution of users and communities to outcomes and public value', *Voluntas*, **3** (4), 1119–1138.

Brandsen, T., Steen, T. and Verschuere, B. (2018), *Co-Production and Co-Creation: Engaging Citizens in Public Service Delivery*, London: Routledge.

Cajaiba-Santana, G. (2014), 'Social innovation: Moving the field forward. A conceptual framework', *Technological Forecasting and Social Change*, **82** (C), 42–51.

Connell, R.W. (1987), *Gender and Power: Society, the Person and Sexual Politics*, London: Polity Press.

Connell, R.W. (2006), 'The experience of gender change in public sector organizations', *Gender, Work and Organization*, **13** (5), 435–452.

Connell, R.W. (2009), *Gender: In World Perspective*, Cambridge: Polity Press.

Connell, R.W. (2012), 'Gender, health and theory: Conceptualizing the issue, in local and world perspective', *Social Science & Medicine*, **74**, 1675–1683.

Donetto, S., Pierri, P., Tsianakas, V. and Robert, G. (2015), 'Experience-based co-design and healthcare improvement: Realising participatory design in the public sector', *The Design Journal*, **18** (2), 227–248.

Fraser, N. (2003), 'Social justice in the age of identity politics: Redistribution, recognition, and participation', in Nancy Fraser and Axel Honneth, *Redistribution or Recognition? A Political Philosophical Exchange*, London: Verso, pp. 7–109.

Fraser, N. (2007), 'Feminist politics in the age of recognition: A two-dimensional approach to gender justice', *Studies in Social Justice*, **1** (1), 23–35.

Fricker, M. (2007), *Epistemic Injustice: Power and the Ethics of Knowing*, Oxford: Clarendon.

Gitlin, T. (1995), *The Twilight of Common Dreams: Why America is Wracked by Culture Wars*, New York: Metropolitan Books.

Graddy-Reed, A. and Feldman, M.P. (2015), 'Stepping up: An empirical analysis of the use of social innovation in response to an economic recession', *Cambridge Journal of Regions, Economy, & Society*, **8** (2), 293–312.

Hämäläinen, T. and Heiskala, R. (eds) (2007), *Social Innovations, Institutional Change and Economic Performance: Making Sense of Structural Adjustment Processes in Industrial Sectors, Regions and Societies*, Cheltenham, UK and Northampton, MA, USA: SITRA and Edward Elgar Publishing.

Honneth, A. (2003), 'Redistribution as recognition: A response to Nancy Fraser', in Nancy Fraser and Axel Honneth, *Redistribution or Recognition? A Political Philosophical Exchange*, London: Verso, pp. 110–197.

Howaldt, J., Domanski, D. and Kaletka, C. (2016), 'Social innovation: Towards a new innovation paradigm', *Revista de Administração Mackenzie*, **17** (6), 20–44.

Howaldt, J. and Schwarz, M. (2010), *Social Innovation: Concepts, Research Fields and International Trends*, Aachen: International Monitoring (IMO).

Kuhlmann, E. and Annandale, E. (eds) (2010), *The Palgrave Handbook of Gender and Healthcare*, Basingstoke: Palgrave Macmillan.

Lindberg, M., Forsberg, L. and Karlberg, H. (2015), 'Gendered social innovation – a theoretical lens for analysing structural transformation in organisations and society', *International Journal of Social Entrepreneurship and Innovation*, **3** (6), 472–483.

Lorber, J. (1994), *Paradoxes of Gender*, New Haven: Yale University Press.

Marques, P., Morgan, K. and Richardson, R. (2018), 'Social innovation in question: The theoretical and practical implications of a contested concept', *Environment and Planning C: Politics and Space*, **36** (3), 496–512.

Massey, A. and Johnston-Miller, K. (2016), 'Governance: public governance to social innovation?', *Policy & Politics*, **44** (4), 663–675.

McCall, L. (2005), 'The complexity of intersectionality', *Signs: Journal of Women in Culture and Society*, **30** (3), 1771–1800.

Mendes, A., Batista, A., Fernandes, L., Macedo, P., Pinto, F., Rebelo, L., Ribeiro, M., Ribeiro, R., Sottomayor, M., Tavares, M. and Verdelho, V. (2012), *Barriers to Social Innovation. A Deliverable of the TEPSIE Project*. Brussels: European Commission, DG Research.

Moulaert, F., Maccallum, D., Mehmood, A. and Hamdouch, A. (eds) (2013), *International Handbook of Social Innovation. Social Innovation, Collective Action and Transdisciplinary Research*, Cheltenham, UK and Northampton, MA, USA: Edward Elgar Publishing.

Newman, J. and Clarke, J. (2009), *Publics, Politics and Power: Remaking the Public in Public Services*, London: Sage.

Osborne, S.P. and Strokosch, K. (2013), 'It takes two to tango? Understanding the co-production of public services by integrating the services management and public administration perspectives', *British Journal of Management*, **24**, S31–S47.

Ostrom, E. (1996), 'Crossing the great divide: Co-production, synergy and development', *World Development*, **24** (6), 1073–1087.

Palmer, V.J. et al. (2019), 'The participatory zeitgeist: An explanatory theoretical model of change in an era of coproduction and co-design in healthcare improvement', *Medical Humanities*, **45** (3), 247–257.

Pol, E. and Ville, S. (2009), 'Social innovation: Buzz word or enduring term?', *The Journal of Socio-Economics*, **38** (6), 878–885.

Rorty, R. (2000), 'Is "cultural recognition" a useful notion for Leftist politics?', *Critical Horizons*, **1** (1), 7–20.

Taylor, C. (1992), *Multiculturalism and 'The Politics of Recognition'*, Princeton: Princeton University Press.

Van Dyck, B. and Van den Broeck, P. (2013), 'Social innovation: A territorial process', in Frank Moulaert, Diana MacCallum, Abid Mehmood and Abdelillah Hamdouch (eds), *International Handbook of Social Innovation. Social Innovation, Collective Action and Transdisciplinary Research*, Cheltenham, UK and Northampton, MA, USA: Edward Elgar Publishing, pp. 131–141.

Van Wijk, J., Zietsma, C., Dorado, S., de Bakker, F.G.A. and Martí, I. (2019), 'Social innovation: Integrating micro, meso and macro level insights from institutional theory', *Business and Society*, **58** (5), 887–918.

Voorberg, W.H., Bekkers, V.J.J.M. and Tummers, L.G. (2015), 'A systematic review of co-creation and co-production: Embarking on the social innovation journey', *Public Management Review*, **17** (9), 1333–1357.

West, C. and Zimmerman, D.H. (1987), 'Doing gender', *Gender & Society*, **1** (2), 125–151.

8. Underrepresented innovators: an assessment of innovation activities in women-led businesses in the UK

Beldina Owalla, Tim Vorley and Elvis Nyanzu

1. INTRODUCTION

Women-led businesses are an important vehicle for worldwide economic growth (Poggesi et al., 2016), as well as a mechanism for better social inclusion, empowerment and wide institutional change (Filculescu, 2016). Innovation is also viewed as an essential part of the entrepreneurial process. However, while there has been an increase in the number of women-led businesses globally, there are substantial differences in the types of ventures created (Kelley et al., 2017). The Global Entrepreneurship Monitor (GEM) 2018/2019 Women's Entrepreneurship report also indicates that women-led businesses are generally less innovative than their male counterparts by approximately 6% (Elam et al., 2019). Moreover, contextual factors such as physical place, religion, culture, social norms have consistently been shown to impact women's entrepreneurial activities (Baughn et al., 2006; DeVita et al., 2014). However, there has been limited research on innovation in women-led enterprises. Likewise, research adopting a gender lens to understand innovation policies and support schemes are limited (Alsos et al., 2013; Kvidal and Ljunggren, 2014).

This chapter focuses on the innovation activities of women-led SMEs in the UK specifically, and how policy initiatives can effectively support female founders' participation in business innovation. We address the following research question: *How are SMEs' innovation activities influenced by gender, ethnicity and place?* Our findings draw on the Longitudinal Small Business Survey (LSBS) data over the period 2015 to 2018, as well as a study undertaken by the Innovation Caucus focused on supporting diversity and inclusion in innovation (Vorley et al., 2020). We adopt an intersectional approach in our analyses that emphasizes the agentic processes and wider structural forces that often impact a social group's positioning and influences their ability to mobilize resources (Owalla et al., 2021; Romero and Valdez, 2016). Such an approach draws attention to the unequal access to resources, opportunities and support within entrepreneurial ecosystems, while highlighting the need for policy initiatives to pay greater attention to the gendered structures influencing women's innovation activities (Brush et al., 2019; Foss et al., 2019).

The remainder of the chapter is organized as follows. In the next section, we review previous studies in this area. We then discuss our methodology, before presenting our results and analysis. The chapter concludes with a discussion of the findings, and provides recommendations for policy initiatives aimed at supporting female founders' participation in business innovation.

2. IMPACT OF GENDER AND DIVERSITY ON INNOVATION

Research highlights the positive impact that gender diversity has on creativity and innovation (Hewlett et al., 2013), on the functional diversity and innovative performance of new venture teams (Dai et al., 2019), and on the radical innovation of R&D teams (Díaz-García et al., 2013). However, for a long time, innovation policy and research has mainly focused on technological product development among large firms in male-dominated sectors (Alsos et al., 2013; Lindberg et al., 2015). The gendered aspects of the innovation phenomenon are therefore relatively underexplored. For example, analysing innovation measurements, Filculescu (2016) finds that when innovation is measured using 'soft' indicators like attitudes towards innovative behaviours, then female founders are found to be more supportive of new ideas, creative methods, and demonstrate greater inclination towards experimentation and risk taking. On the other hand, when 'hard' indicators like patenting activity and R&D expenditure are used to measure innovation, then male-led firms outperform their female counterparts (Filculescu, 2016). The 'stickiness' of masculinity with innovation and the difficulties encountered in broadening discourses and actors involved in innovation, can be attributed to the gender hierarchy created by power structures (Alsos et al., 2013). This gap is still evident in today's innovation-driven economy where women in STEM continue to be marginalized in terms of disparities in salary, resources, laboratory space and so on (Walters and McNeely, 2010).

The hurdles that women in STEM face can be attributed to either psychological factors such as stereotypes and perceptions of STEM fields, or structural factors such as lack of mentors/role models, organizational culture, and societal expectations (Botella et al., 2019; Sitaridis and Kitsios, 2019; Vitores and Gil-Juárez, 2016). Previous studies find that existing stereotypes and perceptions of STEM fields as a male domain, still have a major influence on female and male students' future career aspirations (Kang et al., 2019; Stout et al., 2016). Other research on structural factors indicate that gendered divisions of labour and the pervasive male culture within STEM workplaces, business incubators, and tech cities, results in the marginalization of women innovators; limiting their access to crucial social and financial resources (Hardey, 2019; Herman, 2015; Marlow and McAdam, 2015). For example, the lack of gender diversity in venture capital firms in the UK (39% of London venture funds have no women at all, while 65% have no senior female partners) creates particular challenges for female founders seeking funding (Diversity VC and OneTech, 2019). In 2018, the majority of the UK venture capital funding (83%) went to all-male teams, with mixed and all-female teams receiving 12% and 4% of the investments respectively (British Business Bank et al., 2019).

Furthermore, studies argue for the need to pay greater attention to the heterogeneity of women-led businesses in STEM, and the landscapes in which they operate (Filculescu, 2016; Griffiths et al., 2007; Pettersson and Lindberg, 2013). For example, female ICT professionals are a heterogeneous group from different educational and social backgrounds, and occupying a broad range of positions within the ICT industry in England (Griffiths et al., 2007). Adopting an intersectional perspective therefore allows us to start from the premise that multiple dimensions of identity intersect to create, maintain and reproduce the opportunities of members sharing similar social positions within a highly stratified society (Valdez, 2016). Various studies have drawn upon intersectional perspectives to show how entrepreneurial activities are influenced by gender, class and racialized histories of oppression (Agius Vallejo and Canizales, 2016; Wingfield and Taylor, 2016). While intersectionality is more commonly associated with qualitative studies, quantitative researchers in the education field have also used the 'inter-categorical' complexity approach to analyse how multiple intersecting inequalities such as gender, social background and ethnicity combine to impact education outcomes (Codiroli Mcmaster and Cook, 2019). For example, female students from less advantaged social backgrounds are more likely to study social science, law and business – rather than STEM subjects – compared to their more advantaged peers (Codiroli Mcmaster, 2017; van de Werfhorst, 2017).

Intersectional analyses can therefore contribute to our understanding of the under-representation of minority groups, as well as the structural inequalities impeding their participation in innovation activities (Vorley et al., 2020). Additionally, research indicates that geographical variations in entrepreneurial activity could be related to various place-based structural factors (OECD, 2020). Large urban centres benefit from agglomeration effects that are conducive to business start-up such as large local markets, easier access to public research and education facilities, high quality of human capital and infrastructure, and networking opportunities (OECD, 2020). Moreover, women are socially located within places differently from men and their firms are often constrained to gendered spaces by socio-economic factors (Blake and Hanson,

2005; Carter et al., 2015). In the UK, women-led SMEs were more likely to be found in the education sector (31%) and health services (37%), compared to the ICT (11%), construction and transportation sectors (9%) (Rhodes, 2019). Ethnic minority-led SMEs are also more likely to be in health (9%), retail, accommodation, food service, administration and support (7%) sectors, than in construction and manufacturing (3%) or professional and scientific (4%) sectors (Office for National Statistics, 2018). These SMEs are also most commonly located in London (16%) and West Midlands (8%) regions, than in the South West (2%) and North East (1%) regions (Office for National Statistics, 2018).

The remainder of the chapter focuses on analysing the innovation activities of women-led SMEs in the UK. We also draw on a previous study on supporting diversity and inclusion in innovation (Vorley et al., 2020), to make recommendations on how policy initiatives can more effectively support female founders' participation in business innovation. Having presented the theoretical framework, we discuss our research methodology next.

3. METHODOLOGY

Our data is based on the Longitudinal Small Business Survey (LSBS) data produced by the Department for Business, Energy and Industrial Strategy (BEIS). This annual survey of businesses with fewer than 250 employees was carried out during the period 2015 to 2018. The survey is voluntary, and responses are collected by Computer Assisted Telephone Interviews, conducted by BMG Research Ltd under contract with BEIS. The sampling frame is a combination of the Inter-Departmental Business Register (IDBR) for employers/ VAT-registered businesses and the Dun & Bradstreet database of businesses for the remainder. Over the four years, 29,302 business have taken part at least once, with 2,757 businesses taking part in all four years. For the purpose of this study, we focused on questions relating to: (a) gender and ethnicity of business owners and directors; (b) product innovation – includes introduction of new or significant improvement in some or all goods and services; (c) process innovation – includes introduction of new or significantly improved processes for producing or supplying goods or services, and (d) investment in R&D – this includes the R&D investment of a 2018 cohort during the previous three years.

As our study focuses on SMEs, a total of 35 large firms with over 250 employees were removed from the dataset. We use the OECD definition of SMEs, that is, businesses with fewer than 250 employees and comprising micro (fewer than 10 employees), small (10–49 employees) and medium (50–249 employees) firms (OECD, 2017). The survey results for the remaining 29,267 firms therefore form the core dataset used in the study. Women-led SMEs (WLED) are defined as SMEs led by either a sole business owner/director who identifies as female, or where over 50% of the firm's directors identify as female. A similar definition is used for ethnic minority-led SMEs (MLED). Geographically, the study covers the entire UK, with administrative regions being used as the main spatial unit of analysis. There are nine regions in England, with Wales, Scotland and Northern Ireland being treated as separate regions. As a result, the regional boundaries comprise 12 areas. Descriptive and statistical analyses were completed using SPSS and R.

4.   FINDINGS AND ANALYSIS

The presentation and analysis of the empirical results focuses on analysing the relationships between gender, ethnic diversity and locational characteristics on the innovation activities of women-led SMEs in the UK.

4.1   Regional Distribution of Women-led SMEs

Out of 29,267 SMEs surveyed within the period 2015 to 2018, about 17% (5,058 firms) identified as women-led SMEs (WLED), and only 1% (255 firms) identified as ethnic minority women-led SMEs (MWLED). Regarding firm size, we find that a significant proportion of WLED SMEs comprise micro firms (62%) compared to small (28%) and medium (10%) firms. Similarly, MWLED SMEs are mainly composed of micro firms (58%), rather than small (29%) and medium-sized (13%) firms (see Table 8.1).

There is minimal variation in the regional distribution of WLED SMEs (see Table 8.2), with West Midlands (18.9%), North East (18.1%), London and Scotland (17.5% each) having the highest proportions of WLED SMEs, and Wales (15.9%) and Yorkshire (16.5%) regions having the lowest. However, in the case of MWLED SMEs, there is considerable variation in the regional distribution of firms, with the highest proportions of MWLED SMEs being located in London (3.1%) and West Midlands (1.1%). The proportion of MWLED SMEs in the other regions is much lower and ranges from 0.2 to 0.7%, with an average of 0.4%.

Table 8.1   Sizes of SMEs led by women

Categories	Number of employees	No. of WLED SMEs	No. of MWLED SMEs	Total SMEs
Medium	50–249	523	32	4,400
Small	10–49	1,398	74	7,668
Micro	Less than 10	3,137	149	17,199
Total		5,058	255	29,267

Note: WLED = women-led; MWLED = Ethnic minority women-led.

Table 8.2   *Regional distribution of women-led SMEs*

Regions	Total No. of SMEs	No. of WLED SMEs	WLED SMEs (%)	No. of MWLED SMEs	MWLED SMEs (%)
East Midlands	1,954	341	17.5	11	0.6
East of England	2,902	494	17.0	16	0.6
London	3,397	595	17.5	104	3.1
North East	763	138	18.1	2	0.3
North West	2,387	408	17.1	13	0.5
Northern Ireland	1,567	269	17.2	5	0.3
Scotland	3,123	545	17.5	20	0.6
South East	4,381	741	16.9	36	0.8
South West	3,097	543	17.5	8	0.3
Wales	1,504	239	15.9	3	0.2
West Midlands	2,230	422	18.9	24	1.1
Yorkshire & the Humber	1,962	323	16.5	13	0.7
Total	29,267	5,058		255	

Note: WLED = women-led; MWLED = Ethnic minority women-led. WLED and MWLED percentages are based on total number of SMEs in each region.

4.2   Intersections of Gender, Ethnicity, Place and Innovation

In order to examine the relationship between gender, ethnicity, place and innovation, we analyse WLED and MWLED firms' participation in innovation in the different regions. Innovation is measured as: (i) product innovation, that is, introduction of new or significant improvement in all goods and services; (ii) process innovation, that is, introduction of new or significantly improved processes, and (iii) level of investment in R&D – includes participation in R&D within the three years prior to the survey, and is based on the 2018 cohort (a total 10,529 SMEs) only. The regional distribution of SMEs' innovation activities is presented in Table 8.3.

Analysing the product and process innovation activities of firms over the period, we find that in general, the proportion of WLED SMEs participating in product innovations is less than those participating in process innovation. These findings are similar to the innovation activities of the overall sample of SMEs surveyed (on average 1.3% participate in product innovation and 22.4% participate in process innovation). On average, 1.3% of WLED SMEs participate in some form of product innovation across the different regions. In contrast, an average of 2.2% of MWLED SMEs undertook some form of

Gender, diversity and innovation

Table 8.3   *Regional distribution of SMEs' innovation activities*

Regions	Investment in R&D (2018 cohort only)			Product innovation (goods and services)			Process innovation		
	ALL (%)	WLED (%)	MWLED (%)	ALL (%)	WLED (%)	MWLED (%)	ALL (%)	WLED (%)	MWLED (%)
East Midlands	6.1	5.1	0.0	1.1	0.9	9.1	22.8	20.8	27.3
East of England	6.4	6.9	13.0	0.9	0.8	6.3	22.9	20.4	37.5
London	7.6	6.5	5.0	1.3	1.2	2.9	25.2	23.9	33.7
North East	2.5	1.8	0.0	1.4	2.9	0.0	22.8	25.4	0.0
North West	6.9	8.3	0.0	1.0	1.7	7.7	22.5	19.4	23.1
N. Ireland	7.5	6.0	0.0	2.0	1.1	0.0	20.6	19.3	20.0
Scotland	7.6	4.9	0.0	1.5	1.1	0.0	20.1	15.0	20.0
South East	5.3	5.7	9.0	0.9	1.1	0.0	22.5	21.2	36.1
South West	6.3	4.5	0.0	1.1	1.3	0.0	21.5	18.8	0.0
Wales	3.6	2.9	0.0	1.7	2.1	0.0	22.9	26.8	33.3
West Midlands	6.0	5.3	8.0	1.1	0.7	0.0	21.9	19.0	29.2
Yorkshire & the Humber	5.1	6.0	0.0	1.3	1.2	0.0	23.3	20.1	15.4

Note: ALL = total number of SMEs; WLED = women-led; MWLED = Ethnic minority women-led.

product innovation. This is higher than the level of product innovation among both WLED SMES and the overall sample of SMEs. It is, however, worth noting that MWLED SMEs from only four regions (East Midlands, East of England, London and North West) were included in the survey.

A higher proportion of both WLED and MWLED SMEs participate in process innovation across the different regions. Scotland has the lowest proportion of WLED SMEs participating in process innovation (15%), while Wales and the North East region have the highest proportions (26.8% and 25.4% respectively). In the case of MWLED SMEs, with the exception of the North East and South West regions (where no firms undertaking process innovation activities are included in the survey), Yorkshire has the lowest proportion (15.4%), while East of England and the South East regions have the highest proportions (37.5% and 36.1% respectively). Similar to product innovation, we find that on average a higher proportion of MWLED SMEs participate in process innovation activities (23%) compared to WLED SMEs (20.8%).

With regard to R&D, we find considerable variation in the R&D investment of WLED SMEs' compared to MWLED SMEs. On average, 5.3% of WLED SMEs across the regions invest in R&D. The North East region has the lowest proportion (1.8%) and the North West and East of England regions have the highest proportion of investment in R&D (8.3% and 6.9% respectively). On the contrary, on average 2.9% of MWLED SMEs invest in R&D – based on firms surveyed in four regions (East of England, London, South East and West Midlands) only. Overall, we find that only three regions, namely East of England, London and the South East, have above average proportions of WLED and MWLED SMEs taking part in both process innovations and R&D investments.

5. DISCUSSION

This chapter focuses on understanding the innovation activities of women-led SMEs in the UK by analysing how gender, ethnicity and place intersect to influence the type and level of innovation activities undertaken by SMEs. Our results build on previous studies that highlight the need to pay greater attention to the heterogeneity of women-led businesses and the landscapes in which they operate (Filculescu, 2016; Griffiths et al., 2007; Pettersson and Lindberg, 2013). Despite the fact that only a minority of SMEs are women-led (17%) and the majority of these are micro firms (62%), our findings suggest that women-led SMEs are equally as likely to participate in product innovation, process innovation, and invest in R&D, as other SMEs in the UK.

When considering the heterogeneity of women-led SMEs, our results further indicate that ethnicity and place both play a role in influencing the level of participation in innovation activities. Similar to findings regarding minority-led SMEs in general, our results indicate that the sub-group of MWLED SMEs are more commonly located in London and West Midlands (Office for National Statistics, 2018). This might imply that the wider business community in these locations provide MWLED SMEs some sort of social or cultural capital that facilitates their participation in entrepreneurial activities at higher proportions in these regions. However, this is beyond the scope of our analysis, and would require future studies to analyse the role of social or cultural capital in facilitating women-led SMEs' participation in business innovation, as well as their access to resources and markets within given regions.

Looking at the type of innovation activities SMEs engage in, both WLED and MWLED SMEs are more likely to undertake process innovation and investments in R&D than product innovation. Additionally, despite the wide variation amongst regions, higher proportions of MWLED SMEs are likely to participate in either product or process innovations than WLED SMEs (and SMEs in general). This suggests that firm size (majority being micro firms) might be a constraining factor on the type of innovation activities women-led firms engage in, as micro firms are mainly dependent on the founder's skills, capabilities and ambitions (Gherhes et al., 2016). Process innovations may therefore be easier for such firms to implement than product innovations.

Interestingly, and contrary to prior studies (Filculescu, 2016), our results also suggest that WLED SMEs (with the exception of MWLED SMEs) are equally as likely to invest in R&D as other SMEs in general. Previous studies have indicated that while smaller sized firms are less likely to invest in R&D, those that do, actually invest a larger proportion of their turnover than larger firms (Baumann and Kritikos, 2016; Office for National Statistics, 2018). However, while R&D investments would be expected to result in higher product innovations, this is not the case in our sample. This might be due to the lagged effect of R&D spending on increased product and process innovations (Baumann and Kritikos, 2016; Mañez et al., 2013), and would require longitudinal studies to capture this impact on WLED SMEs' innovation activities.

Our examination of the spatial variation in WLED and MWLED SMEs' level of participation in business innovation revealed that while there are no substantial differences amongst regions, there are wide variations in terms of founder ethnicity, as well as the type and level of innovation activity. The notion that the socio-economic characteristics of a place influences business activities within that place and surrounding areas is not new, and has been extensively investigated within economic geography literature (Dorling, 2010; Hacking et al., 2011). Overall, East England, London and South East regions have higher proportions of WLED SMEs taking part in process innovations and R&D investments. Research indicates that while all regions have comparative strengths in terms of innovation, London and South East regions tend to dominate in terms of key metrics such as R&D expenditure, venture capital, and human capacity in STEM and so on (BIS, 2015). Neighbouring regions such as the East of England and East Midlands also score relatively well on many of these indicators (BIS, 2015). This would suggest possible cluster or spill-over effects that might have a positive impact on women-led SMEs' innovation activities in these regions, but would require further research into how institutional structures might facilitate or hinder such impact. Our findings emphasize the need to pay greater attention to the heterogeneity of women-led businesses, their social positioning within entrepreneurial ecosystems, as well as the regional variations in the nature and intensity of barriers to innovation (Brush et al., 2019).

Policy initiatives also have a crucial role to play in facilitating the engagement of underrepresented groups in business innovation. Our study raises important questions for future policies and programmes, not least the need to pay greater attention to the gendered structures that constrain women's entrepreneurial activities. The regional variation of innovation activities among women-led SMEs highlights the need to tailor policies and support initiatives, and specifically to address the multi-dimensionality of minority groups as well as the intersectionality of social categories. While policy and programmes in the UK have developed a focus on 'Women in Innovation' there remains a need to better understand and intervene in areas where intersectional factors, such as race, ethnicity, class or place, create particular barriers. Such an approach is likely to have positive influences for other groups of entrepreneurs that are classified as disadvantaged due to their social identity. We therefore encourage a blended approach to policy initiatives that includes both targeted support aimed at specific underrepresented groups, and mainstream initiatives that focus on transforming existing hierarchical structures (Vorley et al., 2020).

Despite its contributions to current literature, our study has a number of limitations. First, the sample is based on cross-sectional data over the period 2015 to 2018, and therefore we are not able to identify causal relationships between women-led businesses and participation in innovation. Second, as the survey is voluntary, it does not include a comprehensive list of firms not registered for VAT. Third, self-reporting surveys are mainly subjective and depend on respondents' perception of what is an innovative process or product. Lastly, the findings are based on SMEs in the UK and may not be generalizable to other geographical contexts.

6.   CONCLUSION

Our study builds on existing gender diversity and innovation research[1] by adopting an intersectional approach to understanding how gender, ethnicity and place intersect to influence women-led SMEs' participation in innovation activities. Our analyses which are based on the Longitudinal Small Business Survey (LSBS) data of 29,267 SMEs over the period 2015 to 2018, show that despite their under-representation, women-led SMEs are equally as likely to engage in process innovation, product innovation, and investment in R&D as other SMEs in the UK. We also demonstrate that there is considerable heterogeneity in the level and type of innovation activities undertaken by women-led SMEs. Future studies can build on our research by analysing how intersectional social categories such as ethnicity, race, class, ability status, education and so on, act as enablers or barriers to female founders' participation in business innovation. There is also scope to focus more on women-led technology firms, and to pursue longitudinal studies focused on evaluating the impact of both targeted and mainstream initiatives.

REFERENCES

Agius Vallejo, J. and Canizales, S.L. (2016), "Latino/a professionals as entrepreneurs: how race, class, and gender shape entrepreneurial incorporation", *Ethnic and Racial Studies*, Taylor & Francis, Vol. 39 No. 9, pp. 1637–1656.

Alsos, G.A., Ljunggren, E. and Hytti, U. (2013), "Gender and innovation: State of the art and a research agenda", *International Journal of Gender and Entrepreneurship*, Emerald, Vol. 5 No. 3, pp. 236–256.

Baughn, C.C., Chua, B.-L. and Neupert, K.E. (2006), "The normative context for women's participation in entrepreneruship: A multicountry study", *Entrepreneurship: Theory and Practice*, Vol. 30 No. 5, pp. 687–708.

Baumann, J. and Kritikos, A.S. (2016), "The link between R&D, innovation and productivity: Are micro firms different?", *Research Policy*, Elsevier, Vol. 45 No. 6, pp. 1263–1274.

Blake, M.K. and Hanson, S. (2005), "Rethinking innovation: Context and gender", *Environment and Planning A: Economy and Space*, Sage Publications, Vol. 37 No. 4, pp. 681–701.

Botella, C., Rueda, S., López-Iñesta, E. and Marzal, P. (2019), "Gender diversity in STEM disciplines: A multiple factor problem", *Entropy: An International and Interdisciplinary Journal of Entropy and Information Studies*, Basel, Switzerland, Vol. 21 No. 1 pp. 30–47.

British Business Bank, Diversity VC and BVCA. (2019), *UK VC & Female Founders*. https://www.british-business-bank.co.uk/wp-content/uploads/2019/02/British-Business-Bank-UK-Venture-Capital-and-Female-Founders-Report.pdf.

Brush, C., Edelman, L.F., Manolova, T. and Welter, F. (2019), "A gendered look at entrepreneurship ecosystems", *Small Business Economics*, Vol. 53 No. 2, pp. 393–408.

Carter, S., Mwaura, S., Ram, M., Trehan, K. and Jones, T. (2015), "Barriers to ethnic minority and women's enterprise: Existing evidence, policy tensions and unsettled questions", *International Small Business Journal*, Vol. 33 No. 1, pp. 49–69.

Codiroli Mcmaster, N. (2017), "Who studies STEM subjects at A level and degree in England? An investigation into the intersections between students' family background, gender and ethnicity in determining choice", *British Educational Research Journal*, Wiley Online Library, Vol. 43 No. 3, pp. 528–553.

Codiroli Mcmaster, N. and Cook, R. (2019), "The contribution of intersectionality to quantitative research into educational inequalities", *Review of Education*, John Wiley & Sons, Vol. 7 No. 2, pp. 271–292.

Dai, Y., Byun, G. and Ding, F. (2019), "The direct and indirect impact of gender diversity in new venture teams on innovation performance", *Entrepreneurship: Theory and Practice*, Vol. 43 No. 3, pp. 505–528.

Department for Business Innovation and Skills (BIS). (2015), *Mapping Local Comparative Advantages in Innovation: Framework and Indicators.* Available at: https://www.gov.uk/government/publications/local-enterprise-partnerships-evidence-on-local-innovation-strengths

DeVita, L., Mari, M. and Poggesi, S. (2014), "Women entrepreneurs in and from developing countries: Evidences from the literature", *European Management Journal*, Vol. 32 No. 3, pp. 451–460.

Díaz-García, C., González-Moreno, A. and Sáez-Martínez, F.J. (2013), "Gender diversity within R & D teams: Its impact on radicalness of innovation", *Innovation: Management, Policy and Practice*, Vol. 15 No. 2, pp. 149–160.

Diversity VC and OneTech. (2019), *Venturing into Diversity and Inclusion 2019: Addressing the Diversity Deficit in VC*. https://www.diversity.vc/wp-content/uploads/2019/09/ DI_Report_2019_Web_Version.pdf.

Dorling, D. (2010), "Persistent north–south divides", in N.M. Coe and A. Jones (Eds) *The Economic Geography of the UK*, London: Sage, pp. 12–28.

Elam, A.B., Brush, C.G., Greene, P.G., Baumer, B., Dean, M. and Heavlow, R. (2019), *Global Entrepreneurship Monitor 2018/2019 Women's Entrepreneurship Report*. Global Entrepreneurship Research Association, London.

Filculescu, A. (2016), "The heterogeneous landscape of innovation in female led-businesses – cross-country comparisons", *Management & Marketing*, Vol.11 No.4, pp. 610–662.

Foss, L., Henry, C., Ahl, H. and Mikalsen, G.H. (2019), "Women's entrepreneurship policy research: A 30-year review of the evidence", *Small Business Economics*, Vol. 53 No. 2, pp. 409–429.

Gherhes, C., Williams, N., Vorley, T. and Vasconcelos, A.C. (2016), "Distinguishing micro-businesses from SMEs: A systematic review of growth constraints", *Journal of Small Business and Enterprise Development*, Emerald, Vol. 23 No. 4, pp. 939–963.

Griffiths, M., Moore, K. and Richardson, H. (2007), "Celebrating heterogeneity?: A survey of female ICT professionals in England", *Information, Communication & Society*, Routledge, Vol. 10 No. 3, pp. 338–357.

Hacking, J.M., Muller, S. and Buchan, I.E. (2011), "Trends in mortality from 1965 to 2008 across the English north–south divide: Comparative observational study", *British Medical Journal*, British Medical Journal Publishing Group, Vol. 342, p. d508.

Hardey, M. (2019), "Women's leadership and gendered experiences in tech cities", *Gender in Management*, Emerald, Vol. 34 No. 3, pp. 188–199.

Herman, C. (2015), "Returning to STEM: Gendered factors affecting employability for mature women students", *Journal of Education and Work*, Routledge, Vol. 28 No. 6, pp. 571–591.

Hewlett, S.A., Marshall, M. and Sherbin, L. (2013), "How diversity can drive innovation", *Harvard Business Review*, Vol. 91 No. 12, p. 30.

Kang, J., Hense, J., Scheersoi, A. and Keinonen, T. (2019), "Gender study on the relationships between science interest and future career perspectives", *International Journal of Science Education*, Vol. 41 No. 1, pp. 80–101,

Kelley, D.J., Baumer, B.S., Brush, C., Greene, P.G., Mahdavi, M., Majbouri, M., Cole, M. et al. (2017), *Global Entrepreneurship Monitor 2016/2017 Women's Entrepreneurship Report*, Vol. 9. Global Entrepreneurship Research Association, London.

Kvidal, T. and Ljunggren, E. (2014), "Introducing gender in a policy programme: A multilevel analysis of an innovation policy programme", *Environment and Planning C: Government and Policy*, Sage Publications, Vol. 32 No. 1, pp. 39–53.

Lindberg, M., Forsberg, L. and Karlberg, H. (2015), "Gendered social innovation – a theoretical lens for analysing structural transformation in organisations and society", *International Journal of Social Entrepreneurship and Innovation*, Inderscience Publishers, Vol. 3 No. 6, pp. 472–483.

Mañez, J.A., Rochina-Barrachina, M.E., Sanchis, A. and Sanchis, J.A. (2013), "Do process innovations boost SMEs productivity growth?", *Empirical Economics*, Springer Science & Business Media, Heidelberg, Vol. 44 No. 3, pp. 1373–1405.

Marlow, S. and McAdam, M. (2015), "Incubation or induction? Gendered identity work in the context of technology business incubation", *Entrepreneurship: Theory and Practice*, Vol. 39 No. 4, pp. 791–816.

OECD. (2017), *Entrepreneurship at a Glance 2017*, OECD, https://doi.org/10.1787/entrepreneur_aag-2017-en.

OECD. (2020), *International Compendium of Entrepreneurship Policies*, https://doi.org/10.1787/338f1873-en.

Office for National Statistics. (2018), *Trends in Self-Employment in the UK: Analysing the Characteristics, Income and Wealth of the Self-Employed*.

Owalla, B., Vorley, T., Coogan, T., Lawton Smith, H. and Wing, K. (2021), "Absent or overlooked: Promoting diversity among entrepreneurs with public support needs", *International Journal of Entrepreneurial Venturing*, Inderscience, Vol. 13 No. 3, p. 1.

Pettersson, K. and Lindberg, M. (2013), "Paradoxical spaces of feminist resistance: Mapping the margin to the masculinist innovation discourse", *International Journal of Gender and Entrepreneurship*, Emerald, Vol. 5 No. 3, pp. 323–341.

Poggesi, S., Mari, M. and De Vita, L. (2016), "What's new in female entrepreneurship research? Answers from the literature", *International Entrepreneurship and Management Journal*, Vol. 12 No. 3, pp. 735–764.

Rhodes, C. (2019), *Business Statistics: Briefing Paper Number 06152*.

Romero, M. and Valdez, Z. (2016), "Introduction to the special issue: Intersectionality and entrepreneurship", *Ethnic and Racial Studies*, Taylor & Francis, Vol. 39 No. 9, pp. 1553–1565.

Sitaridis, I. and Kitsios, F. (2019), "Entrepreneurship as a career option for information technology students: Critical barriers and the role of motivation", *Journal of the Knowledge Economy*, Springer, Vol. 10 No. 3, pp. 1133–1167.

Stout, J.G., Grunberg, V.A. and Ito, T.A. (2016), "Gender roles and stereotypes about science careers help explain women and men's science pursuits", *Sex Roles*, Vol. 75 No. 9–10, pp. 490–499.

Valdez, Z. (2016), "Intersectionality, the household economy, and ethnic entrepreneurship", *Ethnic and Racial Studies*, Taylor & Francis, Vol. 39 No. 9, pp. 1618–1636.

van de Werfhorst, H.G. (2017), "Gender segregation across fields of study in post-secondary education: Trends and social differentials", *European Sociological Review*, Vol. 33 No. 3, pp. 449–464.

Vitores, A. and Gil-Juárez, A. (2016), "The trouble with 'women in computing': a critical examination of the deployment of research on the gender gap in computer science", *Journal of Gender Studies*, Vol. 25 No. 6, pp. 666–680.

Vorley, T., Lawton Smith, H., Coogan, T., Owalla, B. and Wing, K. (2020), *Supporting Diversity and Inclusion in Innovation*. Policy Brief, Innovate UK, Supporting Diversity and Inclusion in Innovation report (www.gov.uk).

Walters, J. and McNeely, C.L. (2010), "Recasting Title IX: Addressing gender equity in the science, technology, engineering, and mathematics professoriate", *The Review of Policy Research*, Vol. 27 No. 3, pp. 317–332.

Wingfield, A.H. and Taylor, T. (2016), "Race, gender, and class in entrepreneurship: Intersectional counterframes and black business owners", *Ethnic and Racial Studies*, Taylor & Francis, Vol. 39 No. 9, pp. 1676–1696.

PART II

Innovation policies, initiatives and ecosystems

9. Beyond Siri and Alexa: gender and AI policy

Vidhula Venugopal and Vishal Rituraj

1.   INTRODUCTION

Innovation has emerged as one of the major ways to accelerate economic growth thereby creating developed and prosperous nations (Lundvall, 1992). Innovation is the introduction of novel solutions in response to problems, challenges, or opportunities which arise in the socio-economic environment (Edler & Fagerberg, 2017). On a broader level, innovation policies are policies which are aimed at providing new solutions, which can be practically implemented, to specific challenges that are relevant to the political agenda (Edler & Fagerberg, 2017). The point to note here is that since the definition itself covers the practical implementation of the suggested solution, policy makers need to take all the phases of the innovation process into account, that is, from invention to its practical usage.

Artificial Intelligence (AI) is one of the biggest tools in innovation in the current age. We define AI as "a collection of interrelated technologies used to solve problems autonomously and perform tasks to achieve defined objectives without explicit guidance from a human being" (Dawson et al., 2019, p. 14). Scientific literature classifies artificial intelligence into two subtypes – narrow and general. Narrow AI, which is what we talk about when we discuss AI in the present world, performs a specific function mainly focusing on a single subset of cognitive abilities. General AI, on the other hand, is comparable to human intelligence across a range of fields. To put it succinctly, narrow AI is where we are, and general AI is where we are going.

When we talk about AI in the current scenario, it predominantly relates to automated decision-making systems and algorithms that predict human behaviour. Since such systems function on data provided by humans, there is a significant chance that these decisions will reflect the bias of the programmer or the data from existing structures (Leavy, 2018). This has particular implications for women in general, and aspiring and current women entrepreneurs in particular. For instance, an automated tool to evaluate the suitability of financial assistance for a business idea could potentially be biased against women if it uses the current data which shows that men are disproportionately favoured (Bosma & Kelley, 2018; Coleman et al., 2018). Similarly, other resources such as professional experience can also be impeded if automated resumé screeners are employed, as was the case at Amazon who then had to discontinue the usage of the system as it was biased against women. These issues are over and above the problem of lack of women in programming given the smaller percentage of women in STEM fields (Kuschel et al., 2020). The impact of AI on gender social equality and gender discrimination would be highly dependent on the structures formed as a result of policy and legislation (Dillon & Collett, 2019).

As Hearn and McKie (2008) argue, "the notion of policy can easily appear at first as gender-neutral. Yet not only is much policy and policy development constructed by and through assumptions about gender, but also much policy development can be understood as policy on and about gender and gender relations" (p. 75). The gender neutrality of innovation research has extended to innovation policy as well which "neither challenges nor transforms the gender system" (Andersson et al., 2012). "Male gender bias is common in scientific literature, and when biased knowledge is used as source of innovation ideas, the outcomes can be worse for women" (Lee & Pollitzer, 2016, p. 2). Given this bias, we argue that the policy should catch up to and stay ahead of the technology in adopting regulations that are gendered and can help minimise, if not eliminate, the bias and discrimination based on gender. An important aspect to note here is that "the mere provision of policy does not contribute to gender equality, women's well-being or financial independence, but rather that '… outcomes depend on the premises behind the policies'" (Coleman et al., 2018, p. 2; Pettersson et al., 2017, p. 50). Pettersson et al. (2017), taking the example of entrepreneurship, notes that scholars have argued that the policies do not explicitly address gender, that is, the policies are gender blind. Further, the policies lack the mandate to address the underlying mechanisms that impede gender equality (Ahl & Nelson, 2015, Pettersson et al., 2017). Studies have been conducted to look at gendering of broader innovation policy (Kvidal & Ljunggren, 2014).

The aim of this chapter is to uncover the premises on which the "National Artificial Intelligence Policy" of 19 major countries[1] around the world are based on which, in turn, will help us in answering the following questions. *What is considered to be the output of AI-enabled technologies? Do these policies explicitly address gender? If so, what contexts within AI do they appear in?* In particular, we explore how these broad strokes of policies have specific effects on entrepreneurial behaviour among women in this future landscape. In the following sections of the chapter, we briefly discuss the methodology followed by the results and discussion of three best practices in AI policy formulation.

2.   METHODOLOGY

We collected the available policy documents specifically related to AI and high tech with a focus on AI for 19 countries. The countries were selected based on the availability of policy documents in public domain as many countries do not have an explicit AI policy as yet. All these 19 policy documents can be accessed via the respective countries' official government website. Out of the 19 policy documents only two (Germany and Italy) were not available in English. "Google Translate" tool was used to translate them prior to analysis. The authors recognise the limitations of a tool such as Google Translate. However, for the purpose of understanding the mandates of each policy and for focus on gender, the translations were considered appropriate. The second author analysed the reports to identify the AI policy mandates with most reports stating their mandates explicitly. These mandates were then thematically categorised. The authors analysed the reports independently to identify the focus on gender in these reports. We defined focus on gender as mention of gender, gender bias, and inclusion of gender in shaping strategies for AI. This focus ranged from mere mention of gender or gender bias to a more in-depth look at effects of these biases and ways to mitigate them. The authors followed an iterative process, aggregating the mandates and focus on gender into themes after independent analysis followed by discussions between the two authors. In our analyses, we first focused on the policies' focus on gender more broadly and subsequently explored the specific impact of these policies on entrepreneurship.

Our first step was to distil the mandates from the respective country's official policy document as the mandates set the tone for the entire formulation process (see Appendix for detailed information about the mandates). We focused on the priorities listed as goals of the document. Please see the Appendix for detailed information about the mandates.

3.   RESULTS

The analysis revealed seven broad goals and intent for the policies viz. leadership, military, strategic, economic, education and research, ethics, and inclusion (See Table 9.1 for region-wise list).

Collectively, it was evident that there is a significant emphasis on economic and strategic goals through these policies with a focus on ensuring a trained workforce for the future and technology adoption in all facets of economic and strategic importance. For instance, the Chinese policy underscores the national

Table 9.1   Policy mandates of 19 countries

Country	Policy Document	AI Policy Mandate	Inclusion	Leadership	Military	Strategic	Economic	Ethics	Education & Research
Brazil	Brazil Digital Transformation Strategy	BR1				•			•
		BR2				•			
		BR3				•	•		•
		BR4				•	•		
USA	1. 2016–2019 Progress Report: Advancing Artificial Intelligence R&D	US1		•					
		US2				•			
	2. The National Artificial Intelligence Research and Development Strategic Plan: 2019 Update	US3					•		
		US4			•				
Canada	Annual Report of the CIFAR Pan-Canadian AI Strategy	CA1							
		CA2		•					•
		CA3							•
Denmark	National Strategy for Artificial Intelligence	DK1	•						
		DK2	•					•	
		DK3				•	•	•	
		DK4	•			•			

Country	Policy Document	AI Policy Mandate	Inclusion	Leadership	Military	Strategic	Economic	Ethics	Education & Research
Finland	Finland's Age of Artificial Intelligence	FI1				•	•		
		FI2				•			
		FI3				•	•		
		FI4	•			•			•
France	For a meaningful Artificial Intelligence	FR1							
		FR2	•						
		FR3	•						
		FR4						•	
Germany	Strategie Künstliche Intelligenz der Bundesregierung	DE1		•					
		DE2	•			•		•	
		DE3	•					•	
Italy	Strategia Nazionale per l'Intelligenza Artificiale	IT1					•		•
		IT2					•	•	•
		IT3	•			•	•		
		IT4	•						
		IT5	•					•	
Netherlands	Strategic Action Plan for Artificial Intelligence	NL1	•				•		
		NL2				•	•		
		NL3						•	
Norway	National Strategy for Artificial Intelligence	NO1	•				•		
		NO2	•			•	•		
		NO3						•	

Gender, diversity and innovation

Country	Policy Document	AI Policy Mandate	Inclusion	Leadership	Military	Strategic	Economic	Ethics	Education & Research
Spain	Spanish RDI Strategy in Artificial Intelligence	ES1				•			•
		ES2				•			•
		ES3					•		
		ES4				•	•		•
		ES5				•	•		
		ES6						•	•
Sweden	National approach to artificial intelligence	SE1							•
		SE2						•	•
		SE3					•	•	
		SE4	•						
UK	1. AI in the UK: ready, willing and able?	UK1						•	
	2. Government response to House of Lords Artificial Intelligence Select Committee's Report on AI in the UK: Ready, Willing and Able?	UK2				•	•		
		UK3				•		•	

Country	Policy Document	AI Policy Mandate	Inclusion	Leadership	Military	Strategic	Economic	Ethics	Education & Research
Australia	1. Artificial Intelligence: Solving problems, growing the economy and improving our quality of life	AU1						•	
	2. Artificial Intelligence: Australia's Ethics Framework	AU2	•						
	3. Science & Technology Australia – Digital Economy Strategy	AU3				•	•		
China	1. Next Generation Artificial Intelligence Development Plan Issued by State Council	CN1				•	•		
		CN2				•	•		
	2. China AI Development Report 2018	CN3		•					
		CN4			•				
India	National Strategy for Artificial Intelligence	IN1	•						
		IN2				•	•		
Israel	2018–19 Innovation in Israel overview	IL1				•	•		
		IL2					•		•
		IL3					•		•
		IL4				•	•		•

Gender, diversity and innovation

Country	Policy Document	AI Policy Mandate	Inclusion	Leadership	Military	Strategic	Economic	Ethics	Education & Research
Japan	Artificial Intelligence Technology Strategy	JP1	•			•			
		JP2		•		•	•		
		JP3							•
		JP4	•						
Singapore	National Artificial Intelligence Strategy	SG1							
		SG2					•		
		SG3				•	•		
		SG4		•		•	•		
		SG5				•			

strategy's emphasis on closely integrating AI in all sectors while the Dutch policy emphasises capitalising societal and economic opportunities through the use and development of AI. There is significant effort also being made in educating school children as well as conducting large scale research in these specialised areas. For example, four out of the six priorities in Spain's strategy document involves education and research goals. Inclusion and ethics are distinctly conspicuous in policies of certain countries primarily in Australia, Canada, India, and among countries in Europe. Interestingly, the world's two superpowers emphasise leadership in technology and state their explicit military goals. The US policy notes its focus on "protecting American AI technology base from *attempted acquisition* by strategic competitors and adversarial nations" (emphasis added) while the Chinese policy clearly states the country's intention to become the leading AI power by 2030 and civil–military fusion lying at the heart of the policy. What is important to note here is that inclusion and ethics are absent among the top priorities of these two countries.

It is also significant to note here that inclusion and ethics as alluded to by these policy mandates are broad and do not specifically reflect gender as a key factor. On one hand, countries such as France explicate the need for inclusive AI in terms of use cases and open data policy. On the other hand, countries such as India and Australia approach the AI opportunity primarily to foster social and inclusive growth. With the former, the focus is on building inclusion into the technology and enablers of the technology whereas in the latter, the focus is primarily on inclusion in the outcomes of the technology. UK specifically describes its potential competitive advantage in considering the ethics of AI. Germany and Australia focus on integrating AI more broadly in the ethical, legal, cultural, and institutional contexts that exist presently with Australia particularly noting that ethics for AI should be built on the ethical principles that already exist and should not be a separate doctrine.

3.1   Gender and Policy

Next, we analysed the document to look for specific discussions about gender in the context of AI. We first looked at the focus on gender in numbers (see Table 9.2). However, numbers do not always tell the whole story. There were mentions unrelated to any policy analysis or prescription. Therefore, we analysed the policies further to recognise the themes of the contexts in which these words appear and are associated with policy making. We identified four broader themes around which gender was acknowledged as a factor (see Table 9.2 for a summary).

Many countries acknowledged gender disparity in AI in broad terms. For example, Denmark's policy calls attention to the need to "promote designs that avoid classification discriminating on ethnicity, sexuality, and gender, for

Table 9.2 *Policy and gender*

Country	Gender-based policy instruments					Word Count
	Acknowledgement of gender disparity in AI	Tackling of gender-biased algorithm	Promoting women in STEM workforce/education	Gender equality as a key focus area	"Gender specific" terms'ŏ word count in policy documents	
Brazil*			•			3
Canada		•				4
USA	•	•	•			3
Denmark	•	•				2
Finland						0
France	•	•	•	•		160
Germany						1
Italy						0
Netherlands**		•				9
Norway		•				4
Spain	•	•	•			6
Sweden						0
UK	•	•	•			22
Australia	•	•	•			22
China						15
India		•				3
Israel***	•		•			4
Japan						0
Singapore						0

Notes: * Brazil's official policy document is titled "Brazilian Digital Transformation Strategy" but specifically covers Artificial Intelligence in detail. ** Report to be published by the Netherlands in collaboration with European Commission which will include an opinion on AI and gender. *** Israel's high-tech innovation report does not specifically mention AI. It talks about a generic all-encompassing term "High-Tech".
ŏ The terms were – "Woman", "Women", "Gender", "Female", "Females", "Girl", "Girls".

example". This is further testament to how gender is broadly acknowledged for the most part as a footnote despite women accounting for around half the population in a bid to make policy gender neutral. Gender is also considered as a standalone factor without acknowledging the impact of the intersection of, in this instance, ethnicity, sexuality, and gender. This is problematic not just for women but also for men, even though women are more disproportionately affected by it.

France is the only country to specifically look at gender equality as a key focus area. Its policy acknowledges that despite increasing numbers of women in the scientific and technical sectors, women's involvement in digital technologies remains "something of an exception, with gender balance still very far off". Towards correcting this, France has adopted a holistic nation-wide approach to "promote diversity in technology via a national database aimed at documenting gender inequality in the workplace and the provision of funds devoted to supporting diversity in AI". This is in addition to the focus on encouraging and incentivising more female students in digital subject areas in universities, business schools, and preparatory classes.

Many other countries have acknowledged specific aspects of gender and technology without taking the holistic approach taken by the French. There is a wide acknowledgement of the gender disparity in AI due to fewer women opting for STEM fields. They address a significant issue of having fewer female voices contributing to writing the codes and algorithms that shape the technology. This highlights the lower numbers in educational institutions as well as in the workforce. Countries such as Israel focus on the development of skilled human capital for high-tech and have designed programmes that incentivise "integration of women and underrepresented populations in high-tech".

More widely, the policies discuss gender in the context of biases resulting from the use of existing data for predictions. Out of the six priorities identified in the Spanish policy, the sixth one focuses on analysing the ethics of AI from the perspective of Research, Development, and Innovation (RDI). Within this, the policy discusses the development of AI technologies without "negative bias and gender bias or other forms of discrimination". Other countries such as Denmark subsume algorithmic bias inequality and justice which is one of its six guiding principles for building an AI framework. The wording of the policy, like many of the other countries', leaves much to be desired in ways of tackling gender inequality since the current articulation makes gender seem like one of the many smaller pockets of the population that one must tackle. The Danish policy says that "there will be active work to prevent unwanted bias and promote designs that avoid classification discriminating on ethnicity, sexuality and gender, for example". This push of gender to the background is also clear in policies of many countries in which gender bias is mentioned perfunctorily and finds merely a handful of mentions, if at all, in the whole document. For example, Brazil's policy lists out UN Sustainable Development Goals that can directly or indirectly be influenced by this digital transformation and gender equality (SDG 5) fails to find a place on the list.

Apart from looking through the lens of individual countries, we analysed the countries based on the following regions: the Americas (Brazil, Canada, USA), Europe (Denmark, Finland, France, Germany, Italy, Netherlands, Norway, Spain, Sweden, UK), and the Asia-Pacific (APAC; Australia, China,

India, Israel, Japan, Singapore). There are differences in how countries within a region engage with gender in their respective AI policies as well. For example, in the APAC region, the east Asian countries (China, Japan, Singapore) have minimal focus on gender in their reports. India focuses on tackling gender-biased algorithm and hence shows a focus closer to the outcomes. Israel recognises the gender disparity and focuses on making their workforce more gender-inclusive by promoting women in STEM education and workforce.

In Europe, apart from France, UK and Spain show an increased focus on gender in their policy. However, gender is conspicuously absent in the reports of Finland, Germany, Italy, and Sweden. In the case of Sweden which ranks 3rd in Gender Inequality Index (UNDP, 2019), 4th in Global Gender Gap Index (World Economic Forum, 2019), and 21st in Women's Workforce Equality Index (Council on Foreign Relations, 2018), it can be argued that their policies thus far have created a workplace and education system that could be seen as relatively more gender equal. We cannot, however, generalise with the data available as countries such as France also rank high in these indices (8th, 15th, and 16th respectively) and yet, explicitly address gender related concerns in their AI policies.

3.2   Gender, Entrepreneurship, and Policy

Few countries allude to digital entrepreneurship and AI entrepreneurship as a reality and necessity to help them reach the goals identified in Table 1. However, here again, there is limited focus on gender. This is a double whammy for women entrepreneurs as not only do they not find any favour within discussions of entrepreneurship but also face a disadvantage in most of the themes identified in these policies as listed in tables 1 and 2. These themes impact women entrepreneurship either directly or indirectly. There is significant focus among most of the countries to ensure that they lead in AI either economically, strategically, or militarily. Enablers include digital infrastructure, data, AI education, training, and research, ecosystem to promote development and commercialisation of AI. Gender has to be an important conversation in each of these themes to ensure that women are encouraged and empowered to be in this new space as entrepreneurs.

Overall, with the exception of very few countries, most of the policies do not explicitly engage with gender to an extensive degree.

4.   DISCUSSION

Our analysis finds that the favoured outputs of the AI policies are economic and strategic. Such outputs, for instance, an economic agenda, can subordinate women by giving precedence to economic growth while silencing feminist approaches to growth (Coleman et al., 2018, p. 4). We argue that such 'gender-neutral' mandates for policies in high technology spaces invariably continue and at times exacerbate gender parity across different economic and social spaces of progress. Looking through a gender lens is, therefore, imperative. We believe policy makers should heed to Brandwein's call – "all policy issues are of concern to women" (1995, p. 252).

Gender equality efforts grounded on the basis of gender research have been found to be more effective and sustainable as compared to those that disregard gender research (Fürst, 2009), but policy makers and practitioners look for tools which are convenient and easy to use rather than those grounded on gender research when integrating gender in policy implementation (Warren, 2007). In a detailed study of women's entrepreneurship policy, Foss et al. (2019) have arrived at the conclusion that there has been no marked change in the implications of women's entrepreneurship policy research over the last 30 years. The study finds that most policy interventions are focused on fixing the skill gaps between men and women (Foss et al., 2019). Furthermore, the study mentions that almost all the policy recommendations are framed with the objective of economic growth. Women's well-being and equality have not been the ultimate aims.

In the case of AI, a policy to encourage more start-ups in the space may seem gender neutral. However, the policy is built on the premise that men and women have equal opportunities to embark on an entrepreneurial journey in the field. Given the fewer number of women in STEM fields, the smaller percentage of women entrepreneurs, and the systemic obstacles such as access to funding and so on, faced by these women entrepreneurs, the policy is unequal in the opportunities it affords men and women.

Developing an AI ecosystem akin to the current entrepreneurial ecosystem is ignoring the implicit biases that exist in the present system. There will be pipeline issues with fewer women intending to be entrepreneurs for reasons such as gender stereotyping and varying socialisation experiences and expectations that drive women away from STEM subjects. Other issues such as lack of access to funds, mentorship, and labour market discrimination will also persist without specific interventions within the policies to circumvent these. In an AI ecosystem built on present data, it is not just that these differences persist, but they are exacerbated by the use of algorithms running on present biased data as well as being designed without the inclusion of women to enable any changes in the said design. It is indeed a vicious cycle where, without the involvement of women, the design will not change and without a proactive, conscious design change of the system, more women cannot participate.

Further, when it comes to AI, biases stemming from the use of existing data which are biased have significant consequences to women. Take the health sector as an example. Studies usually exclude pregnant women and women on birth control from their samples. This data then results in medical advice that is unsuitable and potentially dangerous for a vast number of women. These biased data also extend to scenarios such as safety feature designs like the seat belts in cars in which data is obtained using a crash test dummy modelled on a male.

With the exception of the French policy which explicitly focuses on developing inclusive and diverse AI (Villani, 2018), all policies more or less look at gender as a peripheral issue in varying degrees. There is an acknowledgement of potential bias and the need to encourage women to enter STEM fields. However, these allusions to gender are also very sparse. We take the case of women entrepreneurship specifically to illustrate how ignoring gender while formulating AI policy and addressing its various elements has detrimental effects on women in particular and society at large.

We highlight three approaches to suggest a starting point for reimagining and reformulating AI policy. We arrive at these by looking at the policies of countries which have higher degrees of focus on gender in their mandates and overall policies. These are by no means exhaustive. The broader principles of social good and sustainability should definitely be embedded in the policy like many countries have done. Our argument is that wilful ignorance of around half of the world's population in the formulation of policies is a slippery slope that leads to ignorance of all differences from the male normative idea of society.

Reframing AI ethics with an equality and equity focus: The Australian policy clearly points to the hundreds of years of work done by philosophers, ethicists, political leaders, and academics to debate ethical concepts and frame human rights accordingly. As such, it argues for using "existing ethics in context" and not reinventing ethics. Every policy should recognise the embeddedness of all actors in society. In this regard, the Australian policy goes on to explicate the risk of AI confusing fairness with equality and equity:

> Algorithms can't necessarily treat every person exactly the same either; they should operate according to similar principles in similar situations. But while like goes with like, justice sometimes demands that different situations be treated differently. When developers need to codify fairness into AI algorithms, there are various challenges in managing often inevitable trade-offs and sometimes there's no "right" choice because what is considered optimal may be disputed.

It is important to also note that the concept of fairness, for instance, is not restricted to gender alone but extends to other categories which intersect with genders such as race, ethnicity, and sexuality.

Reframing AI technology as a tool for social good instead of a goal: Many countries, most notably the US and China, approach AI with the goal of becoming "leaders" in the technology. It would be good for countries to pause and recognise that AI is just a tool and the end goal of increased development in technology should be societal good and not cutting-edge technology for technology's sake. The French policy specifically delineates two key areas of consideration viz., inclusive and diverse AI and AI for a more ecological economy. Having these two among the underlying philosophy of AI development ensures that people and planet are both served by the advancement in technology.

Reframing ethics to include gender ethics: Most policies focus on ethics as a separate consideration for AI. As discussed earlier with the Australian example, there is a need to reframe ethics and it is significant to include gender in this new reframing. The Spanish policy is a step in this direction. Within its sixth priority of analysing the ethics of AI from the perspective of RDI (Research, Development, and Innovation), the policy includes the removal of gender bias and other forms of discrimination. While most policies discuss privacy issues, and "Black Box" phenomenon (having little or no understanding of what happens between data input and result output), gender is subsumed under one among many potential biases. There is substantially more discussion on ethics of self-driving cars, for instance, than the exacerbation of systemic biases based on gender. Further, bringing gender to the front in ethics conversations ensures that any new technology's legitimisation must pass the gender test well before the conversations are had post application as is currently done.

Additionally, while reframing their policies, it is important for countries to take a relook at the language used. The French policy is a standout example on the language used in the formulation which clearly includes everyone in the first instance instead of a post-hoc requirement of including "non-mainstream" groups. Viewing gender as one of the many groups looking to be included in the ambit is wilfully ignoring around half of the world's population. This is highlighted by language as used by the Danish policy as illustrated previously.

5.   CONCLUSION

Gender neutrality in policy has been criticised and the need for looking at policy through a gendered lens cannot be underscored enough (McPhail, 2003). This chapter looks at the policies in the emerging area of AI which has significant implications for women. Based on our analysis, we recommend that countries should engage with gender while framing policies for the use of AI. Towards this we recommend three approaches – reframing AI ethics with an equality and equity focus, reframing AI technology as a tool for social good instead of a goal; and reframing ethics to include gender ethics. These are a few of the initial recommendations for countries while reframing their AI policy. It is, however, important to note that this is just the start. Each individual has intersecting identities of gender, race, ethnicity, economic capacity, sexuality, and so on. The next step would be to ensure that the policies are truly embedded in and reflective of the society it aims to serve. A step in this right direction would be to first acknowledge and include women who are rightly described as holding up half the sky, according to a Chinese proverb.

NOTE

1. We analysed policy documents of 19 countries across Europe (10), Asia-Pacific & Middle-east (6), and Americas (3). The countries are Denmark, Finland, France, Germany, Italy, Netherlands, Norway, Spain, Sweden, United Kingdom (UK), Australia, China, India, Israel, Japan, Singapore, Brazil, USA, and Canada.

REFERENCES

Ahl, H. & Nelson, T., 2015. How policy positions women entrepreneurs: A comparative analysis of state discourse in Sweden and the United States. *Journal of Business Venturing, 30*(2), pp. 273–291.

Andersson, S., Berglund, K., Gunnarsson, E. & Sundin, E., 2012. *Promoting Innovation – Policies, Practices and Procedures*, s.l.: VINNOVA – Verket för Innovationssystem/Swedish Governmental Agency for Innovation System.

Bosma, N. & Kelley, D., 2018. *Global Entrepreneurship Monitor 2018/19 Global Report*, s.l.: GEM.

Brandwein, R.A., 1995. Women in social policy. *Encyclopedia of Social Work* (19). Washington DC: NASW Press.

Canadian Institute For Advanced Research, Canada. 2020. *Pan-Canadian AI Strategy.* Viewed on 29 January 2021. https://cifar.ca/ai/

China Institute for Science and Technology Policy, Tsinghua University, China. 2018. *China AI Development Report 2018.* Viewed on 29 January 2021. http://www .iresearchchina.com/content/details8_42904.html

Coleman, S., Henry, C., Orser, B. & Foss, L., 2018. Policy support for women entrepreneurs' access to financial capital: Evidence from Canada, Germany, Ireland, Norway, and the United States. *Journal of Small Business Management*, pp. 1–27.

Council on Foreign Relations, 2018. Women's Workplace Equality Index. Viewed 2021 https://www.cfr.org/legal-barriers/country-rankings/

Dawson, D., Schleiger, E., Horton, J., McLaughlin, J., Robinson, C., Quezada, G., Scowcroft, J. & Hajkowicz, S., 2019. *Artificial Intelligence: Australia's Ethics Framework.* Viewed on 29 January, 2021. https://consult.industry.gov.au/strategic -policy/artificial-intelligence-ethics-framework/supporting_documents/ArtificialIn telligenceethicsframeworkdiscussionpaper.pdf

Department of International Cooperation Ministry of Science and Technology (MOST), China. 2017. *Next Generation Artificial Intelligence Development Plan.* Viewed on 29 January 2021. http://fi.china-embassy.org/eng/kxjs/P020171025789108009001 .pdf

Dillon, S. & Collett, C., 2019. AI and Gender – four proposals for future research. Cambridge: The Leverhulme Centre for the Future of Intelligence.

Edler, J. & Fagerberg, J., 2017. Innovation policy: What, why, and how. *Oxford Review of Economic Policy*, *33*(1), pp. 2–23.

Foss, L., Henry, C., Ahl, H. & Mikalsen, G. H., 2019. Women's entrepreneurship policy research: A 30-year review of the evidence. *Small Business Economics*, *53*(2), pp. 409–429.

Fürst, H. G., 2009. Utvärdering behovet av genusperspektiv-om innovation, hållbar tillväxt og. *Vinnova Rapport*, Volume 16.

General Secretariat of Scientific Policy Coordination, Ministry of Science, Innovation, and Universities, Spain. 2019. *Spanish RDI Strategy in Artificial Intelligence.* Viewed on 29 January 2021. https://www.ciencia.gob.es/stfls/MICINN/Ciencia/Ficheros/Estrategia_Inteligencia_Artificial_EN.PDF

Government of the Federal Republic of Germany, Germany. 2018. *Strategie Künstliche Intelligenz der Bundesregierung.* Viewed on 29 January 2021. https://www.ki-strategie-deutschland.de/home.html

Government of the United Kingdom, United Kingdom. 2018. *AI in the UK: ready, willing and able? – government response to the select committee report.* Viewed on 29 January 2021. https://www.gov.uk/government/publications/ai-in-the-uk-ready-willing-and-able-government-response-to-the-select-committee-report

Hearn, J. and McKie, L., 2008. Gendered policy and policy on gender: The case of 'domestic violence'. *Policy & Politics*, *36*(1), pp. 75–91.

Israel Innovation Authority, Israel. 2018. *2018–2019 Innovation In Israel.* Viewed on 29 January 2021. https://innovationisrael.org.il/en/news/israel-innovation-authority-2018-19-report

Kuschel, K., Ettl, K., Diaz-Garcia, C. & Alsos, G. A., 2020. Stemming the gender gap in STEM entrepreneurship – insights into women's entrepreneurship in science, technology, engineering and mathematics. *International Entrepreneurship and Management Journal*, pp. 1–15.

Kvidal, T. & Ljunggren, E., 2014. Introducing gender in a policy programme: A multilevel analysis of an innovation policy programme. *Environment and Planning C: Government and Policy*, *32*(1), pp. 39–53.

Leavy, S., 2018. *Gender Bias in Artificial Intelligence: The Need for Diversity.* Proceedings of the 1st International Workshop on Gender Equality in Software Engineering, Dublin, pp. 14–16.

Lee, H. & Pollitzer, E., 2016. *Gender in Science and Innovation as Component of Inclusive Socioeconomic Growth.* London: Gender Summit.

Lundvall, B.-A., 1992. *National Systems of Innovation.* London: Pinter Publishers.

McPhail, B.A., 2003. A feminist policy analysis framework: Through a gendered lens. *The Social Policy Journal*, *2*(2–3), pp. 39–61.

Ministry of Economic Affairs and Climate Policy, Netherlands. 2019. *Strategic Action Plan for Artificial Intelligence.* Viewed on 29 January 2021. https://www.government.nl/documents/reports/2019/10/09/strategic-action-plan-for-artificial-intelligence

Ministry of Economic Affairs and Employment, Finland. 2017. *Finland's Age of Artificial Intelligence.* Viewed on 29 January, 2021. https://julkaisut.valtioneuvosto.fi/bitstream/handle/10024/160391/TEMrap_47_2017_verkkojulkaisu.pdf

Ministry of Economical Progress, Italy. 2019. *Strategia nazionale per l'intelligenza artificiale.* Viewed on 29 January 2021. https://www.mise.gov.it/index.php/it/strategia-intelligenza-artificiale/contesto

Ministry of Enterprise and Innovation, Sweden. 2019. *National Approach to Artificial Intelligence.* Viewed on 29 January 2021. https://www.government.se/4a7451/

contentassets/fe2ba005fb49433587574c513a837fac/national-approach-to-artificial
-intelligence.pdf

Ministry of Finance and Ministry of Industry, Business, and Financial Affairs, Denmark. 2019. *National Strategy for Artificial Intelligence.* Viewed on 29 January 2021.   https://en.digst.dk/policy-and-strategy/denmark-s-national-strategy-for-artificial-intelligence/

National Science & Technology Council, USA. 2019. *2016-2019 Progress Report: Advancing Artificial Intelligence R&D.* Viewed on 29 January 2021. https://www.nitrd.gov/pubs/AI-Research-and-Development-Progress-Report-2016-2019.pdf

National Science & Technology Council, USA. 2019. *The National Artificial Intelligence Research and Development Strategic Plan: 2019 Update.* Viewed on 29 January 2021. https://www.nitrd.gov/pubs/National-AI-RD-Strategy-2019.pdf

NITI Aayog, India. 2018. *National Strategy for Artificial Intelligence.* Viewed on 29 January 2021. https://niti.gov.in/national-strategy-artificial-intelligence

Norwegian Ministry of Local Government and Modernisation, Norway. 2020. *National Strategy for Artificial Intelligence.* Viewed on 29 January 2021. https://www.regjeringen.no/contentassets/1febbbb2c4fd4b7d92c67ddd353b6ae8/en-gb/pdfs/ki-strategi_en.pdf

Pettersson, K., Ahl, H., Berglund, K. & Tillmar, M., 2017. In the name of women? Feminist readings of policies for women's entrepreneurship in Scandinavia. *Scandinavian Journal of Management, 33*(1) pp. 50–63.

Science & Technology, Australia. 2017. *Digital Economy Strategy.* Viewed on 29 January 2021. https://scienceandtechnologyaustralia.org.au/wp-content/uploads/2017/12/Science-Technology-Australia-Digital-Economy-Strategy-Submission.pdf

Select Committee on Artificial Intelligence, House of Lords, United Kingdom. 2018. *AI in the UK: ready, willing and able?.* Viewed on 29 January 2021. https://publications.parliament.uk/pa/ld201719/ldselect/ldai/100/100.pdf

Smart Nation, Singapore. 2019. *National Artificial Intelligence Strategy – Advancing our smart nation journey.* Viewed on 29 January 2021. https://www.smartnation.gov.sg/why-Smart-Nation/NationalAIStrategy

Strategic Council for AI Technology, Japan. 2017. *Artificial Intelligence Technology Strategy.* Viewed in July 2020. http://www.nedo.go.jp/content/100865202.pdf

The Government of Brazil, Brazil. 2018. *Brazilian Digital Transformation Strategy.* Viewed on 29 January 2021. https://www.gov.br/mcti/pt-br/centrais-de-conteudo/comunicados-mcti/estrategia-digital-brasileira/

United National Development Programme. 2020. *Human Development Report 2020: The Next Frontier - Human Development and the Anthropocene.* Viewed on 15 March 2022, https://hdr.undp.org/sites/default/files/hdr2020.pdf

Villani, C., 2018. *For a meaningful artificial intelligence: Towards a French and European strategy.* Viewed on 29 January 2021. https://www.aiforhumanity.fr/pdfs/MissionVillani_Report_ENG-VF.pdf

Warren, H., 2007. Using gender-analysis frameworks: Theoretical and practical reflections. *Gender and Development*, 15(2), pp. 187–198.

World Economic Forum. 2019. *Global Gender Gap Report 2020.* Viewed on 29 January 2021. http://reports.weforum.org/global-gender-gap-report-2020/

APPENDIX: LIST OF AI POLICY MANDATES

BR1 – Promote education training for the digital environment

BR2 – Focus on cybersecurity, privacy and data protection

BR3 – Digital education has been considered vital for Brazil's digital transformation strategy. The focus has been given on changing the education curricula from the grassroots level

BR4 – Internationalisation of Brazilian companies in the digital economy

CA1 – Increase the number of researchers and skilled graduates in the field of AI

CA2 – Develop global thought leadership on the economic, ethical, policy and legal implications of advances in artificial intelligence

CA3 – Support a national research community on artificial intelligence

US1 – Continued American Leadership in AI of paramount importance

US2 – Promoting the trust of American people in AI

US3 – Training a workforce capable of using AI in their occupations

US4 – Protecting American AI technology base from attempted acquisition by strategic competitors and adversarial nations

DK1 – Denmark envisions to be a front runner in the responsible development and use of AI

DK2 – Use of AI to supplement human decision making (not replace) without compromising their social values

DK3 – Danish businesses to achieve growth through developing and using AI

DK4 – The public sector should use artificial intelligence to offer world-class services

FI1 – Enhancement of business competitiveness through the use of AI

FI2 – Effective utilization of data in all sectors

FI3 – Ensure top-level expertise and attract top experts

FI4 – Build the world's best public services

FR1 – Improve AI education and training ecosystem to nurture and attract top AI talent

FR2 – Focus on developing inclusive and diverse AI

FR3 – Establishing an open data policy for the implementation of AI applications (currently data availability is skewed towards a handful of large operators)

FR4 – Develop an ethical framework for transparent and fair use of AI applications

DE1 – Making Germany and Europe global leaders on the development and use of AI technologies and securing Germany's competitiveness in the future

DE2 – Safeguarding the responsible development and use of AI which serves the good of society

DE3 – Integrating AI in society in ethical, legal, cultural and institutional terms in the context of a broad societal dialogue and active political measures

IT1 – Improving AI-related skills and competences at all education levels and creating lifelong learning and reskilling opportunities for the labour force

IT2 – Fostering AI research and innovation to enhance the competitiveness of the entrepreneurial ecosystem

IT3 – Establishing a regulatory and ethical framework to ensure a sustainable and trustworthy AI

IT4 – Developing a data infrastructure to fuel AI developments

IT5 – Improving public services through wider adoption and use of AI applications

NL1 – Capitalising on societal and economic opportunities through the use and development of AI

NL2 – Creating the right conditions for support and growth of AI R&D

NL3 – Strengthening the policy foundations so that AI applications are developed within legal and ethical frameworks and the national safety (of citizens, government and businesses) remains protected

NO1 – Sharing of data is a theme that runs throughout the report

NO2 – Norway will invest in AI in areas where they have distinct advantages (strong research and business communities), such as health, seas and oceans, public administration, energy and mobility

NO3 – The report focuses on the objective of developing AI based on ethical principles, respect for data protection and good cybersecurity

ES1 – Towards an organisational structure that allows the development of an RDI (Research Development and Innovation) System in AI and the assessment of its impact

ES2 – Establish strategic areas where to develop RDI activities in AI

ES3 – Define and develop actions that allow the transfer of knowledge

ES4 – Develop a system to promote cross-disciplinary and vocational training in Artificial Intelligence

ES5 – Develop a digital data ecosystem and enhance infrastructures

ES6 – Analyse the ethics of AI from the perspective of RDI (Ethics is given the last priority)

SE1 – Education and training: Sweden needs a strong AI component in non-technical programmes to create the conditions for broad and responsible application of the technology

SE2 – Research: Sweden needs both strong basic research and strong applied research in AI to ensure knowledge and skills supply in the field

SE3 – Ethics: Sweden needs to develop rules, standards, norms and ethical principles to guide ethical and sustainable AI and the use of AI

SE4 – Data: Sweden needs to continue the work on making data available to serve as infrastructure for AI use in areas where it adds value

UK1 – The report acknowledges that the UK cannot compete with the US or China in terms of funding or people but suggests the country may have a competitive advantage in considering the ethics of AI.

UK2 – "People" are at the core of UK's AI strategy – focus on growing STEM and digital training skills

UK3 – Focus is on creating an open data ecosystem with the view that large companies which have control over large quantities of data must be prevented from becoming overly powerful within this landscape

AU1 – Special emphasis on creating an ethics framework for AI

AU2 – AI should be developed to benefit individuals, society and the environment (Australia's AI strategy uniquely focuses on enhancing natural resource management using AI)

AU3 – The report stresses the need to train and educate an entire new AI specialist workforce

CN1 – AI to be the backbone of China's industrial upgradation and economic transformation

CN2 – The national strategy emphasises closely integrating AI in all sectors of the Chinese economy or "intelligentisation"

CN3 – Become leading AI power by 2030

CN4 – Civil-military fusion lies at the heart of China's AI policy

IN1 – #AIforAll The strategy paper focuses on how India can leverage AI to ensure social and inclusive growth

IN2 – The strategy paper states that India should become the "garage" or AI solutions provider for 40% of the world comprising of emerging and developing economies

IL1 – Objective is to reinforce research infrastructure in AI fields in academia and to turn Israeli research universities into AI excellence centres. Currently, the most advanced AI algorithms are developed by academia and serve as the basis for ground-breaking applications in the industry

IL2 – Another objective is to nurture all the human capital in the AI field

IL3 – Development of R&D infrastructure that would serve both academia and industry – particularly computing power and data infrastructure

IL4 – Penetration of AI tech in all branches of the economy – not just future high-tech industries

JP1 – Realization of Society 5.0 through effective utilization of AI

JP2 – Japan should improve its international presence and radically strengthen its industrial competitiveness

JP3 – To create a sustainable society that incorporates diversity

JP4 – For Japan to take a leadership role in building international research, education, and social infrastructure networks in the AI field, and to accelerate AI-related R&D, human resource development, the achievement of SDGs, etc.

SG1 – Enable rapid commercialisation of fundamental AI research and deployment of AI solutions

SG2 – Address the shortfall in the quantity and quality of talent across the entire range of AI-related job roles

SG3 – Enable quick and secure access to high-quality, cross-sectoral datasets

SG4 – Strengthen trust (citizens) in AI technologies to enable an environment for test-bedding, developing, and deploying AI solutions

SG5 – Work with international partners to shape the international AI discourse and develop the other horizontal enablers

10. Targeting in targeted funds: how inclusion policies and programs can exclude intended beneficiaries

Katindi Sivi

1.   INTRODUCTION

Africa's bulging youth population and the unprecedented levels of unemployment now and in the future have been of significant concern to policy makers. In Kenya, the data shows a 200% growth rate of the working age population between 1999 and 2009 with a corresponding labor force participation rate that shrank to 76% in the same period (RoK, 2018). The country has therefore been inadequate in successfully transitioning the 800,000 youth joining the job market annually to secure decent employment opportunities (RoK, 2017). The most severely affected by unemployment are young people aged between 15 and 34 who form 85% of all the unemployed individuals – basically the youth in the country as defined by the Constitution. However, female unemployment in all youth age cohorts, was on average two times higher compared to that of their male counterparts. Living in rural areas and with a disability compounds the issue further. The unemployment crisis is buttressed by a decreasing formal sector employment, a growing informal sector and an economy that has a very small wage sector. A continued exponential growth of the working age population projected to grow one and half times (150%) by 2030 and double (214%) by 2045 in Kenya (Sivi, 2020) makes the future crisis even bigger.

Youth unemployment, which is framed as a form of social exclusion of the youth from productive opportunities is one of the major concerns at international, regional and local levels that warrants urgent responses because of the potential negative effects; key among them being political instability (Sivi, 2016). As a result, a plethora of policy recommendations have been designed and tons of resources poured out by different agencies. In Kenya since the 2008 post-election violence and the 2013 elections, government and donor related trainings and employment programs show an investment of well over USD 3 billion (Mwongera, 2019). At the international level, the 2030 Agenda for Sustainable Development, which Kenya is a signatory to, in its Goal 8 commits to promote sustained, inclusive, and sustainable economic growth, full and productive employment, and decent work for all have been instituted. Specific targets incorporated into this goal include, but are not limited to, achieving full employment for young people (8.5); substantially reducing the proportion of youth not in employment, education, or training (8.6); as well as developing and operationalizing a global strategy for youth employment by 2020 (8.b) (ILO, 2018). At the regional level, African Heads of State and Government declared 2009–2018 the Decade of Youth Development in Africa to accelerate youth empowerment for sustainable development (Union, 2011).

At the national level, the Kenya government has a Constitutional provision to ensure the right to equal treatment including right to equal opportunities in political, economic, cultural and social spheres. The Constitution gives effect to the realization of the rights guaranteed in Article 27(6) which obligates the state to take legislative and other measures, including affirmative action programs and policies designed to redress any disadvantages suffered by individuals or groups because of past discrimination (RoK, 2013). The corresponding youth un/employment interventions, designed to execute these wider policy proposals, therefore have adopted affirmative action programming. These measures incorporate policies, institutional frameworks, plans and funding mechanisms that seek to target the most vulnerable lot – the youth, women and people with disability, on the matter of unemployment and include them into productive roles.

The two most prominent approaches used include: the entrepreneurship track that is now synonymous with an easy to enter, small capital base, often survival retail trading that is not viable or value-adding innovative businesses that create other opportunities; and the financing track that, among other things, provides very minimal, unviable risk capital for startups that would not otherwise be funded through formal lending channels. The repayment rates are also very low with about 75% of the 'businesses' lasting only two years at best (Sivi, 2020). Conceptually, social exclusion therefore includes: the 'conditions of deprivation' – which are multiple and interconnected; 'the process' of deprivation – which is enabled by the flaws in the political, social, cultural, or economic systems; as well as 'the outcome' of deprivation – which exposes the extent of deprivation people experience (Babajanian and Hagen-Zanker, 2012).

The main objective of this chapter is therefore to examine conditions, process and outcomes of one of Kenya's targeted affirmative action funds, the Women Enterprise Fund (WEF). The work explores the issue of intersectionality, with respect to age, region, and socio-economic status to show how these can further sideline those already left out of the productive role, such as young female entrepreneurs. In order to determine the extent WEF disbursements benefited those who need the funds most, categorical targeting which includes further defining of the classifications to be applied when choosing eligible beneficiaries that would ideally meet the goals of the fund, was applied. A beneficiary calculation sheet was generated based on certain assumptions about the fund, the census data and the WEF disbursements to all Kenya's 47 counties from inception to date to generate the ideal disbursement by county, age and people with disability. From the analysis, it is clear that the lack of targeting can negate the ultimate goals of affirmative action funds. The fund allocations over the last 13 years indicate that WEF may have advantaged already privileged women entrepreneurs and disadvantaged those who needed the resources most.

The chapter begins with a brief literature review of unemployment as social exclusion and the affirmative action policies and programs. Expansive empirical data follows on the correlation between youth unemployment, education levels and informal micro-enterprises predominantly owned by women. Affirmative action programs in Kenya are also discussed, before findings from the data analysis are presented. The chapter concludes with recommendations on how WEF can disburse resources with more equity, to create more jobs and realize high productivity of micro, small and medium enterprises (MSMEs).

2. THEORETICAL FOUNDATIONS OF SOCIAL EXCLUSION AND AFFIRMATIVE ACTION

Lack of permanent employment, earnings, property, credit, and adequate education opportunities persistently exclude unemployed people and deprive them of their capability to live decent lives (Sen, 2000). Social exclusion in this chapter therefore denotes multiple forms of economic and social disadvantages that are caused by various factors, sometimes beyond the control of the individuals like history, culture, gender, age, socio-economic status, levels of education, and geographical location, which manifest in lack of or unequal access to productive opportunities (Burchardt et al., 2002). Conceptually social exclusion therefore includes: the 'conditions of deprivation' – which are multiple and interconnected; 'the process' of deprivation – which is enabled by the flaws in the political, social, cultural, or economic systems; as well as 'the outcome' of deprivation – which exposes the extent of deprivation people experience (Babajanian and Hagen-Zanker, 2012). The resultant effect is hugely differentiated outcomes between and among groups in things like accessing entrepreneurial funds, innovation training opportunities or awarding of contracts within governments (Laderchi, Saith, and Stewart, 2003).

To remedy this persistent inaccessibility of work, special assistance through affirmative action is considered to targeted individuals as a form of anti-discrimination measure (Holzer and Neumark, 2000). It is done to enhance inclusion and participation of the marginalized group who would otherwise continuously be left out if the 'preferential treatment' were not accorded to them for some time so that the playing field eventually levels up for them (Holzer and Neumark, 2000). Loury (2000), however, argues that the targeted groups become beneficiaries of 'positive discrimination' in their favor, to offset the effects of marginalization and thus objects that "two wrongs do not make a right and that while we cannot undo the exclusionary practices of the past, we should not add to this injustice with present-day 'discrimination', however noble its purpose" (p. 240). To this end, affirmative action, which is frequently used as a blanket remedy for past exclusion or unfair outcomes, is therefore controversial and often, a poorly understood policy. However, having both the social exclusion and the affirmative action angles is beneficial for the study as it helps integrate the conditions of deprivation with the processes of inclusion and exclusion to understand outcomes (Kabeer, 2000).

2.1 Youth Unemployment in the Context of Kenya

African countries have been experiencing a bulging youth population – aged between 15 and 34 years old as per the Constitutional definition (RoK, 2020) – and who form 70% of the working age population. Unfortunately, the rapid growth rate of this working age population has been outstripping the jobs created, and causing acutely high proportions of unemployment. Of the unemployed youth, female unemployment was on average two times higher compared to that of their male counterparts. A commonly cited issue underpinning employment status and job competitiveness is skills levels of the population, often derived from levels of education attained. Due to past emphasis on providing basic education, we now have a situation where, in the 21st century, one quarter of Kenya's population has no education. Slightly over half of the population (51%) only has a primary education while only 21% of the population has secondary education. Only about 6% of those with post-secondary education attain university education (RoK, 2018). While there is gender parity in education at the lower levels, there are more males than females who generally proceed to complete higher levels of education. The low number of formerly educated youth reaching higher levels of education structurally excludes the majority of them from getting high level formal jobs that pay well (Sivi, 2013).

Data also shows a big correlation between levels of education, and ownership of formal businesses in Kenya. Cumulatively, most licensed businesses were owned by people with secondary education and above and male ownership of licensed businesses was 1.5 times more than that of women. These formalized businesses, which accounted for 26% of the paid labor force in MSMEs tended to attract or employ significantly less numbers of women.

Conversely, all unlicensed businesses which are synonymous with small-scale trading or informal micro enterprises, were predominantly owned by those with primary education and below and female ownership was two times more than that of men (RoK, 2016). On average, women also engaged two times more in the sectors with most unlicensed businesses like agriculture, waste management, and wholesale and retail. Although female-owned businesses also tended to shut down one and half times more than their male counterparts, they accounted for 81% of employment reported in the MSMEs, and attracted twice the number of female employees (RoK, 2016). The informal micro enterprises have evolved from a temporary safety net where unemployed people engage as they look for employment in the modern wage sector, to a permanent destination for 77% of the youth who cannot find formal jobs (Potts, 2005; Agwaya and Mairura 2019). This explains why one of the highest reasons for starting informal micro enterprises in Kenya has been because people did not have another alternative (RoK, 2016).

The increasing importance of the informal micro enterprises in providing high labor absorption and use of local resources to increase domestic capital (Potts, 2008) has attracted the infusion of small business development services by policy makers and some donor agencies. Their aim has been to create 'entrepreneurship' that helps further absorb the high numbers of unemployed youth (Jeffrey and Dyson, 2013). Unfortunately, there are so many assumptions that come with this kind of conceptualization of youth entrepreneurship.[1] While policy makers and donors imagine bourgeoning businesses that would establish high labor-intensive jobs to grow wage employment, the same policy makers design and support youth programs whose aim is to develop micro, informal Household Enterprises (HEs) that mostly deal with some form of merchandising (Fox and Sohnesen, 2012). The reality is that the market dynamics do not allow these small low productivity micro-businesses to make enough sales to grow, and to employ more people (Bateman and Chang, 2012). HEs therefore transition into survivalist, 'necessity' types of enterprises serving to sustain household livelihoods at reasonably low levels (Fox and Sohnesen, 2012). It is the reason why these informal micro enterprises have very little innovation going on within their businesses. According to RoK (2016), innovation was 3.5 times more in medium enterprises and two times more in small enterprises than in micro businesses across the board, meaning that women-owned businesses had the least innovation taking place within their businesses (RoK, 2016). Among all the innovation levels (of product, process, and marketing), marketing or advertising of goods or services had the least innovation for all the businesses as they depended on the quality of products and clientele satisfaction to get new products in the market, create awareness of their products or services and attract potential customers. About

84% of unlicensed businesses, all operating at micro levels and where there is most female ownership or employment did not advertise.

This data makes it clear that when socio-economic stratification by gender, age, level of education, and even region is done, certain groups of people, in this case the younger women with lower levels of education in rural areas, are relegated to the margins of society compared to others on issues of unemployment, entrepreneurship and innovation. Agwaya and Mairura (2019) argue that apart from the differential access and control over productive resources like education and employment, access to credit and cash income are major underlying sources of inequalities between male- and female-owned businesses. In a democratic country that subscribes to equality of opportunities for all citizens, the marginalized therefore warrant greater and more substantive preferential policies to level the playing field (Alam, 2010).

2.2   Affirmative Action Interventions in Kenya

A plethora of youth employment policies, programs and funds surged after the 2008 post-election violence in Kenya and the 2013 elections. These programs basically adopted the financial set-aside model which incorporates low interest loans to groups to start up small businesses, and the quota system where a certain guaranteed percentage of resources or opportunities are secluded for affected groups for purposes like accessing government procurement opportunities. The main aim of all the initiatives is to include the marginalized in the productive role with the hope that it will enhance empowerment, equality, equity, and non-discrimination in national development processes (RoK, 2020). These affirmative action initiatives include the Women Enterprise Fund (WEF), Youth Enterprise Development Fund (YEDF), Access to Government Opportunities (AGPO), Uwezo Fund, and the National Government Affirmative Action Fund (NGAAF). Other such funds not considered in Table 10.1 include the Constituency Development Fund (CDF); Equalization Fund; and the National Fund for the Disabled.

A summary of the policies, programs and funds in Table 10.1 shows an emphasis on access to financial resources, to women, youth and people with disabilities and they mostly target both formal and informal businesses. In addition to financial access: YEDF offers enterprise business development, marketing and entrepreneurial training / capacity building; WEF offers enterprise business development and market linkages; while the Uwezo fund offers entrepreneurial training / capacity building and mentorship. NGAAF is the only fund supporting social welfare programs such as scholarships, nurturing talent, and preventing Gender Based Violence. AGPO is the only affirmative action initiative that does not offer access to financial support services. Instead it is the only one setting aside 30% of government procurement contracts to

Table 10.1　　Summary of affirmative action funds in Kenya

Affirmative action initiative	Women Enterprise Fund (WEF), 2007	Youth Enterprise Development Fund (YEDF), 2007	Access to Government Opportunities (AGPO), 2013	Uwezo Fund, 2013	National Government Affirmative Action Fund (NGAAF), 2015
Access to finance	✓	✓	×	✓	✓
Enterprise Business Development & Value addition	✓	✓	×	×	×
Marketing and market linkages	✓	✓	×	×	×
Entrepreneurial training / capacity building	×	✓	×	✓	×
Access to 30% government procurement	×	×	✓	×	×
Mentorship	×	×	×	✓	×
Support social welfare e.g. scholarships, nurturing talent, preventing GBV	×	×	×	×	✓
Target groups	Women only	Male and female youth	Women, youth and people with disabilities	Women, youth and people with disabilities	Women, youth and people with disabilities, needy children and the elderly
Target sectors	Informal and formal	Informal and formal	Formal	Informal and formal	Informal and formal

Affirmative action initiative	Women Enterprise Fund (WEF), 2007	Youth Enterprise Development Fund (YEDF), 2007	Access to Government Opportunities (AGPO), 2013	Uwezo Fund, 2013	National Government Affirmative Action Fund (NGAAF), 2015
Amounts disbursed	Since inception: Kshs 17.8 billion with Govt contribution of Kshs. 6 billion				Since inception: Kshs 9.3 billion
No of beneficiaries	Since inception: 1,733,323				Since inception: 5,125,212
Expected growth of beneficiaries (2019/2020 financial year)	2.5%	85.6%	8.1%	18.9%	-

Source: Agwaya and Mairura (2019), RoK (2020).

formal and not informal businesses. According to RoK (2020), women, youths and persons with disabilities entrepreneurs are expected to be awarded tenders worth KSh 17.3 billion, KSh 13.6 billion and KSh 1.9 billion, respectively, in 2019/20. Due to the similar roles funds like the WEF, YEDF and the Uwezo Fund play, there is a proposition to merge them into one fund that will be referred to as the Biashara Kenya Fund (Kiriti-Nganga and Mogeni, 2019).

3.   METHODOLOGY: ANALYTICAL STRATEGY

The decision to improve inclusion and the social welfare of select populations – the youth women and people with disabilities – requires mechanisms of defining beneficiary eligibility in order to effectively achieve the intended results (Conning and Kevane, 1999). While these mechanisms are characterized by: the overall policy framework that dictates implementation in accordance with the operational guidelines; the program design; and the institutional strategy to successfully support the intended beneficiaries (Farrington, Sharp and Sjoblom, 2007), "there is no guarantee that the projects will succeed in their intended objectives or be superior in performance with respect to untargeted programs" (Kilic, Whitney and Winters, 2015, p. 28). It is possible for targeted programs designed to include the marginalized to have ambiguous and opposing effects (Ravallion, 2003). This is because targeted programs are designed to reach those who meet a certain global or general criteria like youth who may be defined by a certain age category like 18–34 or women meaning females above 18 years old. That criteria does not further differentiate the other categories or identities that these groups subscribe to, that may advantage or disadvantage them in accessing productive resources. General program implementation without considering these other sub-categories means that there is no accuracy in beneficiary identification, and resources will not be equitably shared to reach those who need them most, thus introducing exclusion and inclusion errors (Coady, Grosh, and Hoddinott, 2004). The success of these programs therefore lies not in the fact that they are necessarily targeted, but rather in how the targeting is done (Kilic et al., 2015).

Categorical targeting which includes further defining the classifications to be applied when choosing eligible beneficiaries is used in this chapter to assess the Women Enterprise Fund allocations since inception to date. Given that the basic eligibility criteria of WEF is females aged 18 and above in groups or as individuals, further targeting of eligible women will include: young women aged between 18 and 34 due to the established fact that they are most likely to be unemployed; regional targeting (in this case County administrative boundaries) to help with the regions that are lagging behind because of poverty; socio-economic activity – to enable the capturing of those who are not in formal employment; ability – to include people with disabilities; and population – to enable proportionality of disbursements. These categorizations are predominantly informed by the 2019 census data, WEF disbursement data over time as well as the intended goal of the fund. Ideally, however, it should consist of statistical targeting – which is a combination of data, group targeting – which is local community knowledge that is enhanced through stakeholder consultation; and tagging – which consists of needs assessments (Costella and Ovadiya, 2014).

To calculate the number of expected female beneficiaries and project disbursements, I used the beneficiaries' calculation sheet in Table 10.2.

Table 10.2   WEF beneficiary calculation sheet

Variable	Sub-variable	Calculation
Population	Total female population	24,014,716
	Total population below 18	10,862,532
	Women above 18	13,152,184
	WEF target 70% of women above 18	9,206,529
	Exclude number of women potentially in formal jobs estimated at the national average of 30%	2,761,959
	Exclude number of women above 18 in school over the last 10 years	1,269,516
	Estimated number of WEF beneficiaries between inception and 2030, i.e. 23 years (since the program is anchored as a flagship project of government's vision 2030	5,175,054
	Estimated number of annual WEF beneficiaries	225,002
	Estimated number of WEF beneficiaries up to 2020 (13 years)	2,925,031
Persons with disability	PWD beneficiaries in 13 years is 2% of the population.	58,501
Female youth (aged 18–34)	Youth beneficiaries in 13 years calculated at 29.8% of the pop (based on census data)	872,935
Poverty	As given per county by the census data	Varies per county
Geographical region	County administrative boundaries	47
Disbursed loans	As per the WEF accounts of disbursements from 2007 to 2020	
Ideal amounts for disbursements	Calculated on the assumption of one shilling per person hence total WEF disbursements divide by ideal beneficiary population multiplied by specific county populations	

4.   FINDINGS AND ANALYSIS

The data in Table 10.3 shows that there is no co-relation between WEF disbursements and age, ability, regional, socio-economic levels or population considerations. It is also clear that the lack of targeting can negate the fund's ultimate goals which include the meeting SDG 1 and SDG 5 on poverty reduction, gender equality and women empowerment (RoK, 2019). Based on the categorized targeting, the data shows that WEF disbursements should have ideally reached 2.9 million women by year 2020 of implementation if they were to achieve their intended goal by 2030. Based on the current number of total beneficiaries of 1.7 million, it means that the fund has benefited 57% of women, meaning that there are 1.25 million women that have not been ideally reached in thirteen years. The data also shows that WEF's disbursements have no co-relation with population proportions of counties or their poverty levels. Within the 13 years of WEF's implementation, counties like Nyeri cumulatively received 7.5% of the total WEF resources while counties like Turkana, Mandera, and Wajir with similar populations but with poverty levels as high as 84% and above received a cumulative average of 0.5% of WEF resources. One can argue that the absorption capacity of poorer counties might be low but the targeting would help address these barriers so that the women in these regions are lifted to the level of more affluent counties.

In all the WEF reporting, there is no disaggregated data of beneficiaries by level of ability and age yet as demonstrated earlier, these two facts lead to further marginalization of women from productive activities. The calculations show that out of the 2.9 million women that should have benefited by 2020, 58,500 should have been female PWDs and 871,659 should have been female youth, as a means of enhancing WEF's mandate to support women entrepreneurs to start and/or expand businesses for wealth and employment creation. Interestingly, when one compares the population that benefited versus the population that should have benefited from the disbursement per county, the data shows that 34 out of 47 counties under-benefited by 14% to 90%. Nyeri, for example, only benefited 50% of women who should have ideally received loans despite getting the bulk of WEF resources while counties like West Pokot, Trans Nzoia, Migori, Meru and Nairobi benefited less than 15% of the individuals or groups. Thirteen counties, that is, Marsabit, Samburu, Isiolo, Lamu, Tana River, Elgeyo Marakwet, Siaya, Tharaka Nithi, Taita Taveta, Busia, Kirinyaga, Kisumu, and Embu over-benefited by up to 3.4 times. In comparing the actual disbursements by county, versus what should have ideally gone to the counties if better targeting had been done, the data shows that 17 counties were over-resourced with Nyeri county getting about five times more than the ideal resources for half the number of beneficiaries.

Table 10.3   The findings of WEF beneficiaries

County	2019 census pop	% proportion of the population	Actual WEF benefs (07-2020)	Ideal no. of benefs (07-2020)	% diff btwn actual benefs vs ideal	Ideal no. of PWDs benefs	Ideal no. of youth benefs	Poverty	Disbursed WEF Loan Amount (07-2020)	Proportion received per county	Ideal amounts for disbursement	Proportion of over/under disbursement
Nyeri	752,695	1.59	21,986	46,632	47	933	13,896	27.6	1,193,400,000.00	7.5	252,904,694.25	4.72
Kiambu	2,402,834	5.09	30,528	148,864	21	2,977	44,362	24.2	1,159,550,000.00	7.3	807,349,587.94	1.44
Nakuru	2,142,667	4.54	47,778	132,746	36	2,655	39,558	33.5	930,350,000.00	5.9	719,933,761.36	1.29
Nairobi	4,337,080	9.19	27,742	268,698	10	5,374	80,072	21.8	929,598,000.00	5.9	1,457,254,121.95	0.64
Meru	1,535,635	3.25	11,865	95,138	12	1,903	28,351	31.0	671,252,000.00	4.2	515,971,675.31	1.30
Muranga	1,053,059	2.23	38,923	65,241	60	1,305	19,442	33.2	657,658,000.00	4.1	353,826,668.73	1.86
Kakamega	1,861,332	3.94	11,562	115,316	10	2,306	34,364	49.2	626,703,000.00	4.0	625,405,510.00	1.00
Mombasa	1,190,987	2.52	52,579	73,786	71	1,476	21,988	34.8	511,120,450.00	3.2	400,170,325.41	1.28
Homa Bay	1,125,823	2.38	10,996	69,749	16	1,395	20,785	48.4	478,283,200.00	3.0	378,275,292.90	1.26
Bungoma	1,663,898	3.52	25,713	103,084	25	2,062	30,719	47.3	442,513,000.00	2.8	559,067,902.60	0.79
Embu	604,769	1.28	70,322	37,468	188	749	11,165	35.3	439,874,200.00	2.8	203,201,720.53	2.16
Nyandarua	636,002	1.35	33,796	39,403	86	788	11,742	38.8	435,310,000.00	2.7	213,695,974.27	2.04
Kisumu	1,144,777	2.42	108,904	70,923	154	1,418	21,135	39.9	433,550,000.00	2.7	384,643,816.11	1.13
Kirinyaga	605,630	1.28	44,419	37,521	118	750	11,181	25.9	428,689,000.00	2.7	203,491,015.59	2.11
Kitui	1,130,134	2.39	39,872	70,016	57	1,400	20,865	60.4	409,138,000.00	2.6	379,723,784.17	1.08
Kilifi	1,440,958	3.05	45,506	89,272	51	1,785	26,603	58.4	400,188,980.00	2.5	484,160,307.18	0.83
Machakos	1,414,022	2.99	49,510	87,604	57	1,752	26,106	42.6	369,830,000.00	2.3	475,109,840.73	0.78
Kisii	1,260,509	2.67	54,457	78,093	70	1,562	23,272	51.4	333,076,000.00	2.1	423,529,641.14	0.79

County	2019 census pop	% proportion of the population	Actual WEF benefs (07-2020)	Ideal no. of benefs (07-2020)	% diff btwn actual benefs vs ideal	Ideal no. of PWDs benefs	Ideal no. of youth benefs	Poverty	Disbursed WEF Loan Amount (07-2020)	Proportion received per county	Ideal amounts for disbursement	Proportion of over/under disbursement
Kericho	896,863	1.90	23,292	55,564	42	1,111	16,558	39.3	298,450,000.00	1.9	301,344,984.08	0.99
Nandi	883,634	1.87	18,580	54,744	34	1,095	16,314	40.0	286,849,000.00	1.8	296,900,054.60	0.97
Migori	1,108,950	2.35	9,548	68,703	14	1,374	20,474	49.6	275,250,000.00	1.7	372,605,983.41	0.74
Uasin Gishu	1,152,671	2.44	43,353	71,412	61	1,428	21,281	33.8	262,050,000.00	1.7	387,296,191.45	0.68
Makueni	977,015	2.07	34,420	60,530	57	1,211	18,038	60.6	261,919,000.00	1.7	328,275,968.15	0.80
Vihiga	587,189	1.24	7,032	36,378	19	728	10,841	38.9	258,000,000.00	1.6	197,294,859.82	1.31
Trans Nzoia	985,333	2.09	8,388	61,045	14	1,221	18,191	41.2	252,425,000.00	1.6	331,070,807.03	0.76
Busia	886,856	1.88	68,445	54,944	125	1,099	16,373	60.4	250,475,000.00	1.6	297,982,643.06	0.84
Kajiado	1,107,296	2.35	42,415	68,601	62	1,372	20,443	38.0	244,100,000.00	1.5	372,050,241.23	0.66
Bomet	873,023	1.85	42,448	54,087	78	1,082	16,118	51.3	242,360,000.00	1.5	293,334,770.24	0.83
Taita Taveta	335,747	0.71	69,133	20,801	332	416	6,199	50.4	240,154,500.00	1.5	112,810,623.66	2.13
Tharaka-Nithi	391,303	0.83	82,025	24,243	338	485	7,224	41.0	226,850,000.00	1.4	131,477,378.72	1.73
Siaya	989,708	2.10	85,786	61,316	140	1,226	18,272	38.2	212,512,900.00	1.3	332,540,802.23	0.64
Kwale	858,748	1.82	30,420	53,202	57	1,064	15,854	70.7	202,150,000.00	1.3	288,538,385.90	0.70
Baringo	662,760	1.40	17,122	41,060	42	821	12,236	52.2	190,600,000.00	1.2	222,686,632.91	0.86
Laikipia	513,879	1.09	13,519	31,837	42	637	9,487	47.9	180,200,000.00	1.1	172,662,780.24	1.04

County	2019 census pop	% proportion of the population	Actual WEF benefs (07-2020)	Ideal no. of benefs (07-2020)	% diff btwn actual benefs vs ideal	Ideal no. of PWDs benefs	Ideal no. of youth benefs	Poverty	Disbursed WEF Loan Amount (07-2020)	Pro-portion received per county	Ideal amounts for disbursement	Proportion of over/under disbursement
Narok	1,149,379	2.43	44,126	71,208	62	1,424	21,220	41.0	140,300,000.00	0.9	386,190,083.06	0.36
Elgeyo Marakwet	453,403	0.96	88,219	28,090	314	562	8,371	52.7	103,700,000.00	0.7	152,342,910.59	0.68
Wajir	775,302	1.64	8,484	48,033	18	961	14,314	84.2	101,750,000.00	0.6	260,500,621.44	0.39
Tana River	314,710	0.67	32,040	19,497	164	390	5,810	75.6	99,050,000.00	0.6	105,742,214.74	0.94
Nyamira	603,051	1.28	25,051	37,361	67	747	11,134	50.7	99,047,300.00	0.6	202,624,474.41	0.49
Lamu	141,909	0.30	10,694	8,792	122	176	2,620	32.3	93,450,000.00	0.6	47,681,268.32	1.96
Garissa	835,482	1.77	24,046	51,761	46	1,035	15,425	58.9	87,950,000.00	0.6	280,721,035.42	0.31
Isiolo	267,997	0.57	29,710	16,603	179	332	4,948	65.3	86,150,000.00	0.5	90,046,697.99	0.96
Turkana	922,210	1.95	11,374	57,134	20	1,143	17,026	87.5	85,750,000.00	0.5	309,861,548.28	0.28
Samburu	307,957	0.65	30,889	19,079	162	382	5,686	71.4	85,707,000.00	0.5	103,473,214.15	0.83
Marsabit	447,150	0.95	28,537	27,703	103	554	8,255	75.8	57,488,000.00	0.4	150,241,909.45	0.38
Mandera	862,079	1.83	16,852	53,409	32	1,068	15,916	85.8	50,450,000.00	0.3	289,657,598.24	0.17
West Pokot	618,867	1.31	4,424	38,341	12	767	11,426	66.3	38,400,000.00	0.2	207,938,633.06	0.18
Grand Total	47,213,282	100.00	1676830	2925030.60		58500.61	871659		15,863,621,530.00	100.0	15,863,610,956	

Source: Author calculation based on RoK (2019a, 2019b, 2019c, 2019d).

Twenty-six counties were underfunded with five particular counties – Narok, Garissa, Turkana, Mandera, and West Pokot receiving less than 0.3% of the cumulative resources despite very high poverty levels in some of these areas. Kakamega and Nandi counties received amounts equivalent to the ideal resources they should have received by 2020 but for 11% of the beneficiary population while Tana River and Isiolo counties received the ideal amounts they should have received had targeting been done, for double the number of beneficiaries. From the analysis, it is clear that the lack of targeting can negate the funds ultimate goals.

5.   DISCUSSION

This chapter demonstrates that the issue of unemployment is multi-dimensional in nature and thus affects people in very different ways, resulting in double deprivations. Unemployment in Kenya for example is epitomized by young women with low education levels, living in rural areas. The complexity that comes with multiple dispossessions is often not taken into account when defining the problem or formulating policies and programs. Instead, the conceptualization is simplistic, logical, linear and on top of that political, which negates the neutrality and results in outcomes that either do not adequately resolve the problem or lead to unintended consequences among some of the beneficiaries. This means that while working towards the inclusion of youth, women and people with disability as marginalized groups, it is possible to advantage the privileged members among these groups while structurally excluding the sub-groups that need the intervention the most.

The quota system approach which is based on a certain guaranteed percentage of public resources or procurement opportunities to the affected group is the default setting of affirmative action programs in Kenya and most of Africa. Holzer and Neumark (2000) argue that this model of affirmative action results in distribution but ignores allocative efficiency which induces distortions in as far as it treats the target populations as homogenous groups and does not take into account the sub-categories of the target populations suffering further deprivations. As indicated in Table 10.1, a variety of disadvantages and barriers – of being young, of being female, and of living in rural areas reasonably show that the playing field is not level across the groups when it comes to entrepreneurship and job opportunities. When the policies are therefore applied in a blanket way without consciously targeting the sub-groups that have multiple deprivations, the affirmative action programs do not necessarily act to prohibit various forms of discrimination within groups of the target audience (Crosby, Iyer, and Sincharoen, 2006). In this case, the laws and programs instead act to undermine the very tenets of affirmative action and in fact generate reverse discrimination. This claim is confirmed by Burger and Jafta's (2010) assertion that affirmative action policies and programs have had marginal effects in reducing employment gaps and were much less significant in bringing about changes in labor market outcomes like policies that improved access to quality education for the same groups. While generally it is these disadvantages that are the basis for affirmative action policies and programs, they also become the very disadvantages that limit the abilities of minority groups of youth from competing for the opportunities provided on an equal footing with their counterparts.

Micro enterprise entrepreneurship which, through the affirmative action funds are structured as a critical pathway from unemployment, but where policies and programs are designed to perpetuate low value enterprising, located in low value markets, have led to market saturation and stagnation (Kiraka, Kobia and Katwalo, 2013). Unless MSMEs innovate through new product development and access to higher value markets as well as innovate through enhancing organization efficiency and effectiveness in their internal operations to give them a competitive edge over other sector players, WEF funded MSMEs will not achieve their intended purposes (Kiende, Mukulu and Odhiambo, 2019).

6. RECOMMENDATIONS

In conclusion, it is evident that having affirmative action policies and fund allocations in place is not always sufficient in achieving effective inclusion. Targeting in targeted funds has to be done if affirmative action funds are to achieve their objectives. It is therefore crucial to first, incorporate detailed and comprehensive gender disaggregated data, which is a vital ingredient in category targeting, within the whole process from policy framing and design to routine evaluations and also for impact on the position of women with respect to equality or 'life opportunities' (Henry et al., 2017) in order to capture and address the multiple dimensions of deprivation. Second, consciously design affirmative action policies and initiatives that establish formal small and medium enterprises with adequate resourcing and training components for youth, women and people with disabilities to enhance innovation of processes and products while creating value-based market linkages.

Third, it is crucial for organizations to use the targeting processes when implementing affirmative action programs to constantly monitor their own performance and devise corrections if they find themselves falling short of the intended goals. This is often done through different sets of data modeling and calculations to minimize the errors of inclusion and exclusion (Crosby et al., 2006). Fourth, to maximize effectiveness, clear and persuasive communication to identify barriers that solidify exclusion and demonstrate how these barriers are effectively eliminated within the program to positively change the lives of the target beneficiaries, legitimizes the affirmative action initiatives and it often attracts additional program support (Guinier, 2003).

NOTE

1. Entrepreneurship is loosely and often used to refer to any small business activity. However, Langevang and Gough (2012) argue that the term needs to be reserved for those who introduce radical innovations and transformational change in societies.

REFERENCES

Agwaya, R. and Mairura, S., 2019. Discussion Paper No. 226 of 2019 on Gender Productivity Gap in Kenyan Informal Enterprises.

Alam, M.S., 2010. Social exclusion of Muslims in India and deficient debates about affirmative action: Suggestions for a new approach. *South Asia Research*, *30*(1), pp.43–65.

Babajanian, B. and Hagen-Zanker, J., 2012. Social protection and social exclusion: An analytical framework to assess the links. *Background Note*. London: ODI.

Bateman, M. and Chang, H.J., 2012. Microfinance and the illusion of development: From hubris to nemesis in thirty years. *World Economic Review*, Volume 1, pp.13–36.

Burchardt, T., Le Grand, J., Piachaud, D., Hills, J. and Grand, L., 2002. Understanding social exclusion. London School of Economics.

Burger, R. and Jafta, R., 2010. Affirmative action in South Africa: An empirical assessment of the impact on labour market outcomes. *CRISE (Centre for Research on Inequality, Human Security and Ethnicity) Working Paper*, *76*, pp.9–36.

Coady, D., Grosh, M. and Hoddinott, J., 2004. *Targeting of transfers in developing countries: Review of lessons and experience*. Washington, DC: The World Bank.

Conning, J. and Kevane, M., 1999. Community based targeting mechanisms for social safety nets. *Mimeograph*. Department of Economics, Santa Clara University.

Costella, C. and Ovadiya, M., 2014. *Targeting households vulnerable to disasters and climate change* (No. 91777). Washington, DC: The World Bank.

Crosby, F.J., Iyer, A. and Sincharoen, S., 2006. Understanding affirmative action. *Annu. Rev. Psychol.*, *57*, pp.585–611.

Farrington, J., Sharp, K. and Sjoblom, D., 2007. Targeting approaches to cash transfers: Comparisons across Cambodia, India and Ethiopia. London: ODI.

Fox, L. and Sohnesen, T.P., 2012. *Household enterprises in sub-Saharan Africa – why they matter for growth, jobs, and livelihoods*. Washington, DC: The World Bank.

Guinier, L., 2003. Social change and democratic values: reconceptualizing affirmative action policy. *Western Journal of Black Studies*, *27*(1), 45.

Henry, C., Orser, B., Coleman, S., Foss, L. and Welter, F., 2017. Women's entrepreneurship policy: A 13-nation cross-country comparison. In Manolova, T.S., Brush, C.G., Edelman, L.F., Robb, A. and Welter, F. (Eds.), *Entrepreneurial ecosystems and growth of women's entrepreneurship* (pp. 244–278). Cheltenham, UK and Northampton, MA, USA: Edward Elgar Publishing.

Holzer, H. and Neumark, D., 2000. Assessing affirmative action. *Journal of Economic Literature*, *38*(3), pp.483–568.

International Labour Organization (ILO), 2018. Decent work and the sustainable development goals: A guidebook on SDG labour market indicators.

Jeffrey, C. and Dyson, J., 2013. Zigzag capitalism: Youth entrepreneurship in the contemporary global South. *Geoforum*, (49), pp.R1–R3.

Kabeer, N., 2000. Social exclusion, poverty and discrimination towards an analytical framework. *IDS Bulletin*, *31*(4), pp.83–97.

Kiende, C.K., Mukulu, E. and Odhiambo, R., 2019. Influence of organization innovation on the performance of small and medium women-owned enterprises in Kenya. *Journal of Entrepreneurship & Project Management*, *3*(1), pp.33–49.

Kilic, T., Whitney, E. and Winters, P., 2015. Decentralised beneficiary targeting in large-scale development programmes: Insights from the Malawi farm input subsidy programme. *Journal of African Economies*, *24*(1), pp.26–56.

Kiraka, R.N., Kobia, M. and Katwalo, A.M. (2013). Micro, small and medium enterprise growth and innovation in Kenya: A case of the women enterprise fund. *ICBE-RF Research Report No. 47/13*.

Kiriti-Nganga, T. and Mogeni, D., 2019. *Impact assessment of affirmative action funds in Kenya*. Nairobi: LAP LAMBERT Academic Publishing.

Laderchi, C.R., Saith, R. and Stewart, F., 2003. Does it matter that we do not agree on the definition of poverty? A comparison of four approaches. *Oxford Development Studies*, *31*(3), pp.243–274.

Langevang, T. and Gough, K.V., 2012. Diverging pathways: Young female employment and entrepreneurship in sub-Saharan Africa. *The Geographical Journal*, *178*(3), pp.242–252.

Loury, G.C., 2000. *Social exclusion and ethnic groups: The challenge to economics*. Boston University, Institute for Economic Development.

Mwongera, S. K., 2019. *Youth education, training and employment interventions in Kenya: Rapid baseline and situational analysis*. Unpublished.

Potts, D., 2005. Counter-urbanisation on the Zambian Copperbelt? Interpretations and implications. *Urban Studies*, *42*(4), pp.583–609.

Potts, D., 2008. The urban informal sector in sub-Saharan Africa: From bad to good (and back again?). *Development Southern Africa*, *25*(2), pp.151–167.

Ravallion, M., 2003. *Targeted transfers in poor countries: revisiting the tradeoffs and policy options* (Vol. 3048). World Bank Publications.

Republic of Kenya (RoK), 2013. *The Constitution of Kenya: 2010*. Chief Registrar of the Judiciary.

Republic of Kenya (RoK), 2016. *Micro, Small and Medium Establishment (MSME) Survey: Basic Report*. Kenya National Bureau of Statistics (KNBS), Nairobi.

Republic of Kenya (RoK), 2017. Address by Mr Joe Mucheru, EGH, Cabinet Secretary, Ministry Of ICT, during the launch of studio Mashinani and y254 TV channel at Komarock, Machakos County on Friday 17 March 2017. Ministry of Information, Communications and Technology.

Republic of Kenya (RoK), 2018. *The 2015/16 Kenya Integrated Household Budget Survey (KIHBS): Labour Force Basic Report*. Kenya National Bureau of Statistics (KNBS), Nairobi.

Republic of Kenya (RoK), 2019. *Report of the Pilot Assessment on the Implementation Status and Impact of Affirmative Action Funds in Kenya*. National Treasury and Planning, State Department for Planning.

Republic of Kenya (RoK), 2019a. *2019 Kenya Population and Housing Census: Volume I*.

Republic of Kenya (RoK), 2019b. *2019 Kenya Population and Housing Census: Volume II.*

Republic of Kenya (RoK), 2019c. *2019 Kenya Population and Housing Census: Volume III – Distribution of population by age, sex and administrative units.* Kenya Bureau of Statistics, Nairobi.

Republic of Kenya (RoK), 2019d. Report of the pilot assessment on the implementation status and impact of affirmative action funds in Kenya. The National Treasury and Planning State Department For Planning, Social and Governance Department.

Republic of Kenya (RoK), 2020. *Economic Survey 2020.* Kenya National Bureau of Statistics [KNBS], Nairobi.

Sen, A., 2000. Social Exclusion: Concept, Application, and Scrutiny. *Social Development Paper*, 1, pp. i–54.

Sivi, K., 2013. *Exploring Kenya's Inequality: Pulling Apart or Pooling Together?* Nairobi, Kenya National Bureau of Statistics (KNBS) and Society for International Development (SID).

Sivi, K., 2016. Changing demographics: Is Kenya's political stability guaranteed? In Khan, F., Grundling, E., Ruiters, G., Ndevu, Z. and Baloyi, B. (Eds.), *State, governance and development in Africa* (pp. 80–99). South Africa: UCT Press.

Sivi, K., 2020. *Fear of Monday Morning: A Structural Perspective of Youth Un/ employment and How To Be Future Ready.* PhD Unpublished Manuscript, Regent University, Virginia Beach, USA.

Union, A., 2011. The African Youth Decade 2009–2018 Plan of Action. *Accelerating Youth Empowerment for Sustainable Development: Road Map towards the Implementation of the African Youth Charter.* Addis Ababa, Ethiopia.

Women Enterprise Fund [WEF], 2018. Statement by ENG. Charles Mwirigi, CEO-Women Enterprise Fund. https://www.wef.co.ke/index.php/component/ jdownloads/send/8-program-activities-reports/71-public-accountability-statement -for-fy-2017-2018?Itemid=0/

11. Making gendered science: a feminist perspective on the epistemology of innovation based on science and technology studies

Ilenia Picardi

1. INTRODUCTION

In the last two decades, gender equity in research and innovation has become a priority of the European Research Area (ERA) and a key issue for assessing and grounding accountability in science. The European Commission set three main objectives to foster related changes at scientific and research institutions: gender equality in scientific careers, gender balance in decision-making and the integration of a gender dimension into the content of research and innovation. While several studies have concentrated on the first two aims, analyzing the mechanisms that create gender imbalances in science (Benschop, 2009; van den Brink and Benschop, 2012, 2014; Murgia and Poggia, 2018; Picardi, 2018, 2020; O'Connor and White, 2021), the current work focuses on the last aim, investigating the meanings of gender equity in research and innovation promoted by the European Union (EU) policy.

The European Commission's gender equality strategy defines the integration of a gender dimension into research and innovation content as a primary goal to reaffirm the commitment of European government bodies to gender equality in science (European Commission, 2021a). Moreover, it recommended this theme as a key area in the Gender Equality Plan (GEP), requiring that all public bodies, higher education institutions and research organizations have a GEP in order to receive Horizon Europe funding for calls with deadlines in 2022 and onwards (European Commission, 2021b). This policy is the last stage of a process initiated by national and international institutions in the 1990s to combat women's under-representation in science and technology, for which scholars have identified three different approaches (Schiebinger, 2008; Schiebinger and Schraudner, 2011). During the first stage of this process, government policies on gender equity in research and academia pushed to adopt intervention strategies based on the 'fixing the women' approach. These measures were based mainly on traditional mentoring, researching female role models and building women's networks. They aimed, on the one hand, to encourage girls to undertake scientific studies and, on the other hand, to support women in scientific and technological career paths (Cacace, 2009). In 2009, the experts of *Helsinki group on Gender in Research and Innovation* provided the European Commission with the *Gender and Research Beyond 2009* (European Commission, 2009) document, urging the adoption of a new recommendation by shifting policies' focus from individual women to institutions. Under this push, the Seventh Framework Program changed the commission's activities regarding women in science, promoting structural change and the 'fixing the institution' season (European Commission, 2011).

In the last ten years, European policies have promoted a third approach to encourage gender equality in science. This 'fixing the knowledge' approach focuses on 'overcoming gender bias in science and technology by designing gender analysis into all phases of basic and applied research – from setting priorities, to funding decisions, to establishing project objectives and methodologies, to data gathering, to evaluating results, and transferring ideas to markets' (Schiebinger and Schraudner, 2011, p. 155). In accordance with this perspective, in 2009 Stanford University launched the *Gendered Innovations Project* (European Commission, 2013), with support from the European Commission and the US National Science Foundation, aiming to develop gender and sex analysis methods for natural scientists and engineers (Schiebinger and Schraudner, 2011; Schiebinger et al., 2011). The project developed guidelines to integrate a gender focus into the priorities and questions addressed by scientific and technological research. At the same time, the World Health Organization (WHO) developed a gender-sensitive assessment tool (World Health Organization, 2011), the Organization for the Study of Sexual Differences (OSSD) developed advanced methods of sex and gender analysis for the life and health sciences[1] and, later, the Canadian Institutes of Health Research developed online training modules to integrate sex and gender analysis into biomedical research (Canadian Institutes of Health Research, 2017). Concurrently, peer-review journals have implemented editorial guidelines to use sex and gender analysis as one of assessment's criteria for publication of papers (Tannenbaum et al., 2019).

In this chapter, we explore the concept of *gendered innovation* (GI) that has been promoted recently by EU policies to develop scientific research and technological innovation. Our perspective derives from the field of science and technology studies (STS) in its intersection with feminist epistemology. These perspectives allow us to examine how, in EU policies' discursive practices, *gender* informs the technoscientific governance of researchers and innovation and, reciprocally, how technoscientific governance informs the concept of *gender* and gendered practices among scientific and research institutions. Section two introduces the theoretical framework used in this analysis. The third section presents our methodology and data. The fourth section describes the *technological frame* (Bijker, 1987, 1995) of GI that emerged in this study. Then, the final section discusses our results and presents our conclusions. In concluding, we underline the relevance of an ontological model to present a new focus on the *sociomateriality* of gender innovations.

2. GENDER AND TECHNOSCIENCE IN SCIENCE AND TECHNOLOGY STUDIES PERSPECTIVES AND FEMINIST EPISTEMOLOGY

STS is an interdisciplinary research field which, since the 1970s, has promoted a profound renewal of the sociological, historical and philosophical study of science; its interests in technology and innovation then expanded during the 1980s (Cozza, 2020; Magaudda and Neresini, 2020). From the STS perspective, science and technology are investigated through the unitary concept of *technoscience*. Moreover, they are interpreted as the outcome of social processes by understanding the approaches and methodologies that highlight their practical characteristics and situation in particular contexts.

Within the STS field, the relationship between *gender* and *technoscience* has been analyzed from different perspectives and different conceptions of gender equity developed within feminist literature (Agodi and Picardi, 2020). Feminist STS scholars have shown how women's marginalization from technoscientific communities continuously and profoundly influences design, technical content and the use of technological devices and artefacts. Over the last few decades, these scholars have emphasized women's technical knowledge – for example, by analyzing and re-evaluating technologies of care and everyday life (Cowan, 1976; Stanley, 1995). Consistently with recent perspectives of post-structuralist feminism – which define *gender* in performative terms and as continuously reproduced in social interaction (Butler, 1999) – STS scholars have theorized the relationship between *gender* and *technology* through mutual modelling (Berg, 1996; Faulkner, 2001; Lie, 2003). This approach has analyzed not only gender *in* technology and the gender *of* technology but also gender *as a product of* technology. Moreover, these analyses have fruitfully confronted *practice theory*, which analyses the making of gender through the implementation of gendered practices as an integral part of social processes (Connell, 1987; West and Zimmerman, 1987) and as part of the images, ideologies and distributions of power in various sectors of social and scientific life.

In this work, we adopt the STS notions of *sociomateriality* and *relational ontology* to reconceptualize GI by dismantling the dualism that has continually characterized much of the previous research on gender and science. In accordance with the *symmetry principle*, that suggests that technological elements are shaped by each other, and defines *technological artefacts* symmetrically to humans, as equivalent participants in a network of humans and non-humans (Pickering, 1995; Knorr Cetina, 1997; Schatzki, 2002; Barad, 2003; Latour, 2005), STS scholars have proposed the concept of *sociomateriality* to focus on how meanings and materiality interconnect and interrelate in everyday practices (Barad, 2007; Introna, 2007; Suchman, 2007). This relational ontology presumes that the social and the material are inherently inseparable. As Barad (2003, p. 816) argues, this constitutive *entanglement* does not presume independent or even interdependent entities with distinct and inherent characteristics. This relational ontology rejects 'a dualistic view of agency which claims that agency is located either in the human or in the artefact' (Introna, 2007, p. 3). From this perspective, entities and individuals never pre-exist discretely, with determinate boundaries; rather, they combine or interact with other pre-existing entities and individuals. Moreover, their capacities for action are seen to be enacted in practice. The focus of this perspective is on constitutive entanglements (e.g., configurations, networks, associations, mangles, and assemblages) of humans and technologies. It also posits the social and technical as 'ontologically inseparable from the start' (Introna, 2007, p. 1). Additionally, as Suchman (2007, p. 257) notes, 'The starting place comprises configurations of always already interrelated, reiterated sociomaterial practices.'

Within the theoretical approach of *agential realism* (Barad, 2003), Karen Barad has developed the concept of *apparatuses* to analyze the nature of scientific practices (2007). Barad advances her ontological proposal through a *diffractive* reading of Bohr's analyses of apparatuses which, at the beginning of the last century, revealed the atom's double-wave corpuscular nature, and of Foucault's analyses of *apparatuses* as forms through which biopower can exercise order on bodies, fixing and constraining movements. According to Barad:

> Apparatuses are not inscription devices, scientific instruments set in place before the action happens, or machines that mediate the dialectic of resistance and accommodation between human and nonhuman laboratory actors.... Apparatuses are neither neutral probes of the natural world nor structures that deterministically impose some particular outcome. Significantly, in an agential realism account, the notion of apparatus is not premised on the inherent divisions between the social and the scientific, the human and the nonhuman, nature and culture. Apparatuses are the practices through which these divisions are constituted... Apparatuses are dynamic (re)configurings of the world, specific agential practices/intra-actions/performances through which specific exclusionary boundaries are enacted. (Barad, 2007, p. 169)

Barad uses the concept of *apparatuses* to 'refer to specific material-discursive practices that help to constitute phenomena through the production of knowledge about them' (Orlikowski, 2009, p. 136). From this perspective, phenomena's boundaries and properties are not previously defined ontologically; rather, they are determined only in relation to the observer apparatus's specificity. Thus, apparatuses perform *agential cuts* that stabilize or destabilize distinctions and boundaries within phenomena in practice.

3.   METHODOLOGY AND ANALYSIS

The framework introduced in the previous paragraph defines the theoretical outline through which this study investigates Europe's policies on research, innovation and gender equity. We assume that funding agencies' provisions are themselves technologies that define the frames in which technoscientific knowledge is developed. Thus, European policies on research and innovation can be analyzed as *apparatuses of technoscientific governance of research*. In particular, we investigate the European programme to promote gender dimension in science and GI as *apparatuses* of gender equity's construction in European science.

Therefore, we reconstruct the *technological frame* (Bijker, 1987, 1995) of GI as a set of ideas, theories and practices promoted by the EU policy on gender dimension in research and innovation. To this aim we have analyzed the documents (webpages, reports, papers, videos, webinars, factsheets and images) pertaining to GI published by the European Commission to promote GI and gender diversity in research and innovation. These corpora are analyzed as a set of material-discursive practices that construct gendered meaning in technoscientific research and gender equity in science. In turn, this analysis allows us to investigate how European policies construct the meanings of *gender* and *gender equity* at scientific institutions.

The data used in this research were analyzed qualitatively (Lieblich et al., 1998; Schreier, 2012); to identify actions concealed and abstracted in the texts and focus on their ideological implications, we used critical discourse analysis (van Dijk, 1985; Fairclough, 1992, 2006; Wodak and Meyer, 2009). To explore, classify and analyze the data, we used NVivo software.[2]

The following section explores the *technological frame* of EU policies on gender dimension in research and innovation identifying the *epistemic pitfalls* of this frame through the lenses of STS analysis and feminist epistemology.

4.   EPISTEMIC PITFALLS IN THE TECHNOLOGICAL FRAME OF GENDER INNOVATIONS

Since the first documents introducing the concept (Schiebinger, 2008, 2010a; Schiebinger et al., 2011; Schiebinger and Schraudner, 2011; European Commission, 2013), GI has been described as a process that aims to improve the quality of research, making the technological transfer of research into the market more efficient and productive. The intent is to stimulate innovation in the design of new products, processes, infrastructures, services and technologies in order to promote human well-being and gender equity, meet the needs of complex and diverse user groups and improve competitiveness and sustainability globally.

According to Londa Schiebinger, the principal investigator of *Gendered Innovations Project* (European Commission, 2013):

> Innovation is what makes the world tick. Including gender analysis in science, medicine, and engineering can spark creativity by offering new perspectives, posing new questions, and opening new areas to research. (Schiebinger and Schraudner, 2011, p. 155)

The report *Gendered Innovations. How Gender Analysis Contributes to Research*, published by the European Commission in 2013, defines *gender innovation* as 'processes that integrate sex and gender analysis into all phases of basic and applied research to assure excellence and quality in outcomes' (European Commission, 2013). Schiebinger proposes the use of gender as a quality dimension in the research process and, at the same time, in the transfer of new ideas to the market. The report describes sex and gender bias in science as 'socially harmful and expensive', missing market opportunities:

> In engineering, for example, assuming a male default can produce errors in machine translation. In basic research, failing to use appropriate samples of male and female cells, tissues, and animals yields faulty results. In medicine, not recognizing osteoporosis as a male disease delays diagnosis and treatment in men. In city planning, not collecting data on caregiving work leads to inefficient transportation systems. It is crucially important to identify gender bias and understand how it operates in science and technology. But analysis cannot stop there. The Report Gendered Innovations offered methods of sex and gender analysis to scientists and engineers, Integrating these methods into basic and applied research produces excellence in science, health and medicine, and engineering research, policy, and practice. (European Commission, 2013)

More recently, Nielsen et al. (2018) distinguished three approaches to gender diversity in science: (1) diversity in research teams, (2) diversity in research methods and (3) diversity in research questions. The first approach concerns research teams' composition. It focuses on the different ideas, beliefs and perspectives that women, men and gender-diverse people bring to the team. Meanwhile, the second approach concerns diversifying research methods through gender and sex analysis (GSA). This approach is based on an increasing body of literature that has developed state-of-the-art methods for GSA (Bührer and Schraudner, 2006; Schiebinger and Klinge, 2013; Buitendijk and Maes, 2015; European Commission, 2015; Sánchez de Madariaga and de Gregorio Hurtado, 2016). Moreover, this approach aims to demonstrate that GSA's integration into research design can yield new insights that enhance the external validity and precision of scientific research with human outcomes. Finally, the third approach to gender diversity concerns diversity in research questions. In this context, diversity is evaluated by exploring how new actors' entry into scientific disciplines influences research priorities and agendas, or vice versa (for example, women's entry into traditionally masculine disciplines, such as biomedicine, or men's entry into traditionally feminine disciplines, such as nursing). This approach measures the links between changing gender demographics, research questions and research priorities. It assumes fundamentally that social norms and expectations cultivate variations in the interests and perspectives of women, men and gender-diverse people – and that increased variation in such interests and perspectives can broaden agendas and discoveries.

Source: Authors' own elaboration, based on the work of Nielsen et al. (2018).

Figure 11.1   Technological frame of gender innovations

The technological GI frame that has emerged from this analysis is represented in Figure 11.1. In the following subsections, we underline three *epistemic pitfalls* of this frame from an STS perspective on innovation (Rip and Kemp, 1998; Geels, 2002; Wynne and Felt, 2007; Neresini, 2020), as well as through feminist epistemologies and feminist studies on science and technologies. The first pitfall concerns the *operationalization of gender* in innovation.

Meanwhile, the second pitfall lies in conceiving of GI as *an emergent process* (Orlikowski, 2009). Finally, the third pitfall is the reduction of gender equity to its neoliberal acceptance.

4.1   Operationalizing Gender in Innovation

The introductions to analyzed EU documents on gender dimension in research and innovation effectively clarify the distinction between *sex* and *gender*, and the concepts *gender identities* and *sexual orientations*. However, case studies, methods and research practices reported to support the construction of a gendered dimension in research and innovation particularly emphasize gender diversity as an *attribute*, rather than a *performance*. Therefore, the first pitfall of the technological frame of gendered innovations concerns the *operationalization of gender* in technoscientific research.

In the three approaches to gender diversity in science that Nielsen et al. (2018) observed, gender is operationalized as an attribute of researchers, designers, and the producers, users and consumers of technological innovation, or it can be operationalized as a property of innovation itself (*gendered*). Such approaches centre the focus on gender as *static*, rather than gender as *processual* – as observable in 'making gender' processes and in looking at 'gender in its making' (West and Zimmerman, 1987). STS research has examined how gender informs technology and, at the same time, how technology informs gender. The gender of sociotechnical devices – like other characteristics that connote the *sociomateriality* and symbolic character of technoscience – does not manifest exclusively in design. Rather, it is also configured or reconfigured, even subsequently to products' development and dissemination. For example, this process can take place in marketing, sales, use or consumption. In this sense, STS research has importantly contributed to the deconstruction of the 'designer-user' and 'production–consumption' dichotomies, emphasizing contributions' circularity in the development of technological artefacts (Cowan, 1983). Home appliances since the 1950s exemplify a technology breaking into a domain that is heavily loaded with traditional gendered meanings of social roles. These meanings are imprinted within the technological artefacts in a *gender script* by the designers who, in turn, configure their potential users (Cockburn and Ormrod, 1993; Oudshoorn et al., 2004).

A classic example is the design of the electric refrigerator, which was configured to coincide with single-family homes' spread after World War II. The domestic and public spheres were clearly separated – a distinctive feature of modern society – assigning women additional family management tasks which were, thus, distinct from broader social and service networks (Wajcman, 2004). The technological artefact design contributed to reproducing and strengthening the pre-existent gender order. However, over the past two decades, STS studies have theorized the relationship between gender and technology as a reciprocal modelling relationship (Berg, 1996; Faulkner, 2001; Lie, 2003). Technology, gender and corporeality are not only socially constructed but also interconnected and mutually modelled, resulting from complex and iteratively transformative processes. Scholars analysed several examples of these processes; just to give one example, we can consider the microwave oven, with technology descended from military radar. The microwave oven was originally designed for food preparation in US navy submarines, and later was promoted in the market as a device for men, especially single men, who needed to reheat prepared food. The final form of the microwave, which redefined the gendered character of the user, has resulted from a transformative process in which users – in particular women that appropriated this domestic technology – switched designed targets by the designers (Cockburn and Ormrod, 1993).

In line with this perspective, Judy Wajcman's (2004) *techno-feminist* approach suggests that technological artefacts are both the conditioning element and product of gender relations. Gender relations are materialized in technology, and technological devices have a gender dimension since they exist in sociotechnical systems that are informed by gender relations (Wajcman, 2010). Meanwhile, masculinity and femininity – in turn – acquire meaning and character through their inscription and incorporation into technological devices. Gender relations can be considered to materialize in technological innovation processes, in which masculinity and femininity acquire meaning and character through their inscription and incorporation into technological devices *and* their uses.

4.2   Conceiving Gender Innovation as an Emergent Process

Figure 11.2 presents an example diagram of gender methods applied to an innovation process (European Commission, 2013, p. 2018). This diagram effectively exemplifies the second epistemic pitfall of the GI technological frame: conceptualizing GI as an *emerging process*. Orlikowski (2009) introduces the concept of an 'emergent process' to describe studies that interpret technology as a product of ongoing human interpretations and interactions, thus highlighting the contextually and historically contingent aspect of this process. This conception takes up the widespread idea that innovation results from a process that begins with a scientific discovery that is then applied to a new technological artefact which, ultimately, spreads to society, influencing individuals and transforming their habits, behaviours and culture (Wynne and Felt, 2007; Neresini, 2020). This view, moreover, assumes that technological artefacts and their meanings stabilize during their design. STS scholars have questioned this linear conception of innovation. From the STS perspective, science, technology and society are not separate fields and the discoverers, inventors and users of technology are likewise not so clearly distinct. Innovation is not produced in a space separated from the rest of society and then diffused or transferred to society. Instead, innovation results from a long, reticular process comprising small advances, deviations and decisive turning points. This process cannot be identified or understood without examining the set of actors – often unpredictable – who participate in it. In this way, innovation becomes the emerging product of a large-scale 'collective experimentation', rather than the result of a sudden illumination, an unexpected stroke of luck or a foreseeable technological leap (Wynne and Felt, 2007). The STS literature proposes a co-evolutionary conception of innovation, which includes individual and collective actors, norms, technological objects, scientific knowledge, skills and knowledge that are neither codified nor codifiable.

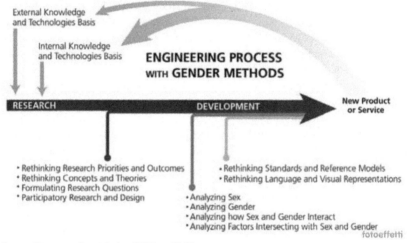

Source: European Commission (2013, p. 2018).

Figure 11.2   Proposed gender innovation method to integrate gender into the engineering innovation process

The approach to GI as an emerging process promoted by the European Commission appears to minimize the continuous and open process of reinterpretation and reworking that modifies and updates technological artefacts during their use over time (Woolgar and Cooper, 1999; Wajcman, 2000). Therefore, the construction of gender and the modification of its meanings are involved in the same processes of technological innovation. As Wajcman (2002, p. 353) notes: 'Technological change is an entirely contingent and heterogeneous process... In this way users can radically change the meanings and the deployment of technologies'. Furthermore, as Winner (1993) observes, focusing on both grounded and contingent interpretations and interactions in technology's design and use, the emerging-process perspective overlooks technology's broader political and social consequences. The focus-centric perspective of the emergent process prevents assigning agency to the distinctive human capacities that interact with human interpretations and social action (Faulkner and Runde, 2009). Therefore, this perspective cannot hypothesize or theorize about technological artefacts' material effects (Orlikowski, 2009). In other words, this conception of GI cannot offer widely applicable insights into how technologies shape organizations and societies – or how they could enhance the gender equity processes they aim to promote.

4.3 Focusing on Gender Equity's Neoliberal Acceptance

According to our analysis, the GI technological frame supported by EU policies is persistently representing science and technology as 'driving forces for economic development and for improving the well-being of individuals and their communities', as already happened in the first decade of this century (Schiebinger, 2010a). It reiterates the conception of technology as 'relatively autonomous driver of organizational change and, as such, that it has significant and predictable impacts on various human and organizational outcomes, such as governance structures, work routines, information flows, decision making, individual productivity and firm performance' (Orlikowski, 2009, p. 129). This view suggests that technological innovation is a unique driver both for economic and social progress.

The European Commission recently remarked upon the connection between gender equity, innovation, business and social needs in its *Gender Equality Strategy*:

> Gender equality is ... an essential condition for an innovative, competitive and thriving European economy. In business, politics and society as a whole, we can only reach our full potential if we use all of our talent and diversity. Gender equality brings more jobs and higher productivity – a potential which needs to be realized as we embrace the green and digital transitions and face up to our demographic challenges. (European Commission, 2020)

As Schiebinger argued:

> Gender bias limits the objectivity and excellence of science and technology, and hence its potential benefits to society... But focusing on bias is not a productive strategy. We need to enhance scientific excellence by mainstreaming gender analysis into science and technology. Gendered innovations [projects] employs gender analysis as a resource to create new knowledge or design. (Schiebinger, 2010b)

Indeed, one of the most significant effects that the GI frame has introduced into discussions is motivating institutional change by prioritizing business opportunities, while shifting themes of equity and social justice to the background. The approach that focuses on GI as a source of market innovation reveals the EU's implicit adoption of a neoliberal perspective on gender equity. This implicit assumption about gender equality, promoted by neoliberal feminism, is the third epistemic pitfall of the EU's GI frame.

According to neoliberal feminism, also known as the 'equal opportunities' perspective, all individuals – regardless of their gender – should have equal rights and equal opportunities to compete in the labour market (Squires, 1999; Verloo, 2005). In this approach, gender equality consists of *achieving* equality; it aims, therefore, to eliminate the barriers that determine women's exclusion from key positions in society without problematizing male gendered norms inscribed in societal organization (Meyerson and Kolb, 2000; Calás and Smircich, 2006). In the feminist debate, this conception of *gender equality* is flanked by other views. One such alternative is the *standpoint perspective* – according to which gender equity's goal is not to integrate women into the current order but, rather, to recognize and reconstruct non-hegemonic gender identities in politics and society while subverting the male-dominated order (Squires, 1999). Another such perspective is *post-equity* (Meyerson and Kolb, 2000), according to which gender is a social practice (not an attribute that characterizes individuals) and gender equity seeks to modify the gender structures and practices that build and re-build gender daily. Gender equity is a multidimensional concept that continually takes on many simple and broader meanings in different times and contexts (Verloo, 2005; Verloo and Lombardo, 2007).

Critical discourse analysis of EU documents reveals the GI technological frame being contaminated by the perspectives of difference or *standpoints* and references to *intersectionality*. However, the neoliberal approach's vision of equal opportunities – and its trusting the market to regulate not only economic well-being but also social development – dominate this frame. GI provides research methodologies to consider the biological characteristics (sex) and socio-cultural factors gendering societal organization. However, few case studies in the GI repertoire (toolkits, guidelines, exemplar projects) directly address the gendered practices embedded in the research process or, more generally, in the social processes through which scientific knowledge is produced, evaluated and circulated – whose relevance has been highlighted by the sociology and epistemology of science and analyzed in the STS context (Harding, 1986; Haraway, 1988, 1997).

The implicit reference of EU policies to the neoliberal theoretical framework, its value and its symbolic dimensions, informs the mainstreaming approach proposed by European Commission documents on research and innovation. This approach, in turn, defines the frameworks in which funding is provided to support interventions for gender equity in academia and research.

5. GENDER'S SOCIOMATERIALITY WITHIN AND THROUGH THE INNOVATION PRACTICES OF TECHNOSCIENTIFIC RESEARCH

In the last decades, scientific institutions have been an arena for profound transformations, redefining scientific research. In this process, competitions to access public funding – framed by governance agencies – continually define not only the aims and meanings of scientific research but also the ideas, values and aims that underlie such research and its social accountability. In this technoscientific governance frame, European research funding agencies have taken on decisive roles in both encouraging and guiding the development of gender equity in science. This chapter has investigated the EU policy on gender in research and innovation, analysing the GI as a specific set of material-discursive practices that constitute the vision and practices of gender equity through knowledge production as an apparatus that helps construct gender equity.

This analysis has emphasized the persistence, within the GI technological frame promoted by the European Commission documents on gender dimension in research and innovation, of a classical, deterministic approach to innovation established in the neoliberal perspective that permeates the Gender Mainstreaming in Europe (Squires, 2005; Verloo, 2005). This frame primarily depicts technologies as homogeneous and stable artefacts which aim to promote well-being and equality as a direct consequence of their use. We have underlined how the idea of technology as a relatively fixed set of stable capabilities obscures the multiple, disordered, complex and dynamic aspects of technologies in practice (de Laet and Mol, 2000). The emphasis on the 'uses' and 'impacts' of GI hides 'the constitutive interweaving and mutual inter-definition of human and material action' (Pickering, 1995, p. 26). In the dominant European frame of GI, the emergent human-centred focus inhibits the assignment of agency to the distinctive technological capabilities that interact with human interpretations and social action (Faulkner and Runde, 2009). This approach fails to grasp the multiple, contingent ways in which human action shapes a technology and the interactions with that technology (Steinkuehler, 2006; Taylor, 2006). This study, therefore, suggests the development of an *entanglement* perspective on the analysis of gender in research. Rather than aiming to understand gender's impact on knowledge or technology, or its interpretations and interactions by developers or human users, this perspective could focus on the dynamic sociomaterial configurations embedded in practices. Moreover, this perspective could add reflexivity to the performativity of specific material-discursive practices that constitute gender equity while simultaneously producing knowledge about gender equity.

Indeed, all practices (including research practices) are configured by some specific sociomateriality. Therefore, to investigate the gender dimension of research and innovation, it is necessary to study dynamic and multiple sociomaterial reconfigurations as they arise in practice, observing gender in the making, in the reticular, complex processes that characterize research and innovation. Finally, our analysis suggests a broader thematization of gender equity's meanings in science. The adoption of best practices for gender equity proposed by European projects' toolkits, guidelines and action plans can risk empty rhetoric and bureaucracy if they are not realized through transformative, sociomaterial scientific practices. Such practices can recognize the value of diversity and inclusiveness through a critical review of gendered and intersectional perspectives, assessing the ambiguities that underlie the institution of science itself across its constituent elements. Gender equity cannot be achieved simply by breaking the *glass ceiling* through acquiring models of excellence that embody individualistic, competitive styles and regarding individuals who do not follow predesigned paths as wasted resources. Instead, gender equity must be built through a long process of construction and deconstruction of daily material-discursive practices that occur alongside academic work, research and innovation processes.

NOTES

1.   https: //www.ossdweb.org/.
2.   NVivo is a CAQDAS (Computer Assisted Qualitative Data Analysis) program produced by Qualitative Software Research for the analysis of texts, images, and multimedia documents.

REFERENCES

Agodi, M. C. and Picardi I. (2020). Genere e corpo. In P. Magaudda and F. Neresini (Eds), *Gli studi sociali sulla scienza e la tecnologia* (pp. 175–190). Il Mulino.
Barad, K. (2003). Posthumanist performativity: Toward an understanding of how matter comes to matter. *Signs, 28*(3), 801–831.
Barad, K. (2007). *Meeting the university halfway: Quantum physics and the entanglement of matter and meaning.* Duke University Press.
Benschop, Y. (2009). The micropolitics of gendering in networking. *Gender, Work & Organization, 16*(2), 217–237.
Berg, A. (1996). *Digital feminism* [doctoral thesis]. Trondheim, Norwegian University of Science and Technology.
Bijker, W. (1995). *Of bicycles, Bakelites, and bulbs. Toward a theory of sociotechnical change.* MIT Press.

Bijker, W. E. (1987). *The social construction of Bakelite. Toward a theory of invention.* In W. E. Bijker, T. P. Hughes and T. Pinch (Eds), *The social construction of technological systems* (pp. 159–187). MIT Press.

Bührer, S. and Schraudner, M. (2006). *Gender-Aspekte in der Forschung: Wie können Gender-Aspekte in Forschungsvorhaben erkannt und bewertet arden?* Frauenhofer IRB Verlag.

Buitendijk, S. and Maes, K. (2015). *Gendered research and innovation: Integrating sex and gender analysis into the research process.* League of European Research Universities.

Butler, J. (1999). *Gender trouble: Feminism and the subversion of identity.* Routledge.

Cacace, M. (2009). *Guidelines for gender: Equality programmes in science. Practising gender equality in science (PraGES).* https://ec.europa.eu/research/swafs/pdf/pub _gender_equality/prages-guidelines_en.pdf.

Calás, M., and Smircich, L. (2006). From the 'women's point of view' ten years later: Towards a feminist organization studies. In S. Clegg, C. Hardy, T. Lawrence and W. Nord (Eds), *The Sage handbook of organization studies* (pp. 284–346). Sage Publications.

Canadian Institutes of Health Research (2017). *Online Training Modules: Integrating Sex & Gender in Health Research.* http://www.cihr-irsc.gc.ca/e/49347.html.

Cockburn, C., and Ormrod, S. (1993). *Gender and technology in the making.* Sage Publications.

Connell, B. (1987). *Gender and power.* Polity Press.

Cowan, R. S. (1976). The 'Industrial Revolution' in the home: Household technology and social change in the twentieth century. *Technology and Culture, 17*(1), 1–23.

Cowan, R. S. (1983). *More work for mother. The ironies of household technology from the open hearth to the microwave.* Basic Books.

Cozza, M. (2020). *Key concepts in science and technology studies.* Studentlitteratur AB.

de Laet, M. and Mol, A. (2000). The Zimbabwe bush pump: Mechanics of a fluid technology. *Social Studies of Science, 30*(2), 225–263.

European Commission. (2009). *Gender and research beyond 2009. Position paper by the Helsinki Group on women in science.* http://ec.europa.eu/research/science -society/document_library/pdf_06/gender-and-research-beyond-2009_en.pdf.

European Commission. (2011). *Structural change in research institutions: Enhancing excellence, gender equality and efficiency in research and innovation.* http://ec .europa.eu/research/sciencesociety/index.cfmfuseaction public.topic&id=1406.

European Commission. (2013). *Gendered innovations. How gender analysis contributes to research.* http://ec.europa.eu/research/sciencesociety/document_library/pdf _06/gendered_innovations.pdf.

European Commission. (2015). *For a better integration of the gender dimension in Horizon 2020 Work Programme 2016–2017.* http://ec.europa.eu/transparency/ regexpert/index.cfm?do=groupDetail.groupDetailDoc&id=18892&no=1.

European Commission (2020). Communication from the Commission to the European Parliament, the Council and the European Economic and Social Committee and the Committee of the Regions. *A Union of Equality: Gender equality strategy 2020–2025.* https://eur-lex.europa.eu/legal-content/EN/TXT/?uri=CELEX%3A52020DC0152.

European Commission. (2021a). *The Commission's gender equality strategy.* https:// ec.europa.eu/info/research-and-innovation/strategy/strategy-2020-2024/democracy -and-rights/gender-equality-research-and-innovation_en.

European Commission. (2021b). *General annexes to Horizon Europe 2021–2022 work programme.* https://ec.europa.eu/info/funding-tenders/opportunities/docs/2021 -2027/horizon/wp-call/2021-2022/wp-13-general-annexes_horizon-2021-2022_en .pdf.

Fairclough N. (1992). *Discourse and social change.* Cambridge: Polity Press, 2006.

Faulkner, P. and Runde, J. (2009). On the identity of technological objects and user innovations in function. *Academy of Management Review, 34*(3), 442–462.

Faulkner, W. (2001). The technology question in feminism: A view from feminist technology studies. *Women's Studies International Forum, 24*(1), 79–95.

Geels, F. W. (2002). Technological transitions as evolutionary reconfiguration processes. A multilevel perspective and a case-study. *Research Policy,* 31, 1257–1274.

Haraway, D. (1988). Situated knowledges. The science question in feminism and the privilege of partial perspective. *Feminist Studies,* 14, 575–609.

Haraway, D. (1997). *Modest_Witness@Second_Millennium_ FemaleMan©_Meets_ OncoMouse™. Feminism and Technoscience.* Routledge.

Harding, S. (1986). *The science question in feminism.* Cornell University Press.

Introna, L. D. (2007). *Towards a post-human intra-actional account of sociomaterial agency (and morality)* (paper prepared for the Moral Agency and Technical Artefacts Workshop). The Hague, Netherlands Institute for Advanced Study.

Knorr Cetina, K. (1997). Sociality with objects: Social relations in postsocial knowledge societies. *Theory, Culture & Society, 14*(4), 1–30.

Latour, B. (2005). *Reassembling the social: An introduction to actor-network-theory.* Oxford University Press.

Lie, M. (Ed.) (2003). *He, she and IT revisited: New perspectives on gender in the information society.* Gyldendal Akademisk.

Lieblich A., Tuval-Mashiach R. and Zilber T. (1998). *Applied social research methods: Narrative research.* Thousand Oaks, CA: Sage Publications.

Magaudda, P. and Neresini, F. (Eds) (2020). *Gli studi sociali sulla scienza e la tecnologia.* Il Mulino.

Meyerson, D. E. and Kolb, D. M. (2000). Moving out of the 'armchair': Developing a framework to bridge the gap between feminist theory and practice. *Organization, 7*(4), 553–571.

Murgia, A. and Poggio, B. (2018). *Gender and precarious research careers: A comparative analysis.* Routledge. https://doi.org/10.4324/9781315201245.

Neresini, F. (2020). L'innovazione tecnologica come processo coevolutivo. In P. Magaudda and F. Neresini (Eds), *Gli studi sociali sulla scienza e la tecnologia* (pp. 59–74). Il Mulino.

Nielsen, M. W., Bloch, C. W. and Schiebinger, L. (2018). Making gender diversity work for scientific discovery and innovation. *Nature Human Behaviour,* 2, 726–734. https://doi.org/10.1038/s41562-018-0433-1.

O'Connor, P. and White, K. (Eds) (2021). *Gender, power and higher education in a globalised world* (pp. 187–207). Palgrave Macmillan. ISBN: 978-3-030-69687-0.

Orlikowski, W. J. (2009). The sociomateriality of organisational life: Considering technology in management research. *Cambridge Journal of Economics, 34*(1), 125–141.

Oudshoorn, N., Rommes, E. and Stienstra, M. (2004). Configuring the user as everybody: Gender and design cultures in information and communication technologies. *Science, Technology, & Human Values, 29*(1), pp. 30–63.

Picardi, I. (2018). *Through the glass labyrinth of science: Mapping gendering processes in academia.* [doctoral thesis]. University of Naples Federico II.

Picardi, I. (2020). *Labirinti di cristallo. Strutture di genere nella ricerca e nell'accademia.* Franco Angeli.

Pickering, A. (1995). *The mangle of practice: Time, agency and science.* The University of Chicago Press.

Rip, A. and Kemp, R. (1998). Technological change. In S. Rayner and E. L. Malone (Eds), *Human Choice and Climate Change* (pp. 327–399). Battelle Press.

Sánchez de Madariaga, I. and de Gregorio Hurtado, S. (Eds) (2016). *Advancing gender in research, innovation and sustainable development.* Fundación General de la Universidad Politécnica de Madrid.

Schatzki, T.R. (2002). *The site of the social: A philosophical account of the constitution of social life and change.* Pennsylvania State University Press.

Schiebinger, L. (2008). *Gendered innovations in science and engineering.* Stanford University Press. http://www.sup.org/books/title/?id=11925.

Schiebinger, L. (2010a). *Gender science technology.* United Nations Division for the Advancement of Women (DAW, part of UN Women), United Nations Educational, Scientific and Cultural Organization (UNESCO). https://www.un.org/womenwatch/daw/egm/gst_2010/.

Schiebinger, L. (2010b). *Gender, science and technology.* United Nations' Expert Group Meeting on Gender, Science, and Technology, September 2010 in Paris. https://www.un.org/womenwatch/daw/egm/gst_2010/presentations/Presentation-Schiebinger-BP1EGMST.pdf.

Schiebinger, L. and Klinge, I. (2013). *GI: How gender analysis contributes to research.* Publications Office of the European Union.

Schiebinger, L. and Schraudner, M. (2011). Interdisciplinary approaches to achieving gendered innovations in science, medicine, and engineering. *Interdisciplinary Science Reviews, 36*(2), 154–167.

Schiebinger, L., Klinge, I., Sánchez de Madariaga, I., Schraudner, M. and Stefanick, M. (2011). *Gendered innovations in science, health & medicine, engineering, and environment.* http://genderedinnovations.stanford.edu/what-is-gendered-innovations.html.

Schreier, M. (2012). *Qualitative content analysis in practice.* Sage Publications.

Squires, J. (1999). *Gender in political theory.* Polity Press.

Squires, J. (2005). Is mainstreaming transformative? Theorizing mainstreaming in the context of diversity and deliberation. *Social Politics: International Studies in Gender, State & Society, 12*(3), 366–388.

Stanley, A. (1995). *Mothers and daughters of invention.* Rutgers University Press.

Steinkuehler, C. (2006). The mangle of play. *Games and Culture, 1*(3), 199–213.

Suchman, L.A. (2007). *Human–machine reconfigurations: Plans and situated actions.* Cambridge University Press.

Tannenbaum, C., Ellis, R. P., Eyssel, F., Zou, J. and Schiebinger, L. (2019). Sex and gender analysis improves science and engineering. *Nature, 575*(7781), 137–146.

Taylor, T. L. (2006). Beyond management: Considering participatory design and governance in player culture. *First Monday*, Special Issue 7. http://www.uic.edu/htbin/cgiwrap/bin/ojs/index.php/fm/article/view/1611/1526.

van den Brink, M. and Benschop, Y. (2012). Gender practices in the construction of academic excellence: Sheep with five legs. *Organization*, 19, 507–524.

van den Brink, M. and Benschop, Y. (2014). Gender in academic networking: The role of gatekeepers in professorial recruitment. *Journal of Management Studies, 51*(3), 460–492.

van Dijk, T. (1985). *Handbook of Discourse Analysis*, 4 vols. New York Academic Press.

Verloo, M. (2005). Displacement and empowerment: Reflections on the concept and practice of the Council of Europe Approach to gender mainstreaming and gender equality. *Social Politics: International Studies in Gender, State & Society*, *12*(3), 344–365. https://doi.org/10.1093/sp/jxi019.

Verloo, M. and Lombardo, E. (2007). Contested gender equality and policy variety in Europe: Introducing a critical frame analysis approach. In M. Verloo (Ed.), *Multiple meanings of gender equality. A critical frame analysis of gender policies in Europe* (pp. 21–49). Central European University Press.

Wajcman, J. (2000). Reflections on gender and technology studies: In what state is the art? *Social Studies of Science*, *30*(3), 447–464.

Wajcman, J. (2002). Addressing technological change: The challenge to social theory. *Current Sociology*, *50*, 347–363.

Wajcman, J. (2004). *Technofeminism*. Polity Press.

Wajcman, J. (2010). Feminist theories of technology. Cambridge Journal of Economics, *34*(1), 143–152. https://doi.org/10.1093/cje/ben057.

West, C. and Zimmerman, D. (1987). Doing gender. *Gender and Society*, *1*(2), 125–151. http://www.jstor.org/stable/189945.

Winner, L. (1993). Upon opening the black box and finding it empty: Social constructivism and the philosophy of technology. *Science, Technology and Human Values*, *18*(3), 362–378.

Wodak R. and Meyer M. (Eds) (2009). *Methods for critical discourse analysis*. Sage Publications.

Woolgar, S. and Cooper, G. (1999). Do artefacts have ambivalence?: Moses' bridges, Winner's bridges and other urban legends in S&TS. *Social Studies of Science*, *29*, 433–449.

World Health Organization. (2011). *Gender mainstreaming for health managers: A practical approach*. World Health Organization.

Wynne, B. and Felt, U. (2007). *Taking European knowledge society seriously*. Directorate-General for Research, European Commission. Office des Publications Officielles des Communautés Européennes.

12. The impact of institutional voids on female innovation in emerging countries

Allan Villegas-Mateos and Rosa Morales

1. INTRODUCTION

Worldwide, women represent about 25% less early-stage entrepreneurial activity in comparison to men (Elam et al., 2019), but how much of this activity is related to innovation? Geographical contexts may influence the recognition of innovation opportunities. Disparities in the distribution of capital and access to networks exist across territories, and these unbalances may affect female participation in innovative entrepreneurial activities (Blake and Hanson, 2005). A problem is that most research focuses on where innovation takes place as opposed to who participates in it (Alsos et al., 2016). Thus, there is a gap in the innovation literature because it pays little attention to gender issues, even though it is highly relevant to analyze gender differences, especially when, in practice, women are at a clear disadvantage in pursuing innovation activities (Brush et al., 2018). Even so, female entrepreneurs are making an increasing contribution to economic growth and therefore policymakers cannot afford to ignore this force (Goyal and Yadav, 2014). In this context, an opportunity-driven early-stage activity rather than a necessity-based early-stage activity in a better situation would achieve higher profits; that is, an improvement of the product thanks to the innovation process, rather than a push to entrepreneurship out of necessity, would create a better position for the entrepreneur, who then has the opportunity to achieve higher profits (Galindo and Méndez, 2014).

Another key fact is the evidence that shows women's share of entrepreneurship in Latin America lags behind more advanced nations in Europe, North America, and Asia (Allen et al., 2008; Amorós and Pizarro, 2007; Terjesen and Amorós, 2010). For emerging economies in general, there is a gap in the literature: attention has been mainly devoted to the analysis of female entrepreneurs' characteristics in developed countries (De Vita et al., 2014).

From an economic perspective, entrepreneurship and innovation are related to economic growth (Galindo and Méndez, 2014). However, a problem is that innovation ecosystems are defined in the literature as "the organizational, political, economic, environmental, and technological system of innovation through which a milieu conductive to business growth is catalyzed, sustained, and supported" (Rubens et al., 2011) and it is assumed that entrepreneurs have the same opportunities for getting resources, participation, and support regardless of their gender. Also, as Oh et al. (2016) mentioned, that definition ignores location and interaction among agents. These elements are key to understanding women's innovative entrepreneurial activities in emerging economies, although the literature highlights that there are not specific market conditions determined by user choice. Innovation ecosystems are defined as a community of interdependent heterogeneous participants targeted at a defined audience (Thomas and Autio, 2020), and traditionally, targeted to technology and product development irrespective of the gender of the entrepreneurs. To identify the participants for innovation ecosystems, facilitating institutions appear among with talent, the density of researchers, entrepreneurs, entrepreneurial culture, access to capital, and a supportive regulatory environment (Oh et al., 2016). Institutions are non-economic components of an innovation ecosystem that can enable idea making, and the introduction and diffusion of innovations (Mercan and Göktas, 2011). If institutions are weak or absent, there are institutional obstacles, known in the literature as institutional voids (Mair and Marti, 2009), that do not facilitate or impede entrepreneurial activities. In addition, as Rodrik (2007) mentions, institutional weaknesses reinforce social inequalities. Hence, we believe that in the case of innovative entrepreneurial activity in emerging economies, institutional voids would increase gender inequality.

This chapter aims to deal specifically with institutional voids to doing business in emerging and Latin American countries, and how they impact women's innovative entrepreneurial activity based on the Global Entrepreneurship Monitor (GEM) and World Bank datasets. It is relevant since academic scholars scientifically reproduce gender equality in their entrepreneurship research: they consider that there are more similarities than there are differences between men and women (Ahl, 2004). Many research studies involving entrepreneurship don't even consider exploring the correlation of gender with the phenomena they test.

The rest of the chapter is structured as follows. The next section reviews the literature regarding institutional voids and their link with business and innovation opportunities for women. The third section presents the methodology of data collection and analysis. In the fourth section different statistical models are developed, and the results are presented. Finally, there is a discussion of the implications of the results and future research directions.

2.   THE IMPACT OF INSTITUTIONAL VOIDS ON INNOVATION

Institutional voids are defined as the lack of or weak institutional facilities and regulations that support the healthy functioning of an economy (Luo and Tung, 2007; Martin et al., 2015). The voids exist in contexts in which institutional arrangements that support markets are either absent or weak (Mair and Marti, 2009), and they may arise from the absence of specialized intermediaries, regulatory systems, and contract-enforcing mechanisms (Chakrabarty and Bass, 2013). Institutional voids are particularly relevant for establishing and growing business in any country since entrepreneurs facing them can choose to either evade or alter the institutional context (McAdam et al., 2018). If institutions are defined as the rules of the game that bound social and economic interactions (North, 1993), then entrepreneurs could decide to accept or change these rules. Also, the evidence suggests that institutional voids can create opportunities for businesses if the systemic conditions are exploited as an advantage (Amankwah-Amoah et al., 2018; McCarthy and Puffer, 2016). The problem is that when formal and informal institutional voids exist, the entrepreneurs lack the social cohesion and normative guides necessary to structure stable entrepreneurial activity (Khoury and Prasad, 2016). Consequently, entrepreneurs are left with limited options to gain access to available market spaces, lack guidance on legitimate operational structures and other venture decisions, and face increased exposure to exploitation and misappropriation (Webb et al., 2019). Nevertheless, institutions underlying the ecosystems can be engaged and exogenously influenced by policy actions (Mercan and Göktas, 2011), but it is important to have a clear objective of who among the currently disadvantaged should be targeted.

The evidence of the effects of institutional voids on individuals in emerging countries remains scarce (McCarthy and Puffer, 2016). Nevertheless, one of the most distinctive characteristics of emerging countries is the existence of institutional voids (Amankwah-Amoah et al., 2018; Khanna and Palepu, 1999; Luo and Chung, 2013; North, 1991). Institutional conditions have consistently been viewed as problems for firms, and much has been written in the international business literature on that topic as well as practices such as networking for getting around these weaknesses (Puffer et al., 2010). Also, Webb et al. (2019) argue that institutional voids shape the outcomes of entrepreneurial activities within society. An example could be that in the cocoa sector of Ghana, corruption creates an institutional void, but some supply chain partners abuse the system to take advantage of others, thus generating entrepreneurial activities (Amankwah-Amoah et al., 2018). Besides, to deal with the presence of institutional voids in the social and cultural context, female entrepreneurs may draw on digital technologies to navigate such voids because the online environment facilitates the pursuit of entrepreneurial intentions in emerging economies (McAdam et al., 2018). Digital entrepreneurship facilitates the navigation and bridging of socio-cultural institutional voids but also provides opportunities for entrepreneurs to alter the existing institutional context directly and indirectly. However, in some countries where institutions are not trustworthy, these alternatives to somehow replace institutional voids are not always a good option (Sydow et al., 2020). Hence, we contribute to the literature of institutional voids in emerging countries by increasing the understanding of their effects on entrepreneurial activities.

Social exclusion, or marginalization, is an informal institutional void that derives from social norms and beliefs that certain individuals, based on their attributes, lack the status to participate in market activities, own property, or engage in trade (Webb et al., 2019). In this context, female entrepreneurs face greater challenges in developing countries simply because of their gender and because such limitations come from deeply ingrained values and traditions in society. At the same time, women in developing countries tend to face challenges that include difficulty in accessing finance, socio-cultural biases against them, low self-esteem, the existence of institutional voids, and lack of skills and entrepreneurial education (Goyal and Yadav, 2014).

Therefore, if we consider that institutional voids are part of an ecosystem that is "the evolving set of actors, activities, and artifacts, and the institutions and relations, including complementary and substitute relations, that are important for the innovative performance of an actor or a population of actors" (Granstrand and Holgersson, 2020, p. 3) it is relevant to consider the entrepreneurial activity output of women and men separately. Regarding the entrepreneurial activity, studies suggest that diverse elements that may be responsible for the gender gap—including individual factors such as women being more averse to taking risks (e.g., Shinnar et al., 2012), environmental elements like inequality levels (Klyver et al., 2013), gender stereotypes (Gupta, 2014), or having difficulty in getting needed resources (Wu, 2012)—may be influential factors that need further analysis.

As individuals, female entrepreneurs make significant contributions to innovation, employment and wealth creation in all economies and are one of the fastest-growing entrepreneurial populations in the world (Goyal and Yadav, 2014). For women, the decision to become an entrepreneur may be mainly related to problems in the workplace (Hoobler et al., 2014; Manolova et al., 2008; Mattis, 2004) or the desire to be more independent and have more time to balance their responsibilities (St-Arnaud and Giguère, 2018). For women, therefore, entrepreneurship may be seen as an opportunity to develop their professional skills. McAdam et al. (2018) confirmed that there is inequality for female entrepreneurs fostered by the presence of institutional voids in the business environment. Additionally, women are associated with weakness and lack of necessary entrepreneurial attributes which generates ontological biases and consequently perpetuates disadvantages for women (Marlow and Swail, 2014). Probably it's associated with more men leading institutions than women. Lastly, women already face difficulties in accessing capital, and dealing with gender stereotypes and with personal responsibilities such as taking care of children and elderly relatives that affect the way women manage their businesses (e.g., Brush et al., 2009; Jennings and McDougald, 2007). Nevertheless, difficulties can also be caused by institutional voids, for example, gaining access to finance: female entrepreneurs do not have access to financial resources because of institutional requirements, among which is entrepreneurship education, that are necessary to both create and grow microenterprises (Chakrabarty and Bass, 2013). In consequence, these types of situations cause female entrepreneurs to become discouraged and turn to informal savings groups or even to finance their projects themselves (Goyal and Yadav, 2014).

Considering the above, the following research questions were developed:

RQ1. *Does the institutional context to create and develop businesses have an impact on female innovative entrepreneurial activities?*

RQ2. *Do women and men have the same opportunities to pursue an innovative entrepreneurial activity in Latin American countries as in other emerging economies?*

3.   STUDY AREA AND RESEARCH METHODOLOGY

We use data from the GEM Adult Population Survey (APS), the World Bank Database Ease of Doing Business Index, and the World Bank Open Data to analyze the effect of institutions on female innovative entrepreneurship. In the GEM APS, we find that the Total Early-stage Activity (TEA) is separated from necessity and opportunity-driven activities at the same time it differentiates those women involved in TEA (Reynolds et al., 2005). We consider the female/male opportunity-driven TEA to be an indicator of the gender-balanced innovative entrepreneurial activity. To measure institutional voids related to the creation and development of businesses by country, we use the Ease of Doing Business Index from the World Bank Database. According to the World Bank, this Index intends to objectively measure business regulations for local firms in 180 countries. The Index comprises measures of processes, time, costs, minimum capital requirements, permissions or licenses, electricity access, properties registration, investor protection, tax payments, foreign trade conditions, and legal contract protection related to the creation of business and business development. If we consider regulations as formal rules that may or may not encourage business, then the Index may be considered as a proxy of institutional voids. The Index ranges from 0 to 1, with 0 being the least friendly business regulation. Thus, we can infer that the lower the Index, the greater the institutional voids and vice versa. The World Bank Open Data is used to collect information on economics and socio-demographic categories.

We gathered the data from countries in which the female/male opportunity-driven TEA was available (see Appendix). This study uses unbalanced panel data with a total of 90 countries and a study period from 2011 to 2017. Given the lack of information for some of the countries in our study, the regression results include data for developed economies and 18 emerging economies, six of which were Latin American countries: Argentina, Brazil, Chile, Colombia, Mexico, and Peru. The total number of observations was 295. To test the research questions, we create a measure of gender-balanced innovative entrepreneurial activity using the female/male opportunity TEA from the GEM APS database that matches the same list of countries. Previous studies (Jafari-Sadeghi, 2020, Terjesen and Amorós, 2010, Verheul et al., 2006) have considered the female/male opportunity TEA; however, as far as we are aware, those studies do not create a dichotomous gender balance measure. This construct is the dependent variable. As an independent variable to measure institutional voids related to the creation and development of businesses by country, we use the Ease of Doing Business Index from the World Bank database. It appears that this Index has not been previously used to analyze how institutional voids affect gender-balanced innovative entrepreneurial activities in emerging countries.

To control for socioeconomic and demographic aspects, we include four variables using the World Bank Open Data. Previous literature (Estrin and Mickiewicz, 2011; Minniti, 2010; Terjesen and Amorós, 2010) includes the Gross Domestic Product (GDP) to analyze whether it affects female entrepreneurship, and, thus, we use it to control for variations in economic activity among countries. The effect of unemployment rates on female entrepreneurial activity has been studied previously (Ascher, 2012; Verheul et al., 2006), but given that there is still no consensus on this effect (particularly on female opportunity entrepreneurial activity), we include two measures of the unemployment rate: total and female unemployment. We follow Kobeissi (2010) and include the fertility rate to control for demographic differences.

Given that the study uses a panel, to control for time and heterogeneity, we include a year dummy and a dummy variable that captures the differences between developed and emerging economies. Due to the sample size and the number of sample countries, we do not include country dummies to avoid losing degrees of freedom when performing econometric analysis. A measure capturing the effect of being a Latin American country was included to test whether being in a Latin American country affects female innovative entrepreneurship. The before-mentioned variables are listed in Table 12.1 in more detail. Table 12.2 reports summary statistics. Since the dependent variable is categorical, we used *probit* models to test the research questions.

Table 12.1   List of variables

Variable	Description
Gender-balanced Innovative Entrepreneurial Activity	This is a dummy variable that takes the value of 1 if the female/male opportunity-driven TEA is greater than 0.82, 0 otherwise
Doing Business Index	Index of ease of doing business
Log GDP	Log of GDP per capita (constant 2010 US$)
Unemployment	Unemployment, total (as a percentage of the labor force)
Female Unemployment	Unemployment, female (as a percentage of the female labor force)
Log Fertility rate	Log of the fertility rate, total (births per woman)
Emerging Countries	This is a dummy variable that takes the value of 1 if a country is an emerging economy, 0 otherwise
Latin America	This is a dummy variable that takes the value of 1 if a country is Latin American, 0 otherwise
Year	Year dummy for each year

Table 12.2   Summary statistics

Variable	Obs	Mean	Std. Dev.	Min	Max
Gender Balance	295	0.8135593	0.3901237	0	1
Doing Business Index	295	68.69153	9.694147	34.9	89.5
Log GDP	268	9.475	1.155808	6.176663	11.609071
Unemployment	248	8.626811	6.371538	0.14	35.15
Female Unemployment	238	9.43695	7.259327	0.03229	41.53
Log Fertility rate	268	2.049199	0.8335935	1.101	5.699
Emerging Economy	295	0.2508475	0.4342375	0	1
Latin American Economy	295	0.0915254	0.2888448	0	1
Year 2011	295	0	0	0	0
Year 2012	295	0	0	0	0
Year 2013	295	0.2	0.4006797	0	1
Year 2014	295	0.2305085	0.421874	0	1
Year 2015	295	0.1932203	0.3954952	0	1
Year 2016	295	0.2067797	0.4056843	0	1
Year 2017	295	0.1694915	0.375823	0	1

4.　　RESULTS

Figure 12.1 shows the box plots for the Easy of Doing Business Index for the whole sample, the sample of emerging economies, and Latin American countries. Given that the Ease of Doing Business Index is a measure of regulations related to the business creation process that entrepreneurs use, it is a proxy of the degree of institutional development or in this case an indicator of the institutional voids. The data shows that both the median and the maximum values of the Index for emerging and Latin American countries are lower than the values for the whole sample. This means that institutional voids are more likely to be greater in the first mentioned economies.

We use a *probit* model to test whether the institutional context affects the probability of having a gender balance in terms of innovative entrepreneurial activities. Table 12.3 summarizes the main results. The coefficients of institutional context (Ease of Doing Business Index) are positive and significant at the 1% level in all our models, meaning that higher values of doing business increase the probability of gender balance in innovative entrepreneurial activities. It is worth noting that even though the sample size decreases, the estimated coefficients for the Ease of Doing Business Index do not lose statistical power. The estimates for the Latin American dummy variable are negative and significant at the 5% and 10% levels. This result means that the probability of having gender balance in terms of innovative entrepreneurship decreases in a Latin American economy. This outcome is not surprising given that, as Figure 12.1 shows, it is likely that a Latin American country exhibits greater institutional voids than other economies, which may impact gender balance in innovative entrepreneurial activities negatively.

The estimates for the emerging economies are positive but not significant, and similar results are obtained in the case of the coefficients of the log of GDP. As for the estimates of the socio-demographic variables, Table 12.3 reports that the coefficients of both unemployment variables (total and female) are negative and significant at the 1% level; the meaning of this finding is that higher rates of unemployment decrease the probability of gender balance in innovative entrepreneurial activity. The estimated coefficients in the case of the log of fertility rate are not significant. These results are relevant since they clarify that entrepreneurial activities are linked to institutional conditions and they contribute to the understanding of the determinants of female entrepreneurship. Furthermore, they contribute to filling the gap in the literature of emerging economies and innovation ecosystems by showing how institutional voids affect gender balance in innovative entrepreneurial activities.

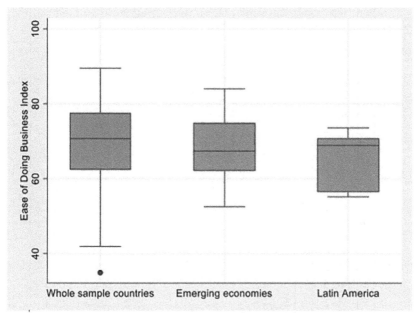

Source: Authors' elaboration based on the World Bank Database Ease of Doing Business Index.

Figure 12.1   Box plots for the Ease of Doing Business Index

5.   DISCUSSION AND IMPLICATIONS

The results are consistent with previous studies that indicate that developing countries face greater institutional voids than developed countries; in the developed countries the entrepreneurs operate with greater certainty under effective formal institutions (Goyal and Yadav, 2014; Puffer et al., 2010; Sydow et al., 2020; Webb et al., 2019). Emerging economies have lower Ease of Doing Business Indexes, and they face less business-friendly regulations. The case of the Latin American countries could be explained by their greater levels of corruption; therefore, doing business becomes more complicated for anyone and it affects entrepreneurial activities. Nevertheless, it is important to highlight the fact that women need to be in an environment where they feel safe and where they have the tools and skills necessary to be successful in their business (Goyal and Yadav, 2014).

These findings imply that there are fewer opportunities for women to pursue innovative entrepreneurial activities in Latin American countries than in the rest of the emerging economies. They also suggest that the regulatory and institutional facilities are weak or lacking to support the healthy functioning of

Table 12.3   Marginal effects (probit models)

	−1	−2	−3	−4	−5
	Gender-balanced Innovative Entrepreneurial Activity	Gender-balanced Innovative Entrepreneurial Activity	Gender-balanced Innovative Entrepreneurial Activity	Gender-balanced Innovative Entrepreneurial Activity	Gender-balanced Innovative Entrepreneurial Activity
	Probit	Probit	Probit	Probit	Probit
	Coefficient (Std. Error)	Coefficient (Std. Error)	Coefficient (Std. Error)	Coefficient (Std. Error)	Coefficient (Std. Error)
Ease of Doing Business Index	0.0096*** (0.0020)	0.0094*** (0.0021)	0.0091*** (0.0021)	0.0130*** (0.0039)	0.0135*** (0.0037)
Emerging Economy		−0.0678 (0.0477)		0.0586 (0.0779)	0.0709 (0.0736)
Latin American Economy			−0.158586** (0.0628274)	−0.1859* (0.0956)	−0.2062** (0.0910)
Log_GDP				0.0188 (0.0328)	0.0129 (0.0321)
Female Unemployment				−0.0078*** (0.0033)	
Unemployment					−0.0098*** (0.0037)
Log_Fertility Rate				0.0299 (0.1124)	−0.0029 (0.1089)
Year Dummies	Yes	Yes	Yes	Yes	Yes
Log-likelihood	−131.57	−130.58	−128.60	−98.84	−100.51

	−1	−2	−3	−4	−5
	Gender-balanced Innovative Entrepreneurial Activity	Gender-balanced Innovative Entrepreneurial Activity	Gender-balanced Innovative Entrepreneurial Activity	Gender-balanced Innovative Entrepreneurial Activity	Gender-balanced Innovative Entrepreneurial Activity
	Probit	Probit	Probit	Probit	Probit
	Coefficient	Coefficient	Coefficient	Coefficient	Coefficient
	(Std. Error)	(Std. Error)	(Std. Error)	(Std. Error)	(Std. Error)
Pseudo R2	0.0728	0.0798	0.0937	0.1723	0.1752
No of Observations	295	295	295	237	248

those economies (Luo and Tung, 2007; Martin et al., 2015). Necessity-based entrepreneurship tends to be greater than opportunity-based entrepreneurship in Latin American countries, so these results confirm the same, but contribute to the understanding that the balance can change with the right institutional conditions in their local innovation ecosystems. In terms of policies, governments must pay special attention since women are the fastest-growing entrepreneurial population in the world and can contribute significantly to innovation among other positive economic outcomes (Goyal and Yadav, 2014).

It is important to highlight that the Ease of Doing Business Index is built upon the analysis of the processes, time, costs, minimum capital requirements, permissions or licenses, electricity access, properties registration, investor protection, tax payments, foreign trade conditions, and legal contract protection that underlie the business creation process that entrepreneurs experience. Consequently, it is an equivalent measure of the degree of institutional development or, in this case, an indicator of the institutional voids.

Therefore, the finding that in Latin America the countries have a negative effect and in the emerging economies they have a positive effect on the female innovative entrepreneurship activities allows the conclusion that the degree of economic development correlates with the institutional framework affecting how innovation is developed. It is possible that the impact on men and women can be different given the same institutional conditions; this is something that requires further study. However, with these results, the recommendation is that governments must first invest in their institutions to create better fundamental conditions for upcoming entrepreneurs whether they are emerging, developed, or Latin American countries.

The main issue in studying Latin America is the scarcity or lack of indicators related to female innovative entrepreneurial activity and other socio-demographic indicators (female educational attainment, school enrollment in terms of the gender parity index) in much of the countries of the regions. Given data constraints, we could focus on only six Latin American countries. More efforts are needed to collect regional information on female innovative entrepreneurial activity that could expand the scope of this study and increase the understanding of female entrepreneurship and the institutional context of other Latin American economies.

Future research could explore other indicators of institutional context as well as include other socio-demographic variables that at the time of this study are not available. Since entrepreneurship is a phenomenon that can be researched from different perspectives, that is, individual determinants or macroeconomic determinants, future research should focus on testing the most relevant indicators of entrepreneurial activity from both perspectives. Entrepreneurship research sometimes encompasses both genders, but with this contribution, we highlight the importance of studying them separately so that countries can make advances in achieving a real gender balance.

REFERENCES

Ahl, H. (2004), *The scientific reproduction of gender inequality: A discourse analysis of research texts on women's entrepreneurship*. Malmö: Liber.

Allen, E., Elam, A., Langowitz, N., & Dean, M. (2008), 'The Global Entrepreneurship Monitor (GEM) 2007 report on women and entrepreneurship'. Babson Park, MA and New York: Babson College and Baruch College.

Alsos, G.A., Hytti, U., & Ljunggren, E. (2016), 'Gender and innovation: An introduction'. In G.A. Alsos, U. Hytti, & E. Ljunggren (Eds.), *Research Handbook on Gender and Innovation* (pp. 3–16). Cheltenham, UK and Northampton, MA, USA: Edward Elgar Publishing.

Amankwah-Amoah, J., Debrah, Y.A., & Nuertey, D. (2018), 'Institutional legitimacy, cross-border trade, and institutional voids: Insights from the cocoa industry in Ghana'. *Journal of Rural Studies*, 58, 136–145. https://doi.org/10.1016/j.jrurstud.2018.01.002

Amorós, J.E., & Pizarro, O. (2007), 'Women entrepreneurship context in Latin America: An exploratory study in Chile'. In M.R. Markovic (Ed.), *The Perspective of Women's Entrepreneurship in the Age of Globalization* (pp. 107–126). Charlotte, NC: Information Age Publishing.

Ascher, J. (2012), 'Female entrepreneurship: An appropriate response to gender discrimination'. *Journal of Entrepreneurship, Management, and Innovation*, 8 (4), 97–114.

Blake, M.K., & Hanson, S. (2005), 'Rethinking innovation: Context and gender'. *Environment and Planning A: Economy and Space*, 37 (4), 681–701.

Brush, C.G., De Bruin, A., & Welter, F. (2009), 'A gender-aware framework for women's entrepreneurship'. *International Journal of Gender and Entrepreneurship*, 1 (1), 8–24.

Brush, C., Edelman, L., Manolova, T., & Welter, F. (2018), 'A gendered look at entrepreneurship ecosystems'. *Small Business Economics*, 53 (2), 393–408. https://doi.org/10.1007/s11187-018-9992-9

Chakrabarty, S., & Bass, A.E. (2013), 'Encouraging entrepreneurship: Microfinance, knowledge support, and the costs of operating in institutional voids'. *Thunderbird International Business Review*, 55 (5), 545–562.

De Vita, L., Mari, M., & Poggesi, S. (2014), 'Women entrepreneurs in and from developing countries: Evidence from the literature'. *European Management Journal*, 32 (3), 451–560. https://doi.org/10.1016/j.emj.2013.07.009

Elam, A., Brush, C., Greene, P., Baumer, B., Dean, M., & Heavlow, R. (2019), 'Global Entrepreneurship Monitor: 2018/2019 women's entrepreneurship report'. London, UK: Babson College, Smith College, and the Global Entrepreneurship Research Association.

Estrin, S., & Mickiewicz, T. (2011), 'Institutions and female entrepreneurship'. *Small Business Economics*, 37 (4), 397.

Galindo, M., & Méndez, M.T. (2014), 'Entrepreneurship, economic growth, and innovation: Are feedback effects at work?' *Journal of Business Research*, 67, 825–829.

Goyal, P., & Yadav, V. (2014), 'To be or not to be a woman entrepreneur in a developing country?'. *Psychosociological Issues in Human Resource Management*, 2 (2), 68–78.

Granstrand, O., & Holgersson, M. (2020), 'Innovation ecosystems: A conceptual review and a new definition'. *Technovation*, 90, 102098.

Gupta, V.A. (2014), 'Gender differences in evaluation of new business opportunity: A stereotype threat perspective'. *Journal of Business Venturing*, 29, 273–288.

Hoobler, J., Lemmon, G., & Wayne, S. (2014), 'Women's managerial aspirations: An organizational development perspective'. *Journal of Management*, 40 (3), 703–730. https://doi.org/10.1177/0149206311426911

Jafari-Sadeghi, V. (2020), 'The motivational factors of business venturing: Opportunity versus necessity? A gendered perspective on European countries'. *Journal of Business Research*, 113, 279–289.

Jennings, J.E., & McDougald, M.S. (2007), 'Work–family interface experiences and coping strategies: Implications for entrepreneurship research and practice'. *Academy of Management Review*, 32 (3), 747–760.

Khanna, T., & Palepu, K. (1999), 'Policy shocks, market intermediaries, and corporate strategy: The evolution of business groups in Chile and India'. *Journal of Economics & Management Strategy*, 8, 271–310. https://doi.org/10.1111/j.1430-9134.1999 .00271.x

Khoury, T.A., & Prasad, A. (2016), 'Entrepreneurship amid concurrent institutional constraints in less developed countries'. *Business and Society*, 55 (7), 934–969. https://doi.org/10.1177/0007650314567641

Klyver, K., Nielsen, S.L., & Evald, M.R. (2013), 'Women's self-employment: An act of institutional (dis)integration? A multilevel, cross-country study'. *Journal of Business Venturing*, 28 (4), 474–488.

Kobeissi, N. (2010), 'Gender factors and female entrepreneurship: International evidence and policy implications'. *Journal of International Entrepreneurship*, 8 (1), 1–35.

Luo, X.R., & Chung, C.N. (2013), 'Filling or abusing the institutional void? Ownership and management control of public family businesses in an emerging market'. *Organization Science*, 24 (2), 591–613. https://doi.org/10.1287/orsc.1120.0751

Luo, Y., & Tung, R. (2007), 'International expansion of emerging market enterprises: A springboard perspective'. *Journal of International Business Studies*, 38, 481–498. https://doi.org/10.1057/palgrave.jibs.8400275

Mair, J., & Marti, I. (2009), 'Entrepreneurship in and around institutional voids: A case study from Bangladesh'. *Journal of Business Venturing*, 24, 419–435.

Manolova, T.S., Brush, C.G., & Edelman, L.F. (2008), 'What do women entrepreneurs want?'. *Strategic Change*, 17, 69–82.

Marlow, S., & Swail, J. (2014), 'Gender, risk, and finance: why can't a woman be more like a man?'. *Entrepreneurship & Regional Development*, 26 (1–2), 80–96. https:// doi.org/10.1080/08985626.2013.860484

Martin, S., Rieple, A., Chang, J., Boniface, B., & Ahmed, A. (2015), 'Small farmers and sustainability: Institutional barriers to investment and innovation in the Malaysian palm oil industry in Sabah'. *Journal of Rural Studies*, 40, 46–58. https://doi.org/10 .1016/j.jrurstud.2015.06.002

Mattis, M.C. (2004), 'Women entrepreneurs: out from under the glass ceiling'. *Women in Management Review*, 19, 154–163.

McAdam, M., Crowley, C., & Harrison, R.T. (2018), 'The emancipatory potential of female digital entrepreneurship: Institutional voids in Saudi Arabia'. *Academy of Management Proceedings*, 1.

McCarthy, D.J., & Puffer, S.M. (2016), 'Institutional voids in an emerging economy: From problem to opportunity'. *Journal of Leadership & Organizational Studies*, 23 (2), 208–219. https://doi.org/10.1177/1548051816633070

Mercan, B., & Göktas, D. (2011), 'Components of innovation ecosystems: A cross-country study'. *International Research Journal of Finance and Economics*, 76, 102–112.

Minniti, M. (2010), 'Female entrepreneurship and economic activity'. *The European Journal of Development Research*, 22 (3), 294–312.

North, D.C. (1991), 'Institutions'. *Journal of Economic Perspectives*, 5 (1), 97–112.

North, D.C. (1993), 'Institutions and credible commitment'. *Journal of Institutional and Theoretical Economics (JITE)/Zeitschrift für die gesamte Staatswissenschaft*, 11–23.

Oh, D., Phillips, F., Park, S., & Lee, E. (2016), 'Innovation ecosystems: A critical examination'. *Technovation*, 54, 1–6. http://dx.doi.org/10.1016/j.technovation.2016.02.004

Puffer, S.M., McCarthy, D.J., & Boisot, M. (2010), 'Entrepreneurship in Russia and China: The impact of formal institutional voids'. *Entrepreneurship: Theory and Practice*, 34, 441–467.

Reynolds, P.D., Bosma, N., Autio, E., Hunt, S., Bono, N.D., Servais, I. et al. (2005), 'Global Entrepreneurship Monitor: Data collection design and implementation 1998–2003' *Small Business Economics*, 24 (3), 205–231. https://doi.org/10.1007/s11187-005-1980-1

Rodrik, D. (2007), *One Economics, Many Recipes: Globalization, Institutions, and Economic Growth*. Princeton University Press.

Rubens, N., Still, K., Huhtamäki, J., & Russell, M.G. (2011), 'A network analysis of investment firms as resource routers in Chinese innovation ecosystem'. *JSW*, 6 (9), 1737–1745.

Shinnar, R.S., Giacomin, O., & Janssen, F. (2012), 'Entrepreneurial perceptions and intentions: The role of gender and culture'. *Entrepreneurship Theory and Practice*, 36, 465–493.

St-Arnaud, L., & Giguère, É. (2018), 'Women entrepreneurs, individual and collective work–family interface strategies and emancipation'. *International Journal of Gender and Entrepreneurship*, 10 (4), 198–223.

Sydow, A., Cannatelli, B.L., Giudici, A., & Molteni, M. (2020), 'Entrepreneurial workaround practices in severe institutional voids: evidence from Kenya'. *Entrepreneurship Theory and Practice*, In press, 1–37. https://doi.org/10.1177/1042258720929891

Terjesen, S., & Amorós, J.E. (2010), 'Female entrepreneurship in Latin America and the Caribbean: Characteristics, drivers and relationship to economic development'. *The European Journal of Development Research*, 22, 313–330. https://doi.org/10.1057/ejdr.2010.13

Thomas, L.D., & Autio, E. (2020), 'Innovation ecosystems in management: An organizing typology'. In R. Aldag (Ed.), *Oxford Research Encyclopedia of Business and Management*. Oxford: Oxford University Press.

Verheul, I., Stel, A.V., & Thurik, R. (2006), 'Explaining female and male entrepreneurship at the country level'. *Entrepreneurship and Regional Development*, 18 (2), 151–183.

Webb, J.W., Khoury, T.A., & Hitt, M.A. (2019), 'The influence of formal and informal institutional voids on entrepreneurship'. *Entrepreneurship Theory and Practice*, 44 (3), 504–526.
Wu, Z.A. (2012), 'Second-order gender effects: The case of US small-business borrowing cost'. *Entrepreneurship Theory and Practice*, 36 (3), 443–463.

APPENDIX

Table 12A.1   List of sample countries

Countries		
Algeria	Hong Kong	Saudi Arabia
Angola	Hungary	Senegal
Argentina	India	Singapore
Australia	Indonesia	Slovakia
Austria	Iran	Slovenia
Barbados	Ireland	South Africa
Belgium	Israel	South Korea
Belize	Italy	Spain
Bolivia	Jamaica	Suriname
Bosnia and Herzegovina	Japan	Sweden
Botswana	Jordan	Switzerland
Brazil	Kazakhstan	Taiwan
Bulgaria	Kosovo	Thailand
Burkina Faso	Latvia	Trinidad and Tobago
Cameroon	Libya	Tunisia
Canada	Lithuania	Turkey
Chile	Luxembourg	Uganda
China	Madagascar	United States
Colombia	Malawi	Uruguay
Costa Rica	Malaysia	Vietnam
Croatia	Mexico	Zambia
Cyprus	Morocco	
Czech Republic	Namibia	
Denmark	Netherlands	
Ecuador	North Macedonia	
Egypt	Panama	
El Salvador	Peru	
Estonia	Philippines	
Finland	Poland	
France	Portugal	
Georgia	Puerto Rico	
Germany	Qatar	
Ghana	Romania	

13. Informal institutional structures and legitimacy perceptions of female innovation in sub-Saharan Africa: a conceptual framework

Priscilla Otuo, Cynthia Forson, Afua Owusu-Kwarteng and Anthony N-Yelkabong

1. INTRODUCTION

The aim of this chapter is to present a conceptual analysis of the salient informal institutional structures that impact on the legitimacy of women's innovation in the sub-Saharan Africa entrepreneurial ecosystem. Employing legitimacy theory (Überbacher, 2014, p.667, Fisher et al., 2017) as a theoretical lens, the chapter seeks to analyse ways in which gendered and other cultural, religious and class-based norms, attitudes and values shape and mediate African female entrepreneurs' engagement with innovation in relation to three essential factors: motivation to innovate, innovation processes (e.g. networking) and innovation outcomes (new products/service) (Alsos et al., 2013, Garud et al., 2013).

As a conceptual contribution, this chapter draws on institutional theory, legitimacy theory, entrepreneurship and innovation theories, exploring evidence from theoretical and empirical contributions on the subjects. The analysis takes a multi-layered perspective and seeks to identify the moderating and shaping effects of these informal structures in the context (societal), setting and situated activity (institutional) and self (individual) levels of social action (Layder, 1993). By introducing the concept of legitimacy, we will demonstrate how informal institutions are relevant to legitimacy perceptions of female innovation within the entrepreneurial landscape and answer the core question: *How do informal institutional structures inform legitimacy perceptions of female innovation in sub-Saharan Africa?*

Studies suggest that the role of informal institutions in female innovation needs to be addressed (Alsos et al., 2013). Alsos et al. (2013) argue that the lack of attention to the subject is due to the "*invisibility of 'people'* in innovation", that is the innovator in the process. The "people" in the context of innovation are actors whose motivation and ability to innovate depends on several factors. These factors include their own self-legitimacy perceptions and those of other key stakeholders (Whittington, 2011, Alsos et al., 2013). Such legitimacy perceptions impact critical aspects of innovation like knowledge sourcing and exchange, potential gains from innovation, opportunities to share innovation outcomes and reception of innovation outcomes (Autio et al., 2014, Brush et al., 2019, Fisher et al., 2017, Thébaud, 2015). Further, although entrepreneurs and entrepreneurial firms may engage in strategies and mechanisms to acquire, maintain and restore their legitimacy (Zimmerman and Zeitz, 2002, Überbacher, 2014, Fisher et al., 2017), the success of these mechanisms are still subject to legitimacy judgements of relevant stakeholders.

Institutional theorists have long argued that legitimacy perceptions hinge on institutional structures (North, 1991, Stenholm and Hytti, 2014, Webb et al., 2020) particularly informal structures. Informal institutional structures include norms and values at varying levels of social action – societal, labour market, family and work settings and even at the individual levels. Informal institutional structures in the sub-Saharan African context include but are not limited to:

a. at the macro level – norms of social obligations, gender role expectations, collectivist orientation, status consciousness and low levels of trust;
b. at the labour market and sectoral levels – reliance on networks, informal leadership structures, particularism, clientelism, patronage and nepotism;
c. at the micro individual level – there are self, family and entrepreneurial logics around womanhood and entrepreneurial identity (Clark, 1997, Moore, 1997, Kuada, 2009, Ratten, 2020).

As these may arise from social and cultural expectations they often are deeply embedded in cultural ideals around gendered behaviours. Previous studies have documented strong connections between informal institutional structures, as those above, and entrepreneurship (Atieno, 2001, Mungai and Ogot, 2012, Ratten, 2020). However, considering that entrepreneurship itself is a gendered phenomenon (Minniti, 2009, Alsos et al., 2013), gender mediates the role of institutional structures within the entrepreneurial landscape. In relation to this, it appears women are more disadvantaged in the context of entrepreneurship (Alsos et al., 2013, Adom and Anambane, 2019, Brush et al., 2019).

Likewise, gender has an effect on firms' innovation (Wang et al., 2011, Ighomereho et al., 2013, Wikhamn and Knights, 2013, Fu et al., 2020). As Wikhamn and Knights (2013, p. 290) posit, "neither organisational life in general nor management innovation in particular can be seen as gender neutral.... for indeed they both tend to reflect and reproduce masculine discourses as normal practice". Empirically, Thébaud (2015) also established that "gender status beliefs" impact on the legitimacy of innovation among female entrepreneurs. Despite the above, it appears discussions have largely ignored ways in which these norms and values may shape and mediate legitimacy perceptions of women (Amine and Staub, 2009, Liu et al., 2019) and therefore their ability to innovate and participate in innovation processes, and benefit from innovation outcomes. Failure to explore gendered aspects of innovation could mean "the nature of innovation is stripped of its contextual influence" (Blake and Hanson, 2005, p. 681).

In this chapter, we extend the existing literature on informal institutions and firm innovation. Specifically, by introducing the concept of legitimacy, we add to the strand of literature on the ways in which institutions impact entrepreneurship (North, 1991, Ahlstrom and Bruton, 2002, Bruton et al., 2010) and female innovation. This study particularly follows prior studies that indicate that legitimacy is a core function of informal institutions (Stenholm and Hytti, 2014). In essence, we build work on existing work by showing that a set of interconnected factors at the macro, meso and individual levels (Blake and Hanson, 2005, Brush et al., 2019) shape legitimacy perceptions of female innovation. Also, contextualising the study in terms of geographical focus benefits readers as several existing studies on legitimacy and entrepreneurship are centred on developed countries.

Overall, our approach in this present study presents a holistic picture of the subject of female innovation and informal institutions. Like all other entrepreneurs, in order for sub-Saharan African women's businesses (including innovative activities) to succeed, they must be perceived as "legitimate" to those institutions and individuals with which they engage and serve. We argue that the likelihood that a woman's innovative behaviour will emerge, be sustained and produce an outcome is a function of three factors. First, the extent that she is deemed credible by the society in which she operates. Second, the institutional framework of the business she owns and her own perceptions of herself. Third, informal norms, values and attitudes. It is also important to address this issue in a region where women dominate the entrepreneurial landscape. Research shows that Africa is the only continent in which female entrepreneurs outnumber their male counterparts (Gaye, 2018). In Ghana for example, Abor and Quartey (2010) suggests women own about 70% of all businesses in Ghana.

The next part of this chapter is a brief examination of the empirical context of female entrepreneurship in sub-Saharan Africa, where at the intersection of culture, religion, class and ethnicity, women experience entrepreneurship differently from men – usually at a disadvantage. We then present an overview of the concept of institutions, establishing connections between institutions and legitimacy. This leads to discussion on the subject of gender and innovation, then to the presentation of the conceptual framework on informal institutions and their impact on legitimacy of female innovation at the societal, firm and individual levels. The chapter concludes by offering recommendations for further research and testing of the framework.

2.   AFRICAN WOMEN IN "ENTREPRENEURSHIP"

Ndemo and Mkalama (2019) have bemoaned the conceptualisation of African female entrepreneurship which has marginalised African women in the glo-balisation research agenda. The authors argue that the sub-Saharan African context is a complex environment for female entrepreneurs. Although they outnumber men in choosing to go into entrepreneurship (Gaye, 2018), their experiences of entrepreneurship are shaped by a number of interrelated factors that are common to their counterparts in other jurisdictions, but which are often qualitatively different (Ndemo and Mkalama, 2019). Entrepreneurship is viewed as a socially legitimate activity for women on the continent and indeed has been hailed as perhaps the panacea to Africa's persistent issues of gender-based poverty and women's economic empowerment (Langevang et al., 2015).

Socio-cultural boundaries that define male and female income-generating activities are being renegotiated as constraints and/or new opportunities arise. The vast majority of women in sub-Saharan Africa run micro businesses in female-dominated sectors such as retail and personal services (so generally tend to hire other women) (Langevang et al., 2015). In these sectors, the barriers to entry are low, competition is rife, profit vulnerability is high, busi-ness failure is common and there are particular challenges in accessing some infrastructure services such as the Internet. Women-owned businesses on the continent generally underperform compared to those owned by their male counterparts (Hallward-Driemeier, 2013) – and achieve slower growth.

Yet, many African female entrepreneurs run high growth innovative businesses and even those who do not, engage in incremental evolutionary processes to improve their business outcomes (Ngoasong and Kimbu, 2019). These outcomes are mostly related to a change or addition of new products, and less common are innovations in services, markets and sources of raw materials (Kiraka et al., 2013). In that regard, Kiraka et al. (2013) have identi-fied innovation drivers and impediments among women-owned businesses in sub-Saharan Africa to include recognition and investment in the appropriate businesses, training and skills, establishing complementary businesses, desire for financial independence, passion for the business, lack of financial knowl-edge and business management skills. Clearly all these drivers are functions of women's ability to engage in activities that enhance their networking and information capital. Again, in most contexts, these opportunities for women and other entrepreneurs are facilitated within the entrepreneurial landscape.

A number of factors shaped by institutional structures impact entrepreneurship within the region and these are discussed later in the conceptual framework. Meanwhile, the next section delves into institutions and their role in forming legitimacy perceptions.

3.   INSTITUTIONS AND LEGITIMACY

Institutions are "the set of political, economic, social, and legal conventions that establish the foundational basis for production and exchange" (Salimath and Cullen, 2010, p. 361). Institutions set the "rules of the game" (North, 1991, p. 98) and are key to the growth and survival of entrepreneurial ecosystems (Acs et al., 2017, Alvedalen and Boschma, 2017, Fuentelsaz et al., 2018). Interactions between these institutional actors give each ecosystem its peculiar configuration (Alvedalen and Boschma, 2017). Institutions further impact entrepreneurial behaviour and vice versa (North, 1991) and their roles vary across regions (Gertler, 2010, North, 1991, Zimmerman and Zeitz, 2002). These institutions can facilitate and impede innovative activities (Powell and Colyvas, 2008, Aldrich and Fiol, 1994).

Informal institutions, in particular, affect entrepreneurial activities. Welter (2002, p. 37) defines informal institutions as *codes of conduct, values and norms, i.e., those attitudes and mental perceptions which are embedded in a society*. She and others argue that they prescribe accepted behaviours to entrepreneurs (Welter, 2002, Welter and Smallbone, 2011). Social relations, for instance, engender trust, improve information flow and ultimately reduce transaction costs (Rauf, 2009). In the African context, Saka-Helmhout et al. (2020) have demonstrated how informal institutions substitute weak formal institutions and complement firm resources for innovation.

Above all, informal institutions prescribe (gendered) behaviours (for both men and women) and influence individual actions and perceptions (Rauf, 2009, Frydrych et al., 2014, Welter et al., 2014, Webb et al., 2020). Unfortunately, informal institutions appear to have more of a disadvantageous influence on women than men (Welter et al., 2014). In weak formal entrepreneurial contexts like sub-Saharan Africa (Atiase et al., 2018) the salience of informal institutions becomes starker (Saka-Helmhout et al., 2020).

Integral to the role of informal institutions is the enhancement of a firm's legitimacy (Bruton et al., 2010, Aldrich and Fiol, 1994) – *a social judgment of acceptance, appropriateness, and/or desirability* (Zimmerman and Zeitz, 2002, p. 414). For Bruton et al. (2010, p. 427), legitimacy is the "right to exist and perform an activity in a certain way" and the social context in which people operate is essential to understanding their legitimacy assessments (De

Clercq and Voronov, 2009, Deephouse et al., 2017). Legitimacy is a resource (Ahlstrom and Bruton, 2002, Zimmerman and Zeitz, 2002, Frydrych et al., 2014) and further provides access to essential resources (Lounsbury and Glynn, 2001). Organisational scholars have relied on legitimacy theory to explore the survival and functioning of new and existing firms (De Clercq and Voronov, 2009, Frydrych et al., 2014, Fisher et al., 2017). Within the entrepreneurship literature, it has been noted that legitimacy enables firms and entrepreneurs to establish relationships with relevant stakeholders (Frydrych et al., 2014).

De Clercq and Voronov (2009, p. 396) refer to firms' need to conform to rules established by norms/institutions in order to gain legitimacy, as "fitting in" and "standing out". Describing entrepreneurial legitimacy as habitus, the authors further assert that newcomers' cultural and symbolic capital enable them to gain legitimacy through fitting in and standing out. Paradoxically however, Navis and Glynn (2011, p. 479) assert that "conformity to established standards is antithetical to entrepreneurship, which tends to be more concerned with novelty, distinctiveness, and nonconformity". Zimmerman and Zeitz (2002) summarise the various strategies, through everyday practice (De Clercq and Voronov, 2009) that firms employ to gain legitimacy as conformance, creation, selection and manipulation.

With evidence from selected farmers in Europe, Stenholm and Hytti (2014) proved that individuals react differently to societal norms and values in the construction of their identities. Some of the farmers studied adhered to social norms so as to secure legitimacy and develop their multiple identities. In the research, farmers that identified as producer-farmers took decisions by taking into consideration community and household perspectives, and not that of the business. This, they perceived, was essential to acquiring legitimacy as producer-farmers. Similarly, García and Welter (2013) work on gender identities highlight that women may adopt varying forms of identities by "doing" or "redoing" gender. As García and Welter (2013, p. 398) note:

> women construct their identity either by building on a perceived dissonance between womanhood and entrepreneurship, or by refuting it. Women can perceive this dissonance either at the personal level or business level; those who do not perceive such dissonance still refer to their femininity when constructing their identity, although this is not such a salient element.

However, the process of acquiring, maintaining and restoring legitimacy is quite complex because all actions that contribute to legitimacy – whether deliberate or not – are judged differently by various stakeholders with various institutional logics (Überbacher, 2014, Fisher et al., 2017). Thus, the criteria used for judging legitimacy may differ depending on the stakeholder (Fisher et al., 2017) as well as the setting.

The above discussion points to the fact that institutions (both formal and informal) influence legitimacy perceptions of individuals, the firm and those of other stakeholders. Clearly, these studies do not fully capture the intricacies of the subject from the developing country context, and sub-Saharan Africa to be specific. Understanding the role of informal institutions in the region may be more relevant in some developing countries like Ghana where innovation is key to the growth and survival of entrepreneurship. Next, we discuss legitimacy and the gendered aspects of innovation. By turning to the legitimacy theory, the chapter aims to establish linkages between informal institutions and female innovation in sub-Saharan Africa.

4.   INNOVATION, LEGITIMACY AND GENDER

Innovation is key to the survival and growth of entrepreneurial firms and regional ecosystems (Ratten, 2020, Autio et al., 2014, Petersen and Kruss, 2019, Blake and Hanson, 2005). It is also critical to the entrepreneurship process (Shane, 2003, Thébaud, 2015, Alsos et al., 2013). Innovation ("the invention, development, and implementation of ideas" (Garud et al., 2013, p. 773)) is important due to the evolving nature of the business environment.

Innovation is even more relevant in a resource-constrained environment (Kodithuwakku and Rosa, 2002, Stenholm and Hytti, 2014). In such settings, the nature of innovation is distinct because of its incremental nature (Garud et al., 2013, Saka-Helmhout et al., 2019). Sometimes described as frugal innovation, they could be just minor additions to already existing products and services (Kumar and Bhaduri, 2014).

Like entrepreneurship (Bird and Brush, 2002, Gupta et al., 2009, Meyer et al., 2017) innovation is a gendered phenomenon (Blake and Hanson, 2005, Ljunggren et al., 2010, Beede et al., 2011, Alsos et al., 2013). As Kingiri (2013, p. 529) writes, "gender as a source of knowledge and power differentials that shape actors' behaviour with respect to access to differing resources can serve as an organising tool for innovation". Yet through a gendered lens innovation is sometimes "conceptualised as technology taking place in manufacturing" (Alsos et al., 2013, p. 243). Accordingly, most studies on innovation are confined to sectors and businesses owned and managed by men which are mostly in the areas of science, technology and engineering (Blake and Hanson, 2005, Ljunggren et al., 2010, Wajcman, 2010, Alsos et al., 2013). As such, the extension of such understandings of innovation to sub-Saharan Africa is problematic given the narrow conceptualisation of African female entrepreneurship (Ndemo and Mkalama, 2019) and the fact that the majority of women entrepreneurs operate within the non-manufacturing sectors, including services and retail (Abor and Quartey, 2010, Adom and Anambane, 2019).

However, the patriarchal, religious and traditional nature of sub-Saharan African society (Amine and Staub, 2009) requires that a study of women in this context must engage with the intersectional impact this has on their lived experiences. The permeation of these structural influences at all levels of social interaction in the region, also requires a multi-level analysis of the phenomenon (Layder, 1993). Although studies on innovation and gender highlight the gendered aspects, however, conceptualisations of gender, entrepreneurship and innovation do not accommodate the multiple hierarchical structures and mechanisms of informal institutions, or entrepreneurial experiences at the intersection of gender, culture and religion. In this chapter we argue that anything else simply paints a partial picture of the dynamics of entrepreneurship and innovation on the sub-continent and the following sections will lay out the argument for the importance of a multi-layered analysis.

5. FRAMEWORK ON THE ROLE OF INFORMAL INSTITUTIONS, FEMALE ENTREPRENEURSHIP AND INNOVATION

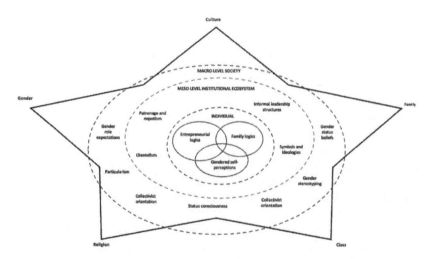

Figure 13.1   *Framework of multi-level informal institutions that impact on women's legitimacy in sub-Saharan Africa*

This section presents a conceptual framework of female innovation, institutions and legitimacy that shows the various levels of institutional effects on female innovation in sub-Saharan Africa: societal, institutional and individual levels at the intersection of culture, family, class, religion and gender as presented in Figure 13.1.

5.1   Societal Level

The level of normative support and legitimacy women entrepreneurs receive is a function of the gender role ideology in any society (Baughn et al., 2006). Informal institutional structures are embedded in the society and reinforced through the processes of socialisation and everyday practices. In sub-Saharan Africa these structures include particularism, gender role expectations, collectivist orientation, gender stereotyping, gender status beliefs and status consciousness (Kuada, 2009, Ratten, 2020) as well as conformity to or departure from these expectations, which impact legitimacy perceptions of female innovation, highlighting the importance of understanding the link between legitimacy perceptions of women and innovation.

Extant literature cites gender role expectations, particularly family roles and responsibilities as one of the critical norms affecting female innovation (Whittington, 2011, Alsos et al., 2013). The ascription of gender roles is typical of many societies worldwide including those in sub-Saharan Africa (Welter et al., 2014) and its role in hampering female entrepreneurship has been confirmed in various parts of sub-Saharan Africa (Madichie et al., 2008, Mordi et al., 2010, Aterido et al., 2011, Ogunsade and Obembe, 2016, Adom et al., 2018). Etim and Iwu (2019), for instance, note that such family and household responsibilities, and gender stereotypes do not allow women enough time to socialise to gain social and other forms of capital or focus on the business.

Additionally, in contemporary Africa, although traditional as well as evangelical Christian and other religious groups can provide an important avenue for social interaction and networking for female entrepreneurs (Kuada, 2009), their ideologies reinforce cultural beliefs about womanhood which discourage women from participating fully in the development of contemporary Africa (Rwafa, 2016, Bawa, 2018). Amine and Staub (2009) show how the social legitimacy of female entrepreneurs across the continent is impacted on by gender status beliefs about a woman's "divine positioning". Inherent in this, is the belief that women are custodians of acceptable traditional/religious beliefs and behaviours. As such, innovation (bucking the trend), viewed as risky behaviour, can sometimes conflict with the quest for women's empowerment (Moyo, 2004). Such gender status beliefs have implications for women's perceptions of themselves as legitimate change agents and in practice, reduces vital capital acquisition for innovation (such as crucial information and networks) as fewer women are able and willing to engage outside the "legitimate" arenas of appropriate female activity.

Moreover, the collectivist orientation coupled with status consciousness (Madubuike, 2015) prevalent in these settings (Beugre and Offodile, 2001, Muchiri, 2011) linked to family ties and informal networks adds another layer of complexity to the problem of perceptions of legitimacy of women. These shape women's choice to conform to, or break the norms. Essentially, departure from widely held views may result in the lack of support for the female entrepreneur and the business. In such instances where the legitimacy of the woman is questioned, "there may be perceptions that women are less legitimate or trustworthy in pursuing entrepreneurial activities and casting doubt over the legitimacy of the whole enterprise" (Brush et al., 2019, p. 399).

Closely linked to this is the issue of gender stereotypes which discourages women from pursuing certain careers or economic activities (Beede et al., 2011, Thébaud, 2015, Adom and Anambane, 2019). In the sub-Saharan context, for instance, female businesses often operate in the informal sectors, particularly retailing and personal services (Adom, 2015, Adom and Anambane, 2019) as a result of these gender stereotypes. For those that engage in entrepreneurial activities, gender stereotypes and role expectations inform decisions regarding the kind of activities women involve themselves in during the entrepreneurship process (Mungai and Ogot, 2012) including those that would lead to business growth, such as innovation-enhancing activities.

Consequently, relevant stakeholders and other actors (whose perceptions of what is legitimate and what is not are shaped by institutional structures) may be reluctant to provide the resources (including support) needed for innovation to take place (Zimmerman and Zeitz, 2002, Fisher et al., 2017). For instance, extended family members in Africa act as critical networks for innovation and entrepreneurship (Buame, 1998, Robson et al., 2009). These family members also approve of a woman's role as an entrepreneur (Liu et al., 2019) and in the context of particularism, patronage and nepotism women are likely to rely on their social networks for support to enable them to overcome challenges they face during the entrepreneurial process (Kuada, 2009). Such networks at the institutional level of operation, may be hesitant to provide such support if the legitimacy of the female innovator and the enterprise is questioned.

5.2   Institutional Level

Societal cultures influence organisational cultures, which, in turn, affect behaviours in organisations (Hofstede and McCrae, 2004). Forms of organisation at the institutional level include both productive and reproductive organisations – work and home – and the informal dynamics and norms of both have implications for women's legitimacy and innovation in their businesses (Langevang et al., 2015). Within the sub-Saharan African context, informality compliments the formal, yet weak, systems and forms complex linkages in almost all aspects of the institutional level (Saka-Helmhout et al., 2020). As such alongside formal practices, in Africa, the institutional level is characterised by patronage and nepotism, clientelism, informal leadership structures and particularism, making perceived legitimacy crucial to gaining access to the informal spaces within the system.

Norms and values held by actors within the entrepreneurial landscape often discourage women from venturing into, and managing larger enterprises (Aterido et al., 2011, Anambane and Adom, 2018). Indeed, Adom (2015, p. 19) takes note of a Ghanaian proverb that declares that "a woman sells eggplant/garden eggs and not gunpowder" implying that there is an expectation that women show modesty when they engage in business. Gender stereotyping combined with particularism and patronage results in women being shut out of networks that provide market information, managerial skills and technical competence, which further affects the size of businesses women run (Belwal et al., 2012). In Africa, the impact of this on performance is more pronounced for female owned businesses (Chirwa, 2008).

Mungai and Ogot (2012, p. 176) write that most African cultures are "of a masculine nature, with masculine notions, stereotypes, values, beliefs and assumptions" and organisational practices often reflect these masculine discourses. In the sub-Saharan context, these include speech prohibitions (Bourey et al., 2012) which may affect confidence in the woman's desire to speak up.It is clear from literature that although women may come up with innovative ideas, these ideas are often not implemented and not considered (Alsos et al., 2013). According to Alsos et al. (2013, p. 244), one reason for this is that "women are not perceived as innovators, and consequently their ideas do not get heard in the first place, or they are deemed inferior to men's ideas and therefore never proceed to the implementation phase". For example, Titi Amayah and Haque (2017) found that in sub-Saharan Africa, women are assumed to lack expertise simply because of their gender and motherhood.

Further, the evaluative criteria used to assess the standard of performance are reflective of status ascriptions (Thébaud, 2015) – this is likely even more so in contexts, such as sub-Saharan Africa, where status consciousness is highly linked to gender roles. The effect on innovation is that innovative activities men engage in are judged on the basis of their already-perceived legitimacy whereas women's are not (Thébaud, 2015). There is evidence that investors, for example, may have different perceptions concerning men and women's legitimacy to engage in innovative activities. In relation to this, Kanze et al. (2018) show that questions investors ask male and female entrepreneurs differ and this affects the outcomes.

At the entrepreneurial level, African women who venture into small-scale businesses may not have growth aspirations and this has consequences on their ability, as well as perceived legitimacy, to engage in innovative activities.

Sustained growth shapes stakeholder judgements regarding the legitimacy of a firm (Zimmerman and Zeitz, 2002) and resource holders and networks within the ecosystem form their legitimacy judgements about actors by considering the nature of economic activity, the size of the business and the industry (Brush et al., 2019). As such, the lack of growth of female-owned African businesses, and perceived lack of growth aspirations may mean that the extent to which these businesses can influence stakeholder perceptions regarding support for innovative activities is limited. This constitutes a major challenge to female innovation in sub-Saharan Africa as women in the region already face challenges securing needed resources such as finance for entrepreneurial activities, let alone innovative ones (Richardson et al., 2004, Aterido et al., 2011).

Organisational practices reflect gender differences and shape legitimacy perceptions (Brush et al., 2019). Masculine discourses and practices are pervasive in most organisations (including those set up to provide support services for women business owners) and Wikhamn and Knights (2013) have argued that they impede the progress and ultimate success of innovation initiatives. For example, Gajigo and Hallward-Driemeier (2010) have demonstrated how clientelism in sub-Saharan Africa results in women being asked for sexual favours when they engage in business transactions. Hallward-Driemeier (2013) suggests that these women are also afraid to go to the authorities to report the harassment due to fear of further harassment. This could keep women from engaging in certain activities (Hallward-Driemeier, 2013), including those that enhance innovation.

Within the domestic space, in Ghana, for example, the time toll exacted from women by gender role expectations has been shown to reduce the time and resources they have to grow their own businesses (Langevang et al., 2015). Langevang and his colleagues argue that women entrepreneurs in Ghana have less time to work on their businesses or engage in marketing expansion activities or to become involved in networking activities that are key to ensuring new sources of finance, new customers and markets, and gaining new knowledge and information (Amine and Staub, 2009). Hence, women are less likely to be innovative or expand their businesses, and they have higher failure rates. Singh et al. (2010) have also argued that due to customary patriarchal norms in force in Nigeria, female entrepreneurs struggle to find acceptance in the market and respect from their customers.

Lastly, Brush et al. (2019) cite symbols and images – within the firm and among stakeholders – as potential sources of gender divisions. Such symbols and images consist of depictions of entrepreneurs as men and women as mothers/homemakers, and this has consequences on the woman's identity. Researching on media representation of women in Nigeria Tijani-Adenle (2016), for example, revealed that narratives and stories on successful female entrepreneurs and leaders often surround their marital status or their homes.

Unfortunately, few female leaders and entrepreneurs featured in the Nigerian media challenged such perceptions but were ready to prove they are legitimate women in terms of being able to manage their homes and families successfully. Regarding this, Tijani-Adenle (2016, p. 402) lamented on how some women interviewees "are always eager to show they are able to do this perfectly, and there are times when women interviewees would volunteer the information without being asked". García and Welter (2013) in their analysis of women entrepreneurs in Spain revealed that those with higher status can change such perceptions by attempting to redo gender and "add value to it". Such actions impact legitimacy perceptions of female entrepreneurs to engage in entrepreneurial activities at the institutional, individual and organisational levels.

5.3   Individual Level

At this level, there are several factors that impact on women's legitimacy and therefore their innovation activities. First, Alam (2011) has revealed that perceived personality traits of an entrepreneur have significant impacts on the firm's legitimacy and innovation capability. Second, the entrepreneur's credentials are positively related to perceived legitimacy, and finally, the entrepreneur's own self-identity can be said to have an impact on self-perceptions of legitimacy, with attendant impacts on self-confidence and risk-taking behaviour.

The idea of entrepreneurs as change agents has received wide acceptance. Related to this, traits theory posits that entrepreneurs are the ones primarily responsible for initiating and sustaining change in society – that entrepreneurs possess certain traits such as risk-propensity and ambition that engender innovation. The entrepreneur's styles of leadership and management have also often been linked to specific organisational practices such as innovation. Alam (2011, p. 56) identified personality traits linked to innovation as "independence of judgment, self-confidence, and attraction to complexity, aesthetic orientation and risk taking". Risk-taking propensity is crucial for small firms' development and success (Antoncic et al., 2012) and innovation is impacted by the risk-taking attitudes and entrepreneurial intensity of the women leaders of firms. Further, given the small sizes of the firms that are owned and managed by women in Africa, it is difficult to distinguish the individual woman's risk-taking attitude and entrepreneurial intensity from that of the firm. Yet the perceived aggressive nature of business and the belief that women business owners must display masculine traits, leads to the perception that in Africa, femininity inherently produces weak leadership (Titi Amayah and Haque, 2017). Consequently, the women who run these firms may be perceived to lack the traits required to initiate innovative ideas or have those ideas taken seriously.

Second, many stakeholder decisions about entrepreneurs are made on the basis of conformance to professional norms and expectations (Zimmerman and Zeitz, 2002). Indeed, Nagy et al. (2012, p. 944) have posited that "credentials related to an entrepreneur's educational accomplishments, social status, industry experience, and family background serve as cues that entrepreneurs are in line with widely recognised norms and expectations developed by stakeholders". However, in sub-Saharan Africa there is high status-consciousness and yet gender role expectations lead to fewer women engaging in the educational system (Hallward-Driemeier, 2013) and gaining the educational, as well as industry experience credentials. Amine and Staub (2009) have argued that this lack of educational opportunities for girls puts adult women at a considerable disadvantage – that it makes them socially subordinate, ill-equipped to resist family pressure to conform to gender role expectations and unable to engage in business on an equal footing with men.

Finally, legitimacy shapes individuals' identity formation, which concerns "who we are" and "what we do" (Navis and Glynn, 2011, p. 479). Largely, identities and images are inextricably linked to rules and norms prescribed by institutional structures. The legitimacy of a woman in her role as a woman is perceived in engaging with her family (Eagly et al., 2000), and the legitimacy of a person in the role of entrepreneur is perceived in networking with other stakeholders (De Clercq and Voronov, 2009). Hamilton (2013) has argued that for women, depending on the culture, there is role conflict between their role as entrepreneur and that of a woman.

Cultures like those in sub-Saharan Africa with steep gender hierarchies expect women to be homemakers. In these regions also, entrepreneurship is seen as a legitimate economic activity. Therefore, female entrepreneurs in sub-Saharan Africa may encounter difficulties navigating through the entrepreneurship process. Many African women face identity struggles in trying to align their identities with norms and values regarding societal and institutional constructions of a female and an entrepreneur (Hamilton, 2013, Liu et al., 2019). In Nigeria for example, Singh et al. (2010) have demonstrated how a large number of men believe that if a woman is independent (in particular, unmarried) and successful, they do not deserve to be considered chaste and respectable and so cannot play the role of good mothers and wives. Family and close network members (e.g. church friends) may rely on the family logic when judging a woman's legitimacy as an entrepreneur whereas business networks rely on entrepreneurial logics when considering her legitimacy as an entrepreneur (Liu et al., 2019). Further, responsibility for ensuring the right balance between the two identities is placed on the individual woman and negative experiences or consequences of the work and family nexus are perceived as a failure of personal responsibility which may simply reinforce the notion that women cannot do both successfully.

6.   CONCLUSION

This chapter set out to answer the core question of how informal institutional structures inform legitimacy perceptions of female innovation in sub-Saharan Africa. Scholars suggest that the legitimacy an entrepreneur experiences affects his or her motivation and access to resources (Überbacher, 2014). We have argued, however, that previous research has presented a fragmented view of female entrepreneurship and innovation in Africa and has not accommodated the multiple hierarchical systems that shape a woman's experience. Instead, we posit that salient factors at the meso, micro and individual levels impact the willingness and ability of women to engage in innovative activities. The argument is situated within the ongoing scholarly discussions on legitimacy, gender, innovation and informal institutions. On the basis of our reasoning, we have presented a conceptual framework of the informal institutions that impact on the legitimacy of female entrepreneurs in Africa and therefore on their ability to innovate and grow their businesses. Our framework shows the various levels of intersectional informal institutional effects on female legitimacy and innovation in sub-Saharan Africa including conflicting family and entrepreneurial norms and logics at the micro level; the relationship between informal and formal dynamics at the meso institutional level and the cultural, religious, gendered, family and class-based social structures at the level of the society.

The framework presented in this chapter also considers the influence of the intersectionality of gender, culture, religion, class and family on legitimacy perceptions of women business innovation. The conceptual model presented allows a consideration of these influences of gender, "religion" and culture on women's legitimacy perceptions, that of their families and firms as well as the broad society within the sub-Saharan African context. The next stage will be to test the framework in the field to determine the comprehensive nature of these influences of women business owners' legitimacy perceptions in innovation. In applying this framework, future studies could examine how women "redo" gender when confronted with challenges posed by informal institutional structures that impact their motivation and ability to engage in, and outcomes of innovative activities. Policy makers may also find this framework useful when addressing issues affecting female innovation in sub-Saharan Africa.

ACKNOWLEDGEMENT

This research was funded through the UKRI Global Challenges Research Fund RECIRCULATE project (ES/P010857/1).

REFERENCES

Abor, J. & Quartey, P. 2010. Issues in SME development in Ghana and South Africa. *International Research Journal of Finance and Economics*, 39, 215–228.

Acs, Z. J., Stam, E., Audretsch, D. B. & O'Connor, A. 2017. The lineages of the entrepreneurial ecosystem approach. *Small Business Economics*, 49, 1–10.

Adom, K. 2015. Recognizing the contribution of female entrepreneurs in economic development in sub-Saharan Africa: Some evidence from Ghana. *Journal of Developmental Entrepreneurship*, 20, 1550003.

Adom, K. & Anambane, G. 2019. Understanding the role of culture and gender stereotypes in women entrepreneurship through the lens of the stereotype threat theory. *Journal of Entrepreneurship in Emerging Economies*, 12, 100–124.

Adom, K., Asare-Yeboa, I. T., Quaye, D. M. & Ampomah, A. O. 2018. A critical assessment of work and family life of female entrepreneurs in sub-Saharan Africa. *Journal of Small Business and Enterprise Development*, 25, 405–427.

Ahlstrom, D. & Bruton, G. D. 2002. An institutional perspective on the role of culture in shaping strategic actions by technology-focused entrepreneurial firms in China. *Entrepreneurship Theory and Practice*, 26, 53–68.

Alam, S. S. 2011. Entrepreneur's traits and firm innovation capability: An empirical study in Malaysia. *Asian Journal of Technology Innovation*, 19, 53–66.

Aldrich, H. E. & Fiol, C. M. 1994. Fools rush in? The institutional context of industry creation. *Academy of Management Review*, 19, 645–670.

Alsos, G. A., Hytti, U. & Ljunggren, E. 2013. Gender and innovation: State of the art and a research agenda. *International Journal of Gender and Entrepreneurship*, 5, 236–256.

Alvedalen, J. & Boschma, R. 2017. A critical review of entrepreneurial ecosystems research: Towards a future research agenda. *European Planning Studies*, 25, 887–903.

Amine, L. S. & Staub, K. M. 2009. Women entrepreneurs in sub-Saharan Africa: An institutional theory analysis from a social marketing point of view. *Entrepreneurship and Regional Development*, 21, 183–211.

Anambane, G. & Adom, K. 2018. Assessing the role of culture in female entrepreneurship in contemporary sub-Saharan society: Insights from the Nabdam District of Ghana. *Journal of Developmental Entrepreneurship*, 23, 1850017.

Antoncic, B., Auer Antoncic, J. & Gantar, M. 2012. Risk-taking propensity of entrepreneurs and their non-persistence in entrepreneurship. Advances in Business-Related Scientific Research Conference, 5–7.

Aterido, R., Beck, T. & Iacovone, L. 2011. *Gender and finance in sub-Saharan Africa: Are women disadvantaged?* The World Bank.

Atiase, V. Y., Mahmood, S., Wang, Y. & Botchie, D. 2018. Developing entrepreneurship in Africa: Investigating critical resource challenges. *Journal of Small Business and Enterprise Development*, 25, 644–666.

Atieno, R. 2001. *Formal and informal institutions' lending policies and access to credit by small-scale enterprises in Kenya: An empirical assessment.* The African Economic Research Consortium.

Autio, E., Kenney, M., Mustar, P., Siegel, D. & Wright, M. 2014. Entrepreneurial innovation: The importance of context. *Research Policy*, 43, 1097–1108.

Baughn, C. C., Chua, B. L. & Neupert, K. E. 2006. The normative context for women's participation in entrepreneurship: A multicountry study. *Entrepreneurship Theory and Practice*, 30, 687–708.

Bawa, S. 2018. "Feminists make too much noise!": Generational differences and ambivalence in feminist development politics in Ghana. *Canadian Journal of African Studies/Revue canadienne des études africaines*, 52, 1–17.

Beede, D. N., Julian, T. A., Langdon, D., McKittrick, G., Khan, B. & Doms, M. E. 2011. Women in STEM: A gender gap to innovation. *Economics and Statistics Administration Issue Brief.*

Belwal, R., Tamiru, M. & Singh, G. 2012. Microfinance and sustained economic improvement: Women small-scale entrepreneurs in Ethiopia. *Journal of International Development*, 24, S84–S99.

Beugre, C. D. & Offodile, O. F. 2001. Managing for organizational effectiveness in sub-Saharan Africa: A culture-fit model. *International Journal of Human Resource Management*, 12, 535–550.

Bird, B. & Brush, C. 2002. A gendered perspective on organizational creation. *Entrepreneurship Theory and Practice*, 26, 41–65.

Blake, M. K. & Hanson, S. 2005. Rethinking innovation: context and gender. *Environment and Planning A*, 37, 681–701.

Bourey, C., Stephenson, R., Bartel, D. & Rubardt, M. 2012. Pile sorting innovations: Exploring gender norms, power and equity in sub-Saharan Africa. *Global Public Health*, 7, 995–1008.

Brush, C., Edelman, L. F., Manolova, T. & Welter, F. 2019. A gendered look at entrepreneurship ecosystems. *Small Business Economics*, 53, 393–408.

Bruton, G. D., Ahlstrom, D. & Li, H. L. 2010. Institutional theory and entrepreneurship: Where are we now and where do we need to move in the future? *Entrepreneurship Theory and Practice*, 34, 421–440.

Buame, S. K. 1998. *Entrepreneurship: A contextual perspective. Discourses and praxis of entrepreneurial activities within the institutional context of Ghana.* Lund University Press.

Chirwa, E. W. 2008. Effects of gender on the performance of micro and small enterprises in Malawi. *Development Southern Africa*, 25, 347–362.

Clark, G. 1997. Market queens: Innovation within Akan tradition. *Annals of the New York Academy of Sciences*, 810, 173–201.

De Clercq, D. & Voronov, M. 2009. Toward a practice perspective of entrepreneurship: Entrepreneurial legitimacy as habitus. *International Small Business Journal*, 27, 395–419.

Deephouse, D. L., Bundy, J., Tost, L. P. & Suchman, M. C. 2017. Organizational legitimacy: Six key questions. In R. Greenwood, C. Oliver, T. Lawrence & R. Meyer (Eds), *The Sage handbook of organizational institutionalism* 4, 27–54. Sage Publications.

Eagly, A. H., Wood, W. & Diekman, A. B. 2000. Social role theory of sex differences and similarities: A current appraisal. In T. Eckes & H. M. Trautner (Eds), *The developmental social psychology of gender*, 123–174. Lawrence Erlbaum.

Etim, E. & Iwu, C. G. 2019. A descriptive literature review of the continued marginalisation of female entrepreneurs in sub-Saharan Africa. *International Journal of Gender Studies in Developing Societies*, 3, 1–19.

Fisher, G., Kuratko, D. F., Bloodgood, J. M. & Hornsby, J. S. 2017. Legitimate to whom? The challenge of audience diversity and new venture legitimacy. *Journal of Business Venturing*, 32, 52–71.

Frydrych, D., Bock, A.J., Kinder, T. & Koeck, B. 2014. Exploring entrepreneurial legitimacy in reward-based crowdfunding. *Venture Capital*, 16, 247–269.

Fu, Y., Liu, R., Yang, J., Jiao, H. & Jin, Y. 2020. "Lean in": The moderating effect of female ownership on the relationship between human capital and organizational innovation. *Journal of Intellectual Capital*, 22, 792–814.

Fuentelsaz, L., Maicas, J. P. & Mata, P. 2018. Institutional dynamism in entrepreneurial ecosystems. In A. O'Connor, E. Stam, F. Sussan & D. B. Audretsch (Eds), *Entrepreneurial ecosystems: placed-based transformations and transitions*, 38, 45–65.

Gajigo, O. & Hallward-Driemeier, M. 2010. Entrepreneurship among new entrepreneurs. *World Bank Mimeo*. Washington DC: World Bank.

Garcia, M.-C. D. & Welter, F. 2013. Gender identities and practices: Interpreting women entrepreneurs' narratives. *International Small Business Journal*, 31, 384–404.

Garud, R., Tuertscher, P. & Van de Ven A. H. 2013. Perspectives on innovation processes. *Academy of Management Annals*, 7, 775–819.

Gaye, D. 2018. Female entrepreneurs: The future of the African continent. *The World Bank*.

Gertler, M. S. 2010. Rules of the game: The place of institutions in regional economic change. *Regional Studies*, 44, 1–15.

Gupta, V. K., Turban, D. B., Wasti, S. A. & Sikdar, A. 2009. The role of gender stereotypes in perceptions of entrepreneurs and intentions to become an entrepreneur. *Entrepreneurship Theory and Practice*, 33, 397–417.

Hallward-Driemeier, M. 2013. *Enterprising women: Expanding economic opportunities in Africa*. World Bank Publications.

Hamilton, E. 2013. The discourse of entrepreneurial masculinities (and femininities). *Entrepreneurship & Regional Development*, 25, 90–99.

Hofstede, G. & McCrae, R. R. 2004. Personality and culture revisited: Linking traits and dimensions of culture. *Cross-Cultural Research*, 38, 52–88.

Ighomereho, O. S., Agbalajobi, T. D. & Edegwa, K. 2013. Gender influence on access to innovation resources in Nigeria. *International Journal of Humanities and Social Science*, 3, 216–227.

Kanze, D., Huang, L., Conley, M. A. & Higgins, E. T. 2018. We ask men to win and women not to lose: Closing the gender gap in startup funding. *Academy of Management Journal*, 61, 586–614.

Kingiri, A. N. 2013. A review of innovation systems framework as a tool for gendering agricultural innovations: Exploring gender learning and system empowerment. *The Journal of Agricultural Education and Extension*, 19, 521–541.

Kiraka, M., Kobia, M. & Katwalo, A. 2013. *Micro, small and medium enterprise growth and innovation in Kenya*. Longhorn Publishers.

Kodithuwakku, S. S. & Rosa, P. 2002. The entrepreneurial process and economic success in a constrained environment. *Journal of Business Venturing*, 17, 431–465.

Kuada, J. 2009. Gender, social networks, and entrepreneurship in Ghana. *Journal of African Business*, 10, 85–103.

Kumar, H. & Bhaduri, S. 2014. Jugaad to grassroot innovations: Understanding the landscape of the informal sector innovations in India. *African Journal of Science, Technology, Innovation and Development*, 6, 13–22.

Langevang, T., Gough, K. V., Yankson, P. W., Owusu, G. & Osei, R. 2015. Bounded entrepreneurial vitality: The mixed embeddedness of female entrepreneurship. *Economic Geography*, 91, 449–473.

Layder, D. 1993. *New strategies in social research: An introduction and guide.* Polity Press.

Liu, Y., Schott, T. & Zhang, C. 2019. Women's experiences of legitimacy, satisfaction and commitment as entrepreneurs: embedded in gender hierarchy and networks in private and business spheres. *Entrepreneurship & Regional Development,* 31, 293–307.

Ljunggren, E., Alsos, G. A., Amble, N., Ervik, R., Kvidal, T. & Wiik, R. 2010. Gender and innovation. *Learning from regional VRI-projects. NF-report,* 2, 2010.

Lounsbury, M. & Glynn, M. A. 2001. Cultural entrepreneurship: Stories, legitimacy, and the acquisition of resources. *Strategic Management Journal,* 22, 545–564.

Madichie, N. O., Nkamnebe, A. D. & Idemobi, E. I. 2008. Cultural determinants of entrepreneurial emergence in a typical sub-Sahara African context. *Journal of Enterprising Communities: People and Places in the Global Economy,* 2, 285–299.

Madubuike, S. C. 2015. Culture, gender and identity: Images and realities in Igbo community, Nigeria. *International Invention Journal of Arts and Social Sciences,* 2, 44–51.

Meyer, V., Tegtmeier, S. & Pakura, S. 2017. Revisited: How gender role stereotypes affect the image of entrepreneurs among young adults. *International Journal of Gender and Entrepreneurship,* 9, 319–337.

Minniti, M. 2009. *Gender issues in entrepreneurship.* Now Publishers.

Moore, M. 1997. Societies, polities and capitalists in developing countries: A literature survey. *The Journal of Development Studies,* 33, 287–363.

Mordi, C., Simpson, R., Singh, S. & Okafor, C. 2010. The role of cultural values in understanding the challenges faced by female entrepreneurs in Nigeria. *Gender in Management: An International Journal,* 25, 5–21.

Moyo, F. L. 2004. Religion, spirituality and being a woman in Africa: Gender construction within the African religio-cultural experiences. *Agenda,* 18, 72–78.

Muchiri, M. K. 2011. Leadership in context: A review and research agenda for sub-Saharan Africa. *Journal of Occupational and Organizational Psychology,* 84, 440–452.

Mungai, E. N. & Ogot, M. 2012. Gender, culture and entrepreneurship in Kenya. *International Business Research,* 5, 175–183.

Nagy, B. G., Pollack, J. M., Rutherford, M. W. & Lohrke, F. T. 2012. The influence of entrepreneurs' credentials and impression management behaviors on perceptions of new venture legitimacy. *Entrepreneurship Theory and Practice,* 36, 941–965.

Navis, C. & Glynn, M. A. 2011. Legitimate distinctiveness and the entrepreneurial identity: Influence on investor judgments of new venture plausibility. *Academy of Management Review,* 36, 479–499.

Ndemo E. B. & Mkalama, B. 2019. Globalization: Do African women entrepreneurs matter? *International Journal of Management & Entrepreneurship Research,* 1, 89–104.

Ngoasong, M. Z. & Kimbu, A. N. 2019. Why hurry? The slow process of high growth in women-owned businesses in a resource-scarce context. *Journal of Small Business Management,* 57, 40–58.

North, D. C. 1991. Institutions. *Journal of Economic Perspectives,* 5, 97–112.

Ogunsade, I. A. & Obembe, D. 2016. The influence of informal institutions on informal sector entrepreneurship: A study of Nigeria's hand-woven textile industry. *Journal of Small Business & Entrepreneurship,* 28, 413–429.

Petersen, I.-H. & Kruss, G. 2019. Promoting alignment between innovation policy and inclusive development in South Africa. *Development Southern Africa,* 36, 351–375.

Powell, W. W. & Colyvas, J. A. 2008. Microfoundations of institutional theory. In R. Greenwood, R. Suddaby, C. Oliver & K. Sahlin (Eds), *The Sage handbook of organizational institutionalism*, 276–298. Sage Publications.

Ratten, V. 2020. African entrepreneurship. *Small Enterprise Research*, 1–7.

Rauf, M. 2009. Innovations and informal institutions: An institutionalist approach to the role of social capital for innovation. *Journal of Academic Research in Economics*, 25–34.

Richardson, P., Howarth, R. & Finnegan, G. 2004. *The challenges of growing small businesses: Insights from women entrepreneurs in Africa*. International Labour Office Geneva.

Robson, P. J., Haugh, H. M. & Obeng, B. A. 2009. Entrepreneurship and innovation in Ghana: enterprising Africa. *Small Business Economics*, 32, 331–350.

Rwafa, U. 2016. Culture and religion as sources of gender inequality: Rethinking challenges women face in contemporary Africa. *Journal of Literary Studies*, 32, 43–52.

Saka-Helmhout, A., Chappin, M. & Vermeulen, P. 2019. Multiple paths to firm innovation in sub-Saharan Africa: How informal institutions matter. *Organization Studies*, 0170840619882971.

Saka-Helmhout, A., Chappin, M. & Vermeulen, P. 2020. Multiple paths to firm innovation in sub-Saharan Africa: How informal institutions matter. *Organization Studies*, 41, 1551–1575.

Salimath, M. S. & Cullen, J. B. 2010. Formal and informal institutional effects on entrepreneurship: A synthesis of nation-level research. *International Journal of Organizational Analysis*, 18, 358–385.

Shane, S. A. 2003. *A general theory of entrepreneurship: The individual–opportunity nexus*. Cheltenham, UK and Northampton, MA, USA: Edward Elgar Publishing.

Singh, S., Mordi, C., Okafor, C. & Simpson, R. 2010. Challenges in female entrepreneurial development: A case analysis of Nigerian entrepreneurs. *Journal of Enterprising Culture*, 18, 435–460.

Stenhom, P. & Hytti, U. 2014. In search of legitimacy under institutional pressures: A case study of producer and entrepreneur farmer identities. *Journal of Rural Studies*, 35, 133–142.

Thébaud, S. 2015. Status beliefs and the spirit of capitalism: Accounting for gender biases in entrepreneurship and innovation. *Social Forces*, 94, 61–86.

Tijani-Adenle, G. 2016. She's homely, beautiful and then, hardworking! *Gender in Management: An International Journal*, 31, 396–410.

Titi Amayah, A. & Haque, M. 2017. Experiences and challenges of women leaders in Sub-Saharan Africa. *Africa Journal of Management*, 3, 99–127.

Überbacher, F. 2014. Legitimation of new ventures: A review and research programme. *Journal of Management Studies*, 51, 667–698.

Wajcman, J. 2010. Feminist theories of technology. *Cambridge Journal of Economics*, 34, 143–152.

Wang, L., Ren, S. & Xie, E. 2011. The effect of R&D collaboration on firm's innovation performance. *Studies in Science of Science*, 29, 787–792.

Webb, J. W., Khoury, T. A. & Hitt, M. A. 2020. The influence of formal and informal institutional voids on entrepreneurship. *Entrepreneurship Theory and Practice*, 44, 504–526.

Welter, F. 2002. Trust, institutions and entrepreneurial behaviour. *Entrepreneurial Strategies and Trust*, 37–42.

Welter, F., Brush, C. & De Bruin, A. 2014. The gendering of entrepreneurship context. *Institut für Mittelstandsforschung Bonn (Hrsg.)*. Working Paper, 1, 14.

Welter, F. & Smallbone, D. 2011. Institutional perspectives on entrepreneurial behavior in challenging environments. *Journal of Small Business Management*, 49, 107–125.

Whittington, K. B. 2011. Mothers of invention? Gender, motherhood, and new dimensions of productivity in the science profession. *Work and Occupations*, 38, 417–456.

Wikhamn, B. R. & Knights, D. 2013. Open innovation, gender and the infiltration of masculine discourses. *International Journal of Gender and Entrepreneurship*, 5, 275–297.

Zimmerman, M. A. & Zeitz, G. J. 2002. Beyond survival: Achieving new venture growth by building legitimacy. *Academy of Management Review*, 27, 414–431.

14. Women's entrepreneurship in the inclusive innovation ecosystem in Canada

Wendy Cukier, Guang Ying Mo and Jodi-Ann Francis

1. INTRODUCTION

Entrepreneurship is a key driver of Canada's economic growth, with small and medium enterprises accounting for more than 88.3% of private sector employment (Government of Canada, 2021). Women are becoming a growing proportion of entrepreneurs, but still account for only about 16% of majority owners of SMEs with fewer than 20 employees (Grekou et al. 2018) although they account for almost 38% of self-employed Canadians (Statistics Canada 2019). McKinsey Global Institute (2017) has indicated that bridging gaps between men and women entrepreneurs could add as much as $150 billion to Canada's GDP in 2026. The Government of Canada launched the Women Entrepreneurship Strategy (WES) in 2019, which is a $5-billion investment aiming to double women-owned businesses by 2025. WES is a unique approach globally offering a "whole-of-government" approach to addressing the issue. In addition to providing funds for women-owned businesses – and to offering preferential procurement and support for programs – the government has specifically set aside funds to support the women entrepreneurship ecosystems with investments in organizations offering supports to women entrepreneurs.

Women's entrepreneurship is structurally different from men's. For example, women are more likely to be in services and are less likely to be in technology. Women-owned enterprises are likely to be smaller and underfinanced – and are less likely to be incorporated or high-growth. Women entrepreneurs have different preferences and needs. Yet, this chapter will argue, the ways in which the innovation and entrepreneurship ecosystem operate is based largely on definitions and models that were built by men to support men. A gender and diversity analysis reveals ways in which bias is built into the system.

2.   AN ECOSYSTEM PERSPECTIVE

Innovation is regarded as a key driver of economic growth, and entrepreneurs play an important role in driving innovation. Globally, national governments invest heavily in programs intended to advance innovation and economic growth, and Canada is no exception, investing billions in research and development, incubators and accelerators, and targeting financing (loans, grants and tax breaks) to promote innovation and entrepreneurship. Research has focused on exploring on how innovation happens (Helbing 2012), is measured and fostered (Lounsbury et al. 2019; Valliere 2017) as well as how the components of the innovation ecosystem interact (Stam & Spigel 2016). Recognizing that innovation activities in firms depend heavily on external sources, attention in recent decades has focused on understanding the systems that support or impede innovation – for example formal and informal institutions (laws, regulations, culture), political processes, research infrastructure, financial institutions, skills, and the linkages between them. An innovation ecosystem is understood to be the evolving set of actors, activities, and artifacts, and the institutions and relations, including complementary and substitute relations, that are important for the innovative performance of an actor or a population of actors (Granstrand & Holgersson 2020). Extensive research has focused on understanding how components of this ecosystem work, assessing, for example, investments in R&D, levels of education, technological infrastructure, financing, and more (OECD 2020). The entrepreneur features prominently in this system as the person who created the new combinations that resulted in new products, new methods of production, new sources of supply, the exploitation of new markets, or new business models (Schumpeter 1911/1934). In the words of Drucker (1993) "Entrepreneurs innovate. Innovation is the specific instrument of entrepreneurs" (p. 30). More recently, attention has focused specifically on how these systems support individual entrepreneurs, which several researchers have described as the entrepreneurial ecosystem concept that focuses on the systems that support or impede entrepreneurs. Isenberg (2010) identified nine elements for these ecosystems, and Stam and Spigel (2016) further elaborated the interactional relationships among actors, such as framework conditions (i.e., formal institutions, culture, physical infrastructure, and demand), systemic conditions (i.e., network, leadership, finance, talent, new knowledge, and support services), entrepreneurial outputs (i.e., innovative startups, high-growth startup, and entrepreneurial employee activities), and outcomes (i.e., productivity, income, employment and well-being). The Global Entrepreneurship Monitor (GEM) also considers "enabling conditions" as an aspect of entrepreneurship ecosystems when assessing entrepreneurial intentions across countries in their annual survey.

While there has been extensive research on the structural differences affecting women entrepreneurs, as well as the barriers that they face, less attention has been focused on the ways in which innovation and entrepreneurship ecosystems support or impede their progress. Informed by research on women entrepreneurs and the critical ecological model (Cukier et al. 2014), which offers a systematic approach to gender and diversity analysis, this chapter examines ways in which elements of the innovation and entrepreneurship ecosystems affect women's entrepreneurship. The model offers an approach to gender and diversity analysis, that recognizes the ways in which gender bias and discrimination are embedded at the macro (societal), meso (organizational) and micro (individual) level and their interactions.

The model also recognizes that there are no simple solutions to complex problems and that strategies for change must also address factors at all three levels. For example, at the macro level, government policies (for example childcare) or culture (for example gendered stereotypes) can support or impede inclusion. Similarly, at the organizational level, policies, practice, values, and culture play a role in determining who is included and who is excluded. At the individual level, knowledge, skills, and behaviour also have an impact, for example, on interpersonal relations, including micro-aggressions or micro-affirmations. This critical ecological model can be applied to our understanding of innovation and entrepreneurship ecosystems to expose barriers to women and diverse entrepreneurs and to inform a strategy to level the playing field (Figure 14.1).

3.   COMPONENTS OF THE ENTREPRENEURSHIP ECOSYSTEM

Stam and Spigel's Entrepreneurial Ecosystem Model (2016) distinguishes framework conditions – formal institutions, culture, physical infrastructure, and demand – from what they term systemic conditions, which are required by entrepreneurs, including networks, leadership, finance, talent, new knowledge, and support services. These all, effectively, are the resources or assets entrepreneurs can access. Partially like this model, our model of innovation and entrepreneurship ecosystems in Canada also considers policy, culture, infrastructure and socio-economic conditions at the macro level, but is focused on organizations operating within these conditions that interact to support innovation and entrepreneurship. These entities including post-secondary institutions (sources of new knowledge), startups, established businesses, financial institutions (source of financing), the talent pool, and intermediaries (business support organizations). Some of the major challenges in the ecosystems include fragmentation between the relevant stakeholders, fractured strategies, and uneven implementation. Canada's lack of population density and large geographic area also pose challenges for networking and cause inconsistent adoption of technology. One outcome of this fragmentation can be seen in the slow institutional response in the ecosystems, such as in post-secondary institutions seen by some as being in misalignment with the needs of many regions (Cukier et al. 2016).

4. GENDER ANALYSIS: MACRO-, MESO- AND MICRO-LEVEL ISSUES

To date, there has been limited research examining entrepreneurship ecosystems through a gender or diversity lens. Some researchers have considered aspects of it – such as social capital and networks – for example, Neumeyer and Santos (2018) focus specifically on the effects of venture typology, race, ethnicity, and past venture experience on the social capital distribution of entrepreneurs in two municipal ecosystems in the U.S. Studies also look at other aspects, including institutional norms (Ahl 2016; Estrin & Mickiewicz 2011), gendered social structures (Coleman et al. 2019; Stam & Spigel 2016), and their impacts on gender diversity within the entrepreneurship ecosystems (Brush et al. 2019). Recently, researchers have started to shed light on the impacts of gender diversity on the growth of the ecosystems. For example, Hughes (2017) studies women entrepreneurs' engagement in the ecosystems and their contribution to the economy in Canada. This is particularly the case within the scope of innovation, where there is a greater variation and contingency in the gender gap across countries, regions, and sectors with respect to entrepreneurship (Hughes 2017).

4.1 Macro (Societal) Level

At the broadest level of analysis, societal-level factors, such as government policies, media, culture, and infrastructure, shape opportunities for women entrepreneurs (Shane & Venkataraman 2000). Government policies and programs have a profound impact on shaping opportunities for women whether in terms of regulatory requirements around employment equity, funding eligibility tax policy, procurement, or access to affordable childcare. For example, most government programs focus on incorporated SMEs, on technology, and on growth, which tend to exclude women.

Policies to support small businesses and innovation programs are seldom examined through a gendered lens (Coleman et al. 2019), and as a result, women face systemic barriers in accessing grants and financing as certain industries, primarily those where men dominate, are preferred over others (Eddleston et al. 2016). The focus on STEM, as well as the promotion of men-dominated, high-growth, and export-based businesses, tends to exclude women (Anna et al. 2000; Foss et al. 2018).

Culture, beliefs, and values also play a role in entrepreneurship ecosystems (Jennings & Brush 2013). Notions of entrepreneurship are highly gendered and associated with tech entrepreneurs (Hindle & Moroz 2010). "Think entrepreneur" and most people think Bill Gates, Steve Jobs, and Mark Zuckerberg, even though these are a small proportion of entrepreneurs. These stereotypes are reflected and reinforced in the media and not only shape the design of programs and the experiences of diverse entrepreneurs, but also affect the aspirations of groups who are less likely to see themselves as entrepreneurs (Politis & Dahlstrand 2011). The media's role in romanticizing the entrepreneurial experience, with images of men who have mostly been involved with IT-related innovations while depicting more cultural, home-based, or "lifestyle" visuals as women's domain, acts as a barrier as it perpetuates a gendered view of innovation (Mundy 2014).

Deeper analysis shows how even concepts, such as innovation, become gendered. While innovation is not inherently about making technology – it is about doing differently – the discourse on innovation tends to focus on technology. This gives rise to policies and programs which exclude sectors such as services, or social enterprises in which women and other underrepresented groups, such as Indigenous Peoples, are more likely to participate (Beckton et al. 2018).

4.2   Meso (Organizational) Level

Key stakeholders in ecosystems include financial institutions and venture capitalists, incubators and business intermediaries (including some designed to support women), post-secondary institutions, startups, and established businesses, which are critical customers (Vershinina et al. 2015). Their policies and practices have a profound impact on the opportunities available for women and other diverse groups. Ensuring organizations in an innovation ecosystem are diverse and inclusive requires attention at multiple levels.

Financial institutions, venture investors, and angel funders are important actors in innovation and entrepreneurship ecosystems, and we need to consider their policies and processes. Majority women-owned firms are less aggressive in financing their businesses' growth through debt compared to those owned by men, and, in 2004, majority women-owned enterprises were less likely to get debt financing approved than those owned by men. The approval rates were 79% for women-owned enterprises, and 88% for men-owned enterprises; further, entrepreneurs who are men are more likely to use requested debt financing as a source of working and operating capital than their women counterparts (Jung 2010). In part, this explains why women business owners are less likely to acquire and use different sources of financing to start up their businesses, and are willing to consider sharing equity in their enterprises to fund growth even as their need for external scale up funding increases (Jung 2010).

Additionally, some of this difference in debt financing is the result of stereotyping. Employees, customers, suppliers, and financial institutions treat women business owners as less credible, creating barriers that prevent women from raising funds for their startups and generating financial growth (Vershinina et al. 2015). Although studies suggest that women face more difficulties receiving financing than men (Malmstrom et al. 2017; Saparito et al. 2013), research shows that when we control for a range of factors, the playing field is not as uneven as some might think. Yet evidence remains strong that gender stereotypes perpetuate the perception that the ideal entrepreneur is a man, not a woman (Malmstrom et al. 2017). Capital providers assess the business characteristics of men and women entrepreneurs differently, "to the disadvantage of women" (Eddleston et al. 2016, p. 489).

Incubators, whether linked to a university or standalone, often have policies, processes, and cultures that are not friendly to women and that do not equally benefit women and men. Applied to organizations across Canada, the Diversity Institute's Diversity Assessment Tool (DAT) reveals that most incubators lack governance and strategy, HR processes, metrics, policies, culture, or outreach approaches aimed at attracting, retaining, and supporting women (Cukier & Hassannezhad Chavoushi 2020). Publicly funded, technology incubators and accelerators have become a critical part of the innovation ecosystems in Canada. There is considerable evidence that most are not welcoming places for women entrepreneurs and maintain a status quo advantageous for white male technology entrepreneurs. Women entrepreneurs tend neither to have access to the power brokers in such contexts, nor to be sponsored by them. The benefits of social capital are unequally distributed across women and men, and access to networks is not gender-neutral (Ozkazanc-Pan & Clark Muntean 2018). They also lack proper mentorship for women, as young women have difficulties finding appropriate mentors who can relate to their personal experiences (McGowan et al. 2015). The tech startup ecosystem is mainly characterized by a "bro culture" of alpha males (Korreck 2019), and high-profile scandals have highlighted some of the most egregious cases (Solon & Wong 2017). Women are less inclined to participate in tech entrepreneurship as a result. These masculine cultures are one of the most-cited barriers to women's entrepreneurship – male dominance in the technology sector makes it inhospitable to women and leads to scarcity of women role models for technological breakthroughs (Ezzedeen & Zikic 2012). Role models can help develop an entrepreneurial identity among young women and help them deal with stereotypes embedded in the individual and collective subconscious (Byrne et al. 2019). While new models targeting women are emerging, particularly in post-secondary institutions (Politis & Dahlstrand 2011), most institutional processes in mainstream incubators and accelerators (Orser et al. 2019) exclude women.

Business intermediaries seldom provide services designed for women. A review of 65 programs designed to support small businesses in Ontario found that the programs are not supporting young and small firms as intended through excluding women-owned firms and other underrepresented groups (Dalziel et al. 2014). Another study, which undertook surveys of Ontario incubators' practices using the Diversity Institute's DAT, showed considerable gaps in supports and services tailored to women (Orser et al. 2019). Some specialized entrepreneur and business organizations have emerged to support women, such as Women's Enterprise Organizations of Canada (WEOC). There are also programs targeting women, such as BDC Capital's Women in Technology (WIT) Venture Fund, and women's organizations, such as the YWCA, Canada Women's Foundation, and the Native Women's Resource Centre, that offer programs that support women entrepreneurs, focusing on women's needs and tailoring their services to suit them. However, these represent a fraction of the resources invested in the overall ecosystems and in some cases risk ghettoizing women entrepreneurs as exceptional, like "lady doctors."

Universities, colleges, and other educational institutions play a huge role in the entrepreneurship ecosystems in ways that affect women. The role of universities has significantly changed in recent years. A new generation of entrepreneurial universities goes beyond the traditional role of being centres for teaching, research, and knowledge generation to make contributions to economic and social innovation of societies (Clauss et al. 2018). Governments have changed policies towards universities, helping to provide facilities for research projects and commercializing some academic achievements with the goal of aiding innovation (Clauss et al. 2018). Yet while higher education programs may espouse commitments to diversity and inclusion, their practices often fall short. For example, many universities have an explicit or implicit bias towards STEM disciplines, which tend to have poor representation of women (Mwasalwiba 2010). Societal norms, often replicated in institutions, can affect women's attitudes and intentions, discouraging them from starting businesses either by shaping gender roles (Deacon et al. 2014) or creating exclusive stereotypes (Henry et al. 2013; Ahl & Marlow 2012). The entrepreneurship pedagogy has not been women-friendly (Berglund et al. 2017), and the image of successful entrepreneurs remains masculinized, following societal stereotypes, in general entrepreneurship curriculum. Socially constructed gender stereotypes, which are "about the characteristics and attributes associated with each sex," are among the most important factors that affect men and women's entrepreneurial intentions (Gupta et al. 2009, p. 399).

Undergraduate entrepreneurship education tends to have a low representation of women (Myrah & Currie 2006). Again, intersectionality is important: for example, a recent study found that "the key to successful entrepreneurship education for Indigenous peoples is the combination of an empowering pedagogical approach and socio-culturally relevant content" (Foley 2012, p. 59). In post-secondary institutions, there is a lack of women-friendly entrepreneurial pedagogy (Foss et al. 2018). Although almost 40% of small-business support agencies in Ontario province provide support to help women and diverse groups, only 1 out of 5 (18.9%) offer specific programming; 1 out of 6 (16.2%) offer childcare; 1 out of 10 (10.8%) offer transportation; and 1 out of 20 (5.4%) offer lower/no program costs (Orser et al. 2019).

Metrics, accountability, and transparency are critical to bridging the implementation gap between good intentions and effective actions. But deciding what and how to measure has a profound impact on who gets included and excluded and how we define success. While innovative initiatives with promising outcomes abound, competition for resources and lack of coordination among support organizations creates fragmentation and duplication and limits opportunities for sharing across institutions, jurisdictions, sectors, and departments. Further, the impact of one-off, stand-alone, or pilot programs is unclear (Orser et al. 2013). There is little rigorous research on the impact of programs and what works for whom (Cukier et al. 2011a; Dalziel 2018). Women and Indigenous entrepreneurs often pursue social and community – as well as economic – goals, but these impacts are often not considered in assessments.

4.3   Micro (Individual) Level

At the micro level, the attitudes, skills, choices, and behaviours of individuals in the ecosystems are profoundly important. The individual characteristics and circumstances of entrepreneurs (e.g., knowledge, skills, attitudes, resources, family situation, geographic location) have a profound impact on their ability to spot and seize opportunities (Bae et al. 2014; Cukier et al. 2011b; Hughes 2018). Entrepreneurial self-efficacy, confidence in one's abilities to perform entrepreneurial tasks and to create a business is shaped by many factors, and there is ample evidence of stereotype threat and a confidence gap for women and other diverse entrepreneurs (Greene & Brush 2018; Robichaud et al. 2018). Research shows that perceived incongruity between gender stereotypes and entrepreneurship poses a major barrier to women who are seen as unfeminine if they behave like men and un-entrepreneurial if they behave like women (Balachandra et al. 2019; Eddleston et al. 2016). There is also extensive evidence of unfair treatment, bias, and micro-aggressions in the treatment of women and diverse entrepreneurs from other individuals. And many others, while not perpetrators, are bystanders.

At the end of the day, the attitudes and behaviours both of diverse individuals and others around them have a profound impact (Balachandra et al. 2019). Individual attitudes, capabilities and behaviours are shaped by culturally embedded cognitive frameworks and access to knowledge and experience (Kirzner 2008; Valliere 2011). A combination of personal motivation and attitudes, as well as the supportiveness of surrounding environments, has been found to impact whether or not individuals will exploit an opportunity (Gabarret et al. 2017; Krueger et al. 2000; Segal et al. 2005). At the same time, individuals' treatment of one another – whether through micro-aggressions, intentional or unintentional bias, allyship or sponsorship – affects the daily experience and potential for success of women and diverse entrepreneurs.

The Global Entrepreneurship Monitor (GEM) indicates that low intent among women is a global phenomenon (Kelley et al. 2017), which is shaped in large part by the stereotypes and societal forces described above. The confidence gap well documented in other sectors also plagues women entrepreneurs (Kirkwood 2009). Women entrepreneurs encounter barriers in accessing networking (McGowan et al. 2015), finding mentors (Rosa & Sylla 2016), and balancing family and work (Brush et al. 2009). There is also ample research documenting the barriers in accessing training (Elliott et al. 2020) and lack of encouragement (Korreck 2019).

5.   INTERSECTIONALITY

When one adds an intersectional lens, the barriers are amplified. Intersectionality is vital for unpacking the experiences of people with multiple, marginalized identities. This concept encompasses overlapping layers of various categories of social differences, such as gender, ethnicity, sexuality, disability, and religion, that are mutually constitutive to an individual's experiences in relation to structural inequality and barriers (Crenshaw 1989). Barriers in the three levels for women are exacerbated when women are racialized, have different gender identities or sexual orientation, immigrants, Indigenous, from various racial or ethnic groups, disabled, or when they are older or living in rural areas. For example, immigrant entrepreneurs reported a number of challenges, including a lack of knowledge of Canadian business practices, regulations, culture and norms, a lack of knowledge of – and access to – programs, language barriers, discrimination and bias in competitions, screening processes, and access to funding, and a lack of access to mentoring and networks (Diversity Institute 2017). Indigenous women, especially those who live on reserves, report unique challenges related to infrastructure, access to the same support resources available to mainstream groups, and access to financial support. Additionally, they tend to engage in activities, such as arts and social innovation, that are not recognized as entrepreneurial activities in the mainstream economy, thus further limiting their access to resources to either start or expand their businesses (CCAB 2016). For women with intersectional identities, the narrow definition of entrepreneurs used by the government and many business-support intermediaries is exclusive. For example, Indigenous women are more likely to have goals which include community development, are less likely to incorporate (partly for tax reasons), and do not have employees. The number of Indigenous women entrepreneurs increases dramatically when entrepreneurship includes self-employment (CCAB 2016).

6.   CONCLUSIONS AND IMPLICATIONS

In order to create an inclusive innovation and entrepreneurship ecosystem, we need to apply a gender and diversity lens to understand where the barriers exist and to develop a comprehensive strategy. Using the critical ecological model to include actors at multiple levels into the same framework, our analysis has highlighted ways in which bias can be embedded into policies, practices, and behaviours at all levels.

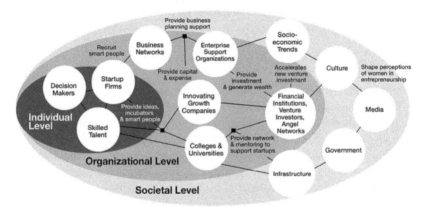

Note: The diagram provides an example of an inclusive innovation and entrepreneurship ecosystem, which consists of multiple actors at various levels. The size of the circles is randomly generated and does not suggest equal weight of the actors as their functions and impacts are constantly changing due to the constant interactions among them in the ecosystem.
Source: Adapted from Cukier and Hassannezhad Chavoushi (2020).

Figure 14.1   The inclusive innovation ecosystem model for entrepreneurship

Although there are no simple solutions to tackling the complex problems, we use the inclusive innovation ecosystem model to make the following recommendations.

From a macro perspective, we need to consider culture – the way we define and value entrepreneurs and the stereotypes that shape assumptions and aspirations. We need to break the association of technology with innovation and entrepreneurship and recognize that there are many forms of innovation and entrepreneurship. We need to ensure that the measures we use to assess entrepreneurship and innovation are not exclusionary – and include, for example, social and cultural impacts. A gender and diversity lens should be applied to address gaps in policy and programming because some concepts and standards often embedded in the policies primarily benefit men. COVID-19 has highlighted the gaps in Canada's social policy, childcare, and eldercare policies. More examination of other issues – for example tax policy which allows entrepreneurs to write off golf memberships as business expenses but not childcare – is needed.

At the meso level, policies and processes needed to be addressed in organizations across the ecosystems – financial institutions, business-support organizations, post-secondary institutions, incubators and accelerators – all need to be more inclusive and accountable. Programs and wrap-around services designed to better respond to meet women's needs – crowdfunding, micro-grants, customized counselling, mentoring, and sponsorship that respond to their needs and preferences, are also required. Business-support organizations need to examine their funding instruments, recruitment and selection practices, forms of support and wrap-around services (such as childcare). Their services or programming should account for the differences among women entrepreneurs, such as differences in age, geography, race and ethnicity, and immigration status, and rigorously assess what works and what does not to develop a coherent strategy that better supports women entrepreneurs from diverse groups. While women-targeted programs and services undoubtedly serve important needs, systems change demands that we apply a gender and diversity lens across organizations in the ecosystems. We need to consider their governance, their human resources policies, their culture, organizational practices, performance metrics and engagement with the ecosystems is critical to advancing diversity and inclusion – the Diversity Institute's Diversity Assessment Tool, for example, has been used to help drive changes in policies and practices (Cukier & Smarz 2012).

There are issues at the micro level too – we know that knowledge, attitudes, and behaviours must be addressed among women entrepreneurs to ensure that individual women are able to see the opportunity that entrepreneurship presents and have access to skills, information, and the support they need to succeed. Additionally, concerted efforts need to be made to address bias among trainers, financiers, business-service providers, VCs and others interacting with women to overcome overt discrimination and micro-aggressions – and to provide the support women entrepreneurs need and deserve.

Canada is one of the few countries in the world that has recognized the importance of tackling change at the ecosystem level, and applying a whole of government approach to think about how to advance women entrepreneurs with all the instruments at its disposal. WES, launched by the Government of Canada, employs a unique "whole of government" approach to support women entrepreneurship ecosystems. But there is more to be done in driving change through the organizations that support entrepreneurs and in tackling cultural bias and stereotypes. Because "if you can't see it, you can't be it".

REFERENCES

Ahl, H & Marlow, S 2012, 'Exploring the dynamics of gender, feminism and entrepreneurship: Advancing debate to escape a dead end?' *Organization*, *19*(5), pp. 543–562.

Anna, AN, Chandler, GN, Jansen, E & Mero, NP 2000, 'Women Business Owners in Traditional and Non-traditional Industries', *Journal of Business Venturing*, *15*(3), pp. 279–303.

Bae, TJ, Qian, S, Miao, C, & Fiet, JO 2014, 'The relationship between entrepreneurship education and entrepreneurial intentions: A meta-analytic review', *Entrepreneurship: Theory and Practice*, *38*(2), pp. 217–254.

Balachandra, L, Briggs, T, Eddleston, K, & Brush, C 2019, 'Don't pitch like a girl!: How gender stereotypes influence investor decisions', *Entrepreneurship Theory and Practice*, *43*(1), pp. 116–137.

Beckton, C, McDonald, J, & Marquis-Bissonnette, M 2018, 'Everywhere, every day innovating: Women entrepreneurs and innovation', The Beacon Agency, viewed 5 September 2020, https://phasenyne.com/wp-content/uploads/2018/04/beacon _Womens_report_eng_web.pdf

Berglund, K, Lindgren, M, & Packendorff, J 2017, 'Responsibilising the next generation: Fostering the enterprising self through de-mobilising gender', *Organization*, *24*(6), pp. 892–915.

Brush, C, De Bruin, A, & Welter, F 2009, 'A gender-aware framework for women's entrepreneurship', *International Journal of Gender and Entrepreneurship*, *1*(1), pp. 8–24.

Brush, C, Edelman, LF, Manolova, T, & Welter, F, 2019, 'A gendered look at entrepreneurship ecosystems', *Small Business Economics*, *53*(2), pp. 393–408.

Byrne, J, Fattoum, S, & Diaz Garcia, MC 2019, 'Role models and women entrepreneurs: Entrepreneurial superwoman has her say', *Journal of Small Business Management*, *57*(1), pp. 154–184.

CCAB 2016, *Promise and prosperity: The 2016 Aboriginal business survey*, Canadian Council of Aboriginal Business, viewed 5 September 2020, https://www.ccab.com/ wp-content/uploads/2016/10/CCAB-PP-Report-V2-SQ-Pages.pdf

Clauss, T, Moussa, A, & Kesting, T 2018, 'Entrepreneurial university: A stakeholder-based conceptualisation of the current state and an agenda for future research', *International Journal of Technology Management*, *77*(1/2/3), pp. 109–144.

Coleman, S, Henry, C, Orser, B, Foss L, & Welter, F 2019, 'Policy support for women entrepreneurs' access to financial capital: Evidence from Canada, Germany, Ireland, Norway, and the United States', *Journal of Small Business Management*, *570*(sup2), pp. 296–322.

Crenshaw, K 1989, 'Demarginalizing the intersection of race and sex: A black feminist critique of antidiscrimination doctrine, feminist theory, and antiracist politics', *University of Chicago Legal Forum*, pp. 139–167.

Cukier, W, Gagnon, S, Lindo, LM, Hannan, C, & Amato, S 2014, 'A [critical] ecological model to enabling change: Promoting diversity and inclusion', In V Malin, J Murphy, & M Siltaoja (Eds.), *Getting things done: Dialogues in critical management studies*, Vol. 2, pp. 245–247. Bingley: Emerald Group Publishing.

Cukier, W, & Hassannezhad Chavoushi, Z 2020, 'Facilitating women entrepreneurship in Canada: The case of WEKH', *An International Journal*, *35*(3), pp. 303–318.

Cukier, W, & Smarz, S 2012, 'Diversity assessment tools: A comparison', *International Journal of Knowledge, Culture & Change Management*, *11*(6), pp. 49–63.

Cukier, W, Smarz, S, & Yap, M 2011b, 'Using the Diversity Audit Tool to assess the status of women in the Canadian financial services sector', *The International Journal of Diversity in Organisations, Communities, and Nations*, *11*(3), pp 15–36.

Cukier, W, Stolarik, K, Ngwenyama, O, & Elmi, M 2016. *Mapping the innovation ecosystem in Eastern Ontario. Towards an inclusive Canadian innovation strategy.* Eastern Ontario Regional Network, viewed 5 February 2021, https://www.ryerson .ca/diversity/reports/Mapping_the_Innovation_Ecosystem_in_Ontario.pdf

Cukier, W, Trenholm, S, Carl, D, & Gekas, G 2011a, 'Social entrepreneurship: A content analysis', *Journal of Strategic Innovation and Sustainability*, *7*(1), pp. 99–119.

Dalziel, M 2018, 'Why are there (almost) no randomized controlled trial-based evaluations of business support programs?' *Palgrave Communications*, *4*(1), pp. 1–9. https://www.nature.com/articles/s41599-018-0069-9

Dalziel, M, Cumming, D, & Wolfe, D 2014, *Report of the expert panel examining Ontario's business support programs.* Report presented to the Ontario Minister of Finance and the Ontario Minister of Economic Development, Employment and Infrastructure.

Deacon, JA, Harris, J, & Worth, L 2014, 'Who leads? Fresh insights into roles and responsibilities in a heterosexual copreneurial business', *International Journal of Gender and Entrepreneurship*, *6*(3), pp. 317–335.

Diversity Institute 2017, *Immigrant entrepreneurship report*, viewed 5 September 2020, https://www.ryerson.ca/content/dam/diversity/reports/ImmigrantEntrepreneur .pdf

Drucker, PF 1993, *Innovation and entrepreneurship.* New York: Harper.

Eddleston, KA., Ladge, JJ, Mitteness, C, & Balachandra, L 2016, 'Do you see what I see? Signaling effects of gender and firm characteristics on financing entrepreneurial ventures', *Entrepreneurship Theory and Practice*, *40*(3), pp. 489–514.

Elliott, C, Mavriplis, C, & Anis, H 2020, 'An entrepreneurship education and peer mentoring program for women in STEM: Mentors' experiences and perceptions of entrepreneurial self-efficacy and intent', *International Entrepreneurship and Management Journal*, *16*(1), pp. 43–67.

Estrin, S & Mickiewicz, T 2011, 'Institutions and female entrepreneurship', *Small Business Economics*, *37*(4), pp. 397–415.

Ezzedeen, SR & Zikic, J 2012, 'Entrepreneurial experiences of women in Canadian high technology', *International Journal of Gender and Entrepreneurship*, *4*(1), pp. 44–64.

Foley, D 2012, 'Teaching entrepreneurship to Indigenous and other minorities: Towards a strong sense of self, tangible skills and active participation within society', *Journal of Business Diversity*, *12*, pp. 59–70.

Foss, L, Henry, C, Ahl, H, & Mikalsen, GH 2018, 'Women's entrepreneurship policy research: A 30-year review of the evidence', *Small Business Economics*, *53*(2), pp. 409–429.

Gabarret, I, Vedel, B, & Decaillon, J 2017, 'A social affair: Identifying motivation of social entrepreneurs', *International Journal of Entrepreneurship and Small Business*, *31*(3), pp. 399–415.

Government of Canada 2021, 'Key small business statistics — 2021', *Innovation, Science and Economic Development Canada*, viewed 19 March 2022, https://www.ic.gc.ca/eic/site/061.nsf/eng/h_03147.html#2.2

Granstrand, O & Holgersson, M 2020, 'Innovation ecosystems: A conceptual review and a new definition,' *Technovation*, *90–91*, viewed 10 February 2021, 10.1016/j.technovation.2019.102098

Greene, P & Brush, C 2018, *A research agenda for women and entrepreneurship: Identity through aspirations, behaviors and confidence*. Cheltenham, UK and Northampton, MA, USA: Edward Elgar Publishing.

Grekou, D, Li, J, & Liu H 2018, '*Women-owned enterprises in Canada*', Statistics Canada, viewed 10 July 2020, https://www150.statcan.gc.ca/n1/pub/11-626-x/11-626-x2018083-eng.htm

Gupta, VK, Turban, DB, Wasti, SA., & Sikdar, A 2009, 'The role of gender stereotypes in perceptions of entrepreneurs and intentions to become an entrepreneur', *Entrepreneurship Theory and Practice*, *33*(2), pp. 397–417.

Helbing, D (Ed.) 2012, *Social self-organization: Agent-based simulations and experiments to study emergent social behavior*. Heidelberg: Springer.

Henry, C, Treanor, L, Sweida, GL, & Reichard, RJ 2013, 'Gender stereotyping effects on entrepreneurial self-efficacy and high-growth entrepreneurial intention', *Journal of Small Business and Enterprise Development*, *20*(2), pp. 296–313.

Hindle, K & Moroz, P 2010, 'Indigenous entrepreneurship as a research field: Developing a definitional framework from the emerging canon', *International Entrepreneurship and Management Journal*, *6*(4), pp. 357–385.

Hughes, KD 2017, *Global entrepreneurship monitor Canada 2015/16 report on women's entrepreneurship*, viewed 5 September 2020, https://thecis.ca/wp-content/uploads/2016/04/GEM-2015-16-Womens-Report-FINAL-Nov-14-2017.pdf

Hughes, KD 2018, *Women's entrepreneurship in Alberta: Insights from the Global Entrepreneurship Monitor*. Calgary: The Centre for Innovation Studies (THECIS).

Isenberg, DJ 2010, 'How to start an entrepreneurial revolution', *Harvard Business Review, 88*(6), pp. 41–50.

Jennings, JE & Brush, CG 2013, 'Research on women entrepreneurs: Challenges to (and from) the broader entrepreneurship literature?' *The Academy of Management Annals*, *7*(1), pp. 663–715.

Jung, O 2010, *Small business financing profiles: Women entrepreneurs*, Small Business and Tourism Branch, Industry Canada, viewed 10 February 2021, https://www.ic.gc.ca/eic/site/061.nsf/vwapj/Profile-Profil_Oct2010_eng.pdf/$file/Profile-Profil_Oct2010_eng.pdf

Kelley, DJ, Baumer, BS, Brush, C, Greene, PG, Mahdavi, M, Majbouri M, Cole, M, Dean, M, & Heavlow, R 2017, 'Women's entrepreneurship 2016/2017 report', viewed 5 July 2020, https://gemorg.bg/wp-content/uploads/2018/02/gem-womens -2016-2017-report-v11df-1504758645.pdf

Kirkwood, J 2009, 'Is a lack of self-confidence hindering women entrepreneurs?' *International Journal of Gender and Entrepreneurship, 1*(2), pp. 118–133.

Kirzner, IM 2008, 'The alert and creative entrepreneur: A clarification', *Small Business Economics, 32*(2), pp. 145–152.

Korreck, S 2019, 'Women entrepreneurs in India: What is holding them back?' *Observer Research Foundation Issue Brief, September* (317), Observer Research Foundation, viewed 5 September 2020, https://www.orfonline.org/research/women -entrepreneurs-in-india-what-is-holding-them-back-55852/

Krueger, NF, Reilly, MD, & Carsrud, AL 2000, 'Competing models of entrepreneurial intentions', *Journal of Business Venturing, 15*(5), pp. 411–432.

Lounsbury, M, Cornelissen, J, Granqvist, N, & Grodal, S 2019, 'Culture, innovation and entrepreneurship', *Organization and Management, 21*(1), pp. 1–12.

Malmstrom, M, Johansson, J, & Wincent, J 2017, 'Gender stereotypes and venture support decisions: How governmental venture capitalists socially construct entrepreneurs' potential', *Entrepreneurship Theory and Practice, 41*(5), pp. 833–860.

McGowan, P, Cooper, SY, Durkin M, & O'Kane, C 2015, 'The influence of social and human capital in developing young women as entrepreneurial business leaders', *Small Business Management, 53*, pp. 645–661.

McKinsey Global Institute 2017, *The power of parity: Advancing women's equality in Canada*, viewed 5 September 2020, https://www.mckinsey.com/featured-insights/ gender-equality/the-power-of-parity-advancing-womens-equality-in-canada

Mundy, L 2014, 7 April, 'The media has a woman problem', *The New York Times*, viewed 5 September 2020, https://www.nytimes.com/2014/04/27/opinion/sunday/ the-media-has-a-woman-problem.html

Mwasalwiba, E 2010, 'Entrepreneurship education: A review of its objectives, teaching methods, and impact indicators', *Education and Training, 52*(1), 20–47.

Myrah, K & Currie, R 2006, 'Examining undergraduate entrepreneurship education', *Journal of Small Business & Entrepreneurship, 19*(3), pp. 233–253.

Neumeyer, X & Santos, S. 2018, 'Sustainable business models, venture typologies, and entrepreneurial ecosystems: A social network perspective', *Journal of Cleaner Production, 172*, pp. 4565–4579.

OECD. 2020, *OECD data*, viewed 10 February 2021, https://data.oecd.org/

Orser, B, Elliott, C, & Cukier, W 2019, *Strengthening ecosystem supports for women entrepreneurs*. Telfer School of Management. University of Ottawa, viewed 5 September 2020, https://www.ryerson.ca/diversity/reports/strengthening_ecosystem _supports_for_women_entrepreneurs/

Orser, BJ., Elliott, C, & Leck, J 2013, 'Entrepreneurial feminists: Perspectives about opportunity recognition and governance', *Journal of Business Ethics, 115*(2), pp. 241–257.

Ozkazanc-Pan, B & Clark Muntean, S 2018, 'Networking towards (in) equality: Women entrepreneurs in technology', *Gender, Work and Organization, 25(*4), pp. 379–400.

Politis, D & Dahlstrand, ÅL 2011, 'Gender and academic entrepreneurship: The effect of structural factors on women entrepreneurship', *Frontiers of Entrepreneurship Research, 31*(8), p. 8.

Robichaud, Y, Cachon, JC, & McGraw, E, 2018. 'Gender comparisons in success evaluation and SME performance in Canada', *Journal of Developmental Entrepreneurship*, *23*(1), 1850004.

Rosa, J & Sylla, D 2016, '*A comparison of the performance of female-owned and male-owned small and medium-sized enterprises*', Government of Canada, viewed 5 September 2020, https://www.ic.gc.ca/eic/site/061.nsf/eng/h_03034.html#sect-2

Saparito, P, Elam, A, & Brush, C 2013, 'Bank–firm relationships: Do perceptions vary by gender?' *Entrepreneurship Theory and Practice*, *37*(4), pp. 837–858.

Schumpeter, JA 1911/1934, *The theory of economic development: an inquiry into profits, capital, credit, interest, and the business cycle*. Piscataway, NJ: Transaction Publishers.

Segal, G, Borgia, D, & Schoenfeld, J 2005, 'The motivation to become an entrepreneur', *International Journal of Entrepreneurial Behaviour & Research*, *11*(1), pp. 42–57.

Shane, S & Venkataraman, S 2000, 'The promise of entrepreneurship as a field of research', *Academy of Management Review*, *25*(1), pp. 217–226.

Solon, O & Wong, J 2017 Jun 21, 'With Uber's Travis Kalanick out, will Silicon Valley clean up its bro culture?' *The Guardian*, viewed 1 February 2021, https://www.theguardian.com/technology/2017/jun/21/uber-travis-kalanick-what-next-silicon-valley

Stam, E & Spigel, B 2016, 'Entrepreneurial ecosystems', *Discussion Paper Series 16-13*, Tjalling C. Koopmans Research Institute, Utrecht School of Economics, viewed 1 February 2020, https://pdfs.semanticscholar.org/17f1/61a6f5c68c4b9aac89a375239658621fe905.pdf?_ga=2.96206364.1255096944.1612882017-640979979.1612882017

Statistics Canada 2019, *Self-employed Canadians: Who and why?* viewed 1 February 2021, https://www150.statcan.gc.ca/n1/pub/71-222-x/71-222-x2019002-eng.htm

Valliere, D 2011, 'Towards a schematic theory of entrepreneurial alertness', *Journal of Business Venturing*, *28*(3), pp. 430–442.

Valliere, D 2017, 'Multidimensional entrepreneurial intent: an internationally validated measurement approach', *International Journal of Entrepreneurial Behavior and Research*, *23*(1), pp. 59–77.

Vershinina, N, Rodionova, Y, & Marlow, S 2015, 'Does an entrepreneur's gender matter for credibility and financing of SMEs?' In V Ramadani, S Gërguri-Rashiti & A Fayolle (Eds), *Female entrepreneurship in transition economies*, pp. 87–111. London: Palgrave Macmillan.

PART III

Conclusion

15. Afterword

Beldina Owalla, Tim Vorley and Helen Lawton Smith

1. INTRODUCTION

Focused on exploring gender, diversity and innovation, the chapters in this edited collection make contributions in three main areas. First, they draw on different theoretical perspectives in order to critique the concept of gender and innovation; second, they examine how gender matters in the innovation process in different geographical, economic and social contexts; and third, they focus on policy and governance issues by analysing interventions and institutions aimed at supporting greater diversity and inclusion within entrepreneurial and innovation ecosystems.

A unifying theme that brings these three areas together is intersectionality. Understood as the intersection of social categories (i.e. ethnicity, class, age, gender, etc.), the intersectional lens can be applied to individuals or groups. Minority groups often experience discrimination or disadvantage, which is typically more acute where there are other intersections (i.e. Black, working class, women). While women comprise half of the world's population, gender is still a primary source of marginalization. This is often compounded by other characteristics, such as race or class, which create further disadvantage.

The contributors to this edited collection, some explicitly and others implicitly, address the question of intersectionality to further emphasize the heterogeneity of women founders. This concluding chapter reflects on the key insights and implications for policy and practice, as well as outlining directions for future research.

2. MAIN INSIGHTS AND CONTRIBUTIONS

2.1 Problematizing Gender and Innovation

The need to rethink the concepts of *gendered innovation* and *gendered social innovation* is explored in two chapters. Problematizing gendered innovation, in

Chapter 11, Picardi explored how adopting the notion of sociomateriality and relational ontology allows us to focus on how meanings and materiality interconnect and interrelate in everyday practices. Innovation is not produced in a separate space from the rest of society, and as such she asserts that we should focus on understanding how gender informs the technoscientific governance of researchers and innovation, and reciprocally, how technoscientific governance informs the concept of gender and gendered practices among scientific and research institutions.

In Chapter 7, Cervia argued that the concept of gendered social innovation is based on a categorical thinking of gender which risks reifying femininity/masculinity, while obscuring cross-cutting axes of subordination. Adopting a relational theory perspective enables us to view gender as a social construct formed and performed within interactions and institutions, that is, gendering social innovations. Using the example of co-production in the healthcare setting, the author shows how a relational approach allows us to consider the co-production process in its reciprocal interrelation at the meso and macro levels; which subsequently define the meaning and outcome of innovation practices introduced at micro level.

While the concepts of gender and innovation are employed widely in the literature, there is a need to ensure that they continue to be employed critically. These chapters remind us as to the importance of continuing to challenge and problematize what are terms and ideas that are often used in ways with assumed meanings. The dominant interpretation of innovation still primarily privileges economic innovations over social innovation, which can create alternative forms of value. In advancing innovation research, there is an opportunity to also better understand these outcomes and impacts of diverse innovators. Problematizing these assumptions will enable us to promote more inclusive innovation that embraces both the diversity of actors and activities involved.

2.2 Gender and Innovation in Different Contexts

Given the crucial role STEM fields play in innovation, understanding women's under-representation in this area has been the focus of several book chapters within this edited collection. These studies have been conducted in different sectoral and geographical contexts. Drawing on social psychology concepts, in Chapter 3, Dotzler and González-Morales reflected on how the current masculinity contest cultures of both STEM and entrepreneurial fields contribute to women's under-representation. They further argue that a shift towards more relational practices and cultures will not only benefit women, but all actors in these fields. Likewise, in Chapter 4, Griffiths et al. explored the academic entrepreneurship setting, and concluded that a masculine culture dominates this context. The chapter found that while male and female academics might face similar challenges across their spinout journeys, the way these challenges are experienced by women is different. Women academic entrepreneurs face multiple and accumulating instances of second-generation gender bias that impacts their access to both resources and opportunities. Moreover, this accumulated disadvantage is amplified by intersecting identity categories.

Institutional biases that uphold a male norm while stereotyping femininity as a deficit are also evident in the technology sector, as Tesfaye and Wainikka argue in Chapter 5. Women in their inventor–innovator–entrepreneur journey face impediments related to intersecting identity categories and structural challenges. As a result, women are placed in a position where their credibility, legitimacy and visibility as innovative entrepreneurs is undermined. The portrayal of women innovators as being riskier investments ultimately limits their access to financial resources. This is a key concern, given that, as shown by Owalla et al. in Chapter 8, despite their limited number and firm size constraints, women-led SMEs are equally as likely to engage in process innovation, product innovation, and investment in R&D as other SMEs in general. The chapter also raises important questions for future policies and programmes, not least the need to pay greater attention to the gendered structures impacting women's entrepreneurial activities.

Gender therefore remains a key inhibitor to innovation and entrepreneurship in both developed and developing economies. In Chapter 6, Tonks and Lawton Smith argued that given the right opportunities starting and growing their businesses, women can overcome social barriers and their own inhibitions to operate in the innovation space. Access to finance plays a critical role in making this a reality, and crowdfunding could be a promising solution to overcoming this barrier. As shown in Chapter 2 by Bort and Meoli, the advantages held by male entrepreneurs in traditional finance dissipate in the crowdfunding context. The authors propose that female innovators utilizing open innovation strategies will experience superior outcomes in rewards-based crowdfunding models. Further research on this alternative source of funding for diverse women innovators, as well as other under-represented groups, would therefore be worthwhile.

As these chapters highlight, understanding context is critical to understanding gender and innovation. While there are common issues and shared challenges, context is critical in determining the extent to which gender and other intersecting categories could be a disadvantage or barrier to being an innovator. In short, context matters. There are of course norms and biases, both conscious and unconscious, that impact women innovators, although these impacts are not uniform. As the chapter authors have shown, there is a need to situate the context before addressing questions of gender and innovation. Understanding how different contexts influence access to financial and social capital, as well as realizing innovation opportunities will enable us to gain a more holistic understanding of the structural and systemic barriers that women innovators face.

2.3   Policy and Governance

The third main area explored by several chapters is that of policy and governance. The foci include reflections on the institutional contexts, as well as the effectiveness of interventions and policies in supporting women's entrepreneurial activities and promoting more inclusive innovation ecosystems. Targeted interventions have been shown to be necessary and successfully implemented, as Tonks and Lawton Smith show in Chapter 6. Furthermore, in Chapter 10, Sivi argued that targeted initiatives also need to ensure that affirmative action interventions actually achieve the intended objectives, and do not see less privileged members of the same target groups disadvantaged. As Sivi concluded, policies and programmes need to better address the complexities that arise due to multiple intersecting categories in their design.

Institutional contexts, as has been shown previously, play a crucial role in enhancing or impeding entrepreneurial and innovation activity. Chapter 12 by Villegas-Mateos and Morales explored the impact of institutional voids in emerging economies on female innovative entrepreneurship activities. The study found that the probability of gender balance in innovative entrepreneurial activity increases with higher values of doing business. The authors concluded that the degree of economic development correlates with the institutional framework, affecting how innovation is developed. Still focused on exploring institutional structures, Otuo et al. present a conceptual analysis of salient informal institutional structures in sub-Saharan Africa entrepreneurial ecosystems in Chapter 13. The discussion presents a framework to explore the multi-layered and intersectional effects of gender, culture, religion, class and family, and demonstrates their relevance for legitimating female innovators.

Chapter 14 argues for the need to apply a gender and diversity lens to all elements in the ecosystem in order to develop a more comprehensive strategy for achieving inclusive innovation and entrepreneurship ecosystems. Cukier et al. applied the critical ecological model in their analysis and highlighted ways in which bias can be embedded into policies, practices and behaviours at macro, meso and micro levels, as well as their interactions. This concern is further explored within the context of AI ecosystems in Chapter 9, which examined how AI policies in 21 countries address gender. Venugopal and Rituraj show that the majority of AI policies favour economic and strategic outputs to the possible detriment of feminist approaches to growth. The authors concluded that developing AI ecosystems akin to current entrepreneurial ecosystems will continue to exacerbate the implicit biases that exist, and recommend greater engagement with gender while framing policies for use of AI.

Policy and governance are of central importance not only in driving innovation, but also in addressing the disparity and disadvantages that women and other under-represented innovators can encounter. The challenge for governments, innovation agencies, and other intermediaries remains to raise awareness and engagement of aspiring innovators from non-majority and under-represented groups. Diversity has come to be recognized as a vital driver of, and catalyst for, innovation, and remains an important focus for future research and policy that is not well understood. Moreover, the focus of inclusive innovation initiatives needs to move beyond focusing on the impact of gender in isolation, to understanding the barriers created by intersecting categories such as race, ethnicity, age, disability and educational background.

3.   IMPLICATIONS FOR POLICY AND PRACTICE

This edited collection highlights a number of issues that are relevant to policy and practice. Some of the challenges highlighted in the various chapters could be addressed through targeted initiatives, however, there also remains a need to pursue a more holistic system-wide approach in order to create inclusive innovation ecosystems. In different contexts this will demand tailoring policies and support initiatives to address specific challenges such as engaging women or ethnic minority groups, as well as intersections of identity categories such as race, ethnicity, class, place and so on. Such an approach needs to recognize the complexity of the problems being addressed, and ensure that strategies for change address the causes of disadvantage and marginalization and not just the symptoms.

Masculinity dominates the innovation culture in many societies, and if innovation is to become more inclusive there is a need to embrace more gendered and intersectional perspectives in the way that policies and programmes are designed, delivered and evaluated. Ensuring greater representation and visibility of under-represented innovators will also go a long way to increase their legitimacy within these contexts. In addition, as has been emphasized previously, initiatives that encourage more relational practices might provide more effective support to women innovators and challenge the prevailing male culture. There is also a need to commit to long-term sustained support for diverse innovators, rather than piecemeal policies and symbolic investments, in order to address these complex and systemic challenges. Furthermore, greater collaboration and coordination is required across the numerous organizations and fragmented initiatives if we are to realize more inclusive economic growth.

4.   MOVING THE DEBATE FORWARD

This edited collection presents a series of cutting-edge insights on innovation, gender and intersectionality, that provides the foundations to move the debate forward from a deficit perspective that primarily focuses on the need for assistance, and invariably conflates agency and structure. Adopting an intersectional lens allows us to further interrogate the heterogeneity of under-represented groups, and with it the interconnectedness of agency and structure. While such a perspective is becoming more common in research, its adoption within policy interventions is still limited. Additionally, future work problematizing the notions of gender and innovation, and associated assumptions regarding what it is and who is involved, will contribute to advancing knowledge in this field.

A better understanding of how under-represented groups are socially positioned within different geographical and institutional contexts, and the corresponding impact this has on their access to resources, legitimacy and power within entrepreneurial and innovation ecosystems, is also necessary for achieving inclusive economic growth. Such comprehensive analyses require not only the collection of broader, more disaggregated data on women and other under-represented innovators in different spatial and geographic contexts, but also a more fine-grained analysis of the data collected.

Lastly, recognizing again the particular importance of context – and the potentially broader range of social, cultural, and institutional factors influencing innovation activities in different places – there is a need for comparative studies that can provide insights into the interplay between gender, innovation and context. Such studies could also contribute to existing knowledge by identifying benchmarks and best practices in promoting inclusive innovation ecosystems in different contexts.

Index